—— *BEYOND* ——
CLEVELAND ON FOOT

—— *BEYOND* ——
CLEVELAND ON FOOT

57 Hikes in Northeast Ohio's Lake, Geauga, Portage, Summit, Medina, Lorain, and Erie Counties

Patience Cameron

Map graphics by Stefanie Erickson

Gray & Company, Publishers
Cleveland

Gray & Company, Publishers
1588 E. 40th St.
Cleveland, OH 44103-2302
info@grayco.com

Library of Congress Cataloging-in-Publication Data:
Cameron, Patience.
Beyond Cleveland on foot : 57 hikes in northeast Ohio's Lake, Geauga, Portage, Summit, Medina, Lorain, and Erie counties / Patience Cameron.
"Companion volume to Cleveland on foot: a guide to walking and hiking in Cleveland and vicinity."
Includes bibliographical references and index.
1. Hiking—Ohio—Guidebooks. 2. Walking—Ohio—Guidebooks.
3. Ohio—Guidebooks. I. Title.
GV199.42.O3C35 1996
796.5'1'09771—dc20   96-25254

ISBN 1-886228-07-8
Printed in the United States of America
10 9 8 7 6 5 4 3 2 1

Photographs by Harry Cameron unless otherwise credited.

Quotations on pages 5, 68, and 230 are from *Walden* by Henry David Thoreau, copyright 1910, Grosset & Dunlap.
Quotations on pages 32 and 214 are from *The Writings of Ralph Waldo Emerson*, copyright 1940 by Random House, Inc.

This book is dedicated to the people who had the foresight to create the county park districts in Lake, Geauga, Portage, Summit, Medina, Lorain, and Erie Counties; to the National Park Service for establishing the Cuyahoga Valley National Recreation Area; to the state of Ohio for administering the area's state parks and nature preserves; and to the dedicated staff members and the host of volunteers who help maintain the parks, trails, historic buildings, and other places that make northeast Ohio a prime area for outdoor recreation.

I also dedicate this book to Ashley and Jonathan and all the other grandchildren in northeast Ohio who enjoy hiking.

I am monarch of all I survey
My right there is none to dispute.
—Henry David Thoreau, *Walden*

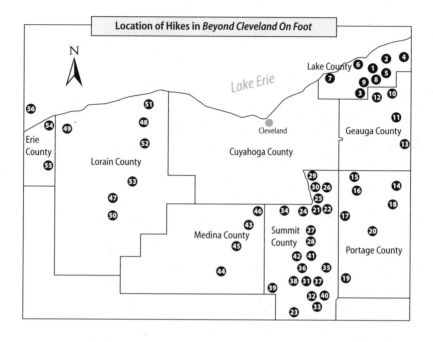

Location of Hikes in *Beyond Cleveland On Foot*

N

Lake Erie

Lake County

Cleveland

Erie County

Lorain County

Cuyahoga County

Geauga County

Medina County

Summit County

Portage County

CONTENTS

CONTENTS (continued)

LIST OF MAPS

LIST OF MAPS (continued)

PREFACE

Beyond Cleveland On Foot is a companion volume to *Cleveland On Foot: A Guide to Walking and Hiking in Cleveland and Vicinity.* That book, first published in 1992 by H & P Publishing Co., contained 33 walks and hikes in urban and suburban Cleveland, including Cleveland Metroparks, Cuyahoga Valley National Recreation Area, and selected state parks and nature preserves, all primarily in Cuyahoga County. It is now out of print. The current second edition of *Cleveland On Foot,* revised, updated, and expanded to 45 walks and hikes, with all-new maps, was published by Gray & Company in 1995.

Beyond Cleveland On Foot follows the same format as our previous books but describes 57 new walks and hikes in seven counties surrounding Cleveland: Lake, Geauga, Portage, Summit, Medina, Lorain, and Erie. While no attempt has been made to include all the possible walks and hikes in the parks and communities of these counties, those described in this book are a thorough sampling of the rich resources we have in our corner of the state.

The walks and hikes are listed by county and organized by degree of difficulty, i.e., easy, moderate, or strenuous. Although my ratings are arbitrary, I have suggested these categories based on the experience of the average walker or hiker. Walks are generally in urban or suburban communities and hikes are on wooded trails in parks or forests. If a trail is also suitable for bicycling or cross-country skiing, that is mentioned in the text. Information about hiking preparation and area resources (included in *Cleveland On Foot*) has been updated and reprinted as a useful aid for both the novice and experienced hiker.

Included in each chapter of *Beyond Cleveland On Foot* are hike distance and approximate hiking time, a description of terrain and special features, directions from the nearest interstate highway, and information about parking and restrooms at the trailhead.

Historical walks in three of northeast Ohio's small towns are included here because of the popularity of urban and suburban walking tours. These are Vermilion in Erie County, Oberlin in Lorain County, and Hudson Village in Summit County. I have provided architectural information, when available, and have consulted with experts to ensure the accuracy of historical information. Geological data has been included to enhance the hiking experience in many of the parks where rock formations are of unusual interest. This information has been verified by the Cleveland Museum of Natural History's Curator of Invertebrate Paleontology, Joseph T. Hannibal, who also supplied the information in Appendix A.

To those who have found *Cleveland On Foot* a valuable resource for the enjoyment of our great outdoors, I hope *Beyond Cleveland On Foot* will enlarge the scope of your hiking adventures and bring many hours of enjoyment.

ACKNOWLEDGMENTS

First and foremost I wish to acknowledge the special contributions to *Beyond Cleveland On Foot* by my husband and co-author of *Cleveland On Foot*, Harry M. Cameron. His help was there whenever I needed it. He walked the trails with me, reviewed chapters after they were written, and supported me in every way. His expert knowledge of the intricacies of word processing was invaluable. I could not have written this book without him.

I am also indebted to many people who helped us put together *Beyond Cleveland On Foot*, but especially:

Flora Burkholder, who supplied the bulk of information for walks and hikes in Lorain and Erie Counties. I am especially indebted to Flora because she prepared detailed maps, trail descriptions, and geological and historical information, and then hiked and re-hiked most of the trails in Lorain and Erie Counties with me. She also reviewed the chapters describing hikes in these counties to ensure their accuracy.

Stefanie Erickson, who created all the maps in this book. Her expert knowledge of computers and her great good humor made the tedious task of map construction much easier.

Charles Briggs, who reviewed several chapters describing hikes in Metro Parks Serving Summit County and walked several trails with me.

Thomas Vince, who reviewed the chapter on Hudson Village for historical accuracy.

Jack Gieck, who provided substantial information and suggestions for, and carefully reviewed, the chapter on Cascade Locks.

Bruce Norton, for his review of the Cascade Locks chapter.

Jennifer Maurer and Edith McNally, who supplied information about Cascade Locks.

Diane Chesnut and Roze Smith, who reviewed the chapter on Vermilion for historical accuracy.

Geoffrey Blodgett, Danforth Professor of History, Oberlin College, who reviewed the walk in Oberlin and supplied valuable textual suggestions.

Ran Taylor, for his review of the Oberlin chapter.

William Gray, for guiding me through Portage Lakes State Park.

Jim Sprague, for the information on Schumacher Woods in Chapter 42.

Patricia Morse, Naturalist, Lake Metroparks, who reviewed maps and chapters describing hikes in Lake Metroparks.

Doreen Brennan, Public Relations, Lake Metroparks, for supplying photographs, and to all the talented photographers in Lake County.

Walter Starcher, Director, Metro Parks Serving Summit County, for reviewing maps and chapters describing hikes in the Metro Parks.

John R. O'Meara, Director, Geauga Park District, who reviewed maps and chapters describing hikes in Geauga Park District.

Gary Gerrone, Naturalist Supervisor, who reviewed maps and chapters describing hikes in Lorain County Metro Parks.

Elinor Polster, who walked many of the trails with me and provided useful information from the hiker's viewpoint.

Joseph T. Hannibal, Curator of Invertebrate Paleontology, Cleveland Museum of Natural History, who helped clarify geological information and supplied the chart in Appendix A.

Daniel T. Melcher, President of the Audubon Society of Greater Cleveland, who supplied substantial help with the chapter on the Aurora Sanctuary.

I also wish to acknowledge the contributions of staff members in all the county park districts who were helpful in supplying information and photographs.

Last, but not least, I wish to express my appreciation to fellow hikers in the Buckeye Trail Association, Cleveland Hiking Club, St. Paul's Walking Group, and others with whom I have spent many pleasant hours enjoying our great outdoors.

DISCLAIMER

This guide was prepared on the basis of the best knowledge available to the author at the time of publication. However, because of constantly changing trail conditions due to natural and other causes, the author disclaims any liability whatsoever for the condition of the trails described herein, for occurrences happening on them, or for the accuracy of descriptions. Users of this guide are cautioned not to place undue reliance upon the continuing validity of the information contained herein and to use this guide at their own risk.

—— *BEYOND* ——
CLEVELAND
ON FOOT

INTRODUCTION

This book has been developed for people who enjoy the outdoors, or want to, and who like to find new ways to explore the world beyond their own front door. *Beyond Cleveland On Foot* is for newcomers to hiking as well as more experienced walkers and hikers who wish to expand the territory with which they are already familiar and comfortable.

Beyond Cleveland On Foot is for newcomers to northeast Ohio, too, as it introduces the region's great variety of natural resources. And it is for people who have lived in metropolitan Cleveland and surrounding counties for many years—possibly all their lives—but who may not yet have discovered the wonderful hiking opportunities that abound in these areas. These hikes are for walkers with varied abilities and interests. They can be enjoyed in as little as an hour or two or as long as a full day.

Please check our descriptions carefully. I hope there are no errors or omissions, but if some have crept in please send me a note in care of the publisher and let me know how to improve this guide for the next edition. Even if the descriptions are satisfactory, I'd like to know that, too.

I encourage you to partake of the special joy that comes from walking and hiking, and the sharpening of the senses that makes one feel more alive. I hope you have as much pleasure taking these walks and hikes as I have had in researching and describing them, and that this guide will be only a start for you on a lifelong hiking adventure.

What is in this guide?

The 57 walks and hikes described here are categorized by county. (Summit County contains subcategories for hikes in Metro Parks Serving Summit County and the Cuyahoga Valley National Recreation Area.) Within each county, the walks and hikes are organized by degree of difficulty for the average walker or hiker, i.e., easy, moderate, or strenuous. Several chapters contain several walks or hikes that may be taken singly or combined for a longer excursion.

Easy Walks usually involve no exertion beyond the pace and distance you set for yourself. Most of the easy walks in this book are in small parks, usually on trails under five miles long, and on terrain that is mostly flat. Others are in the towns of Vermilion, Oberlin, and Hudson Village and entail walking primarily on sidewalks. Easy walks or hikes often have something of historic, scenic, architectural, geological, or other unusual interest to enjoy. They are also generally suitable for children.

Moderate Hikes are usually 5 miles or more in length and entail ascending and descending moderate, or even steep hills for short distances. They may have uneven footing or present obstacles such as stream crossings, but they are generally suitable for average and more experienced hikers in good health.

Strenuous Hikes are usually between 5 and 10 miles and over hilly or rough terrain. Some of these hikes are in remote areas and require carrying a day pack with food and liquid and wearing sturdy boots. On these longer hikes there may be steep ascents and descents and stream crossings without the aid of bridges.

For all hikes described in *Beyond Cleveland On Foot* a note of CAUTION is inserted in the trail descriptions to warn hikers of hazards they need to be especially aware of, i.e., a steep cliff, dangerous erosion on the trail, a swift stream crossing, a bridle trail, an active railroad or road crossing, and any other potential threat to safety or enjoyment.

For any of the walks and hikes described, the prudent hiker, of course, may turn around at any point and return to the car earlier than anticipated. It is especially important to leave the woods when thunder is heard, no matter how distant, as a lightning storm can be very dangerous to the hiker.

Why walk?

Years ago everyone walked out of necessity—to work, to school, to the store. Taking a stroll was a common pastime. Nowadays, having grown up with all sorts of motorized transportation available, we seem to have far less need to walk. But there is value in taking to the woodland trails or even to the neighborhood sidewalks to get away from a frenetic modern lifestyle. Many have learned to love the peacefulness and rhythm of walking and hiking. They appreciate the benefits of physical exercise and the mental relaxation that ensues from participating in this sport. This guide will introduce some of the treasures and pleasures of northeast Ohio that you can easily observe on foot.

When out walking, slow down and observe. Look for wild animals and their footprints, many kinds of birds in all their splendor, a wide variety of ferns, mushrooms, trees, wildflowers, cloud formations, and stunning views.

How do you get started? The most important element is your mental attitude. The hardest part is making a determined effort to get out, perhaps alone or with a friend or an organized group. Once you get past all the excuses you can invent for not walking, you will soon find yourself anxious to go outdoors and begin exploring. There are beautiful days for outdoor exploring in northeast Ohio in every season.

HIKING PREPARATION

Advance planning for a hike is the key to a successful and enjoyable trip. Be Prepared Before You Leave Home. The most basic item to take with you on a hike or walk is a map of the area. Review the chapter in this book for the specific hike you wish to take and study its accompanying map. Sources for trail maps for other areas are listed in the next section, "Hiking Resources."

Next in importance is determining how much time to allow for the walk, what the degree of difficulty is, and how to reach the hiking area. These pointers are enclosed in the box at the beginning of each chapter's hike.

It is also good practice to carry a compass with you. Inexpensive models are available at any outdoor store. Most of the trail descriptions in this book refer to points of the compass and often direct you to head north, east, south, or west rather than make a left or right turn. It is helpful to learn the rudiments of reading a compass. At a minimum, the compass needle, which always points approximately north, will keep you from walking in circles should you lose your way. When you follow the direction in which you wish to go, or another one in consistent relation to it, you will eventually reach a road or other major landmark. You need to know in which direction you are heading when you start out on your hike, so that upon returning you can head in the opposite direction. In the woods, prominent landmarks, such as a stream or rock formation, will aid your orientation to the woods. (Not many trees are unusual enough to serve as a guide or landmark.)

When hiking, comfort is of utmost importance. Most hikers find it helpful to wear clothing in layers that can either be removed or added to as the temperature changes. Cotton keeps the body cooler in hot weather than synthetic fabrics. Wool in cool weather provides the greatest warmth even when it gets wet. Proper socks provide insulation, padding, and skin comfort. Most hikers prefer to wear two pairs—a thick wool outer sock and a thin cotton or propylene inner one.

Boots are the single most important piece of equipment you will acquire and the most difficult to choose. On some easy walks, tennis or walking shoes will be adequate, but on rough terrain and hills, boots with ankle support and a good tread will serve you better.

A beltpack or backpack is necessary for carrying snacks, lunch, water or juice, and extra clothing that you will put on or take off. Try to strike a balance between taking too much and taking too little. Generally, the lighter you go, the better. It is especially important to carry liquids in the pack in all seasons. One can get dehydrated easily without realizing it, even on a winter hike. Basic items to include in the pack are:

- Map
- Compass
- Adhesive strips, tissues
- Moleskin (to apply to sore spots on the feet)
- Insect repellent
- Canteen of water or juice
- Fruit, trail snacks, sandwich
- Pedometer (optional, to determine mileage)
- Small field guides for identifying flowers, trees, or birds.

Safety should be a concern but not a worry. All the hikes in this book are in public places, though sometimes not in heavily populated areas. If you have any doubts about an area, don't continue. This holds true for danger-ous weather conditions such as a sudden thunderstorm. Because there is safety in numbers, it is better to hike with a companion or in a group, so that help will be available in the event of an accident or injury.

On road hikes, make a habit of facing traffic as you walk, and walk in single file if traffic is heavy. On bridle trails when a horse and rider approach, trail safety requires that you stop immediately, step off to the side of the bridle path, and remain quiet and still until they are well beyond you. This behavior prevents a fearful horse from rearing up and injuring you or the rider. On paved all-purpose trails, keep to the right so that faster moving bicyclists and joggers may pass you.

Your own capacity and endurance should guide your pace and the dis-tance, and length of time you hike. The time suggested in these descrip-tions is based upon an average pace of 2-1/2 miles per hour or upon particular features of the hike. On steep hills the going will be somewhat slower. Walking uphill is harder on your heart and lungs, but walking downhill is harder on your knees. Adjust the pace according to your com-fort. A hiking stick is most helpful on hills, both going up and going down. Rest when your body tells you to, but not longer than a few minutes so as not to break your hiking rhythm.

As in every enterprise, using common sense is basic. You will develop trail sense, too. Watch the path for footprints and disturbed vegetation or leaves, especially in the fall when leaves nearly obscure the trail. You will learn to recognize the trail (when there are no trail blazes or markings) by an opening with noticeable clearing and lack of vegetation, or with wildlife tracks or human bootprints. You will gradually recognize these signs. If you feel you have lost the trail, turn around and retrace your steps to the last intersection. Observation is the key, not only for trail safety but for enjoyment, too.

A last reminder—use the carry in/carry out policy. Part of our responsibility in hiking, walking, and enjoying our great outdoors is to carry *out* whatever you carry *in*. Many dedicated hikers take along a small trash bag and routinely pick up litter as they walk. Some hiking clubs and other outdoor organizations regularly schedule trail clean-up hikes. The carry in/carry out philosophy includes carrying out *more* than you carry in. If everyone did this, consider how much we would enhance the walking experience for all.

Blazes

Trails are often marked by a special symbol repeated frequently on trees or posts indicating the trail's route. Sometimes it is the picture of a hiker, jogger, or cross-country skier on a metal marker nailed to the tree. More often, it is a colored patch painted on a tree six to eight feet above the path.

Illustrated below are typical Buckeye Trail blazes encountered on some of the trails described in this book. A single light-blue 2-by-6-inch blaze indicates the hiking trail is straight ahead. Two blazes, one above the other, indicate a turn in the trail: the lower blaze is always fixed and the *upper* blaze indicates the direction of the turn. A variation used for the turn sign is an arrow pointing toward the trail continuation.

Buckeye Trail Tree Blazes

Typical Buckeye Trail blazes: A single blaze indicates the hiking trail is straight ahead. The tree on the right shows two blazes, the upper blaze indicating the direction of the turn and the lower blaze remaining fixed.

HIKING RESOURCES

There are many more walks available in this area than could possibly be included, even in two books. I hope that, after trying the hikes in *Beyond Cleveland On Foot* and *Cleveland On Foot*, you will pursue some of these other hiking opportunities on your own and obtain information from the organizations listed below.

Lake County

General information about Lake County is available from Lake County Visitors Bureau, 216-951-5700, and Lake County History Center, 216-255-8979.

Lake Metroparks

Lake Metroparks consists of 24 parks and recreation areas encompassing more than 5,000 acres of land throughout Lake County. Among these facilities are Lake Farmpark, Children's Schoolhouse Nature Park, Concord Woods Nature Park (park headquarters), Erie Shores Golf Course, Fairport Harbor Lakefront Park, Lakefront Lodge, Lakeshore Reservation, and Pine Ridge Country Club. Penitentiary Glen Reservation features a large nature center and wildlife center. A free publication called *Parks Plus!* is a comprehensive listing of daily activities and programs of all kinds for all ages. In this guide, hikes in Lake Metroparks are described in Chapters 1, 2, 3, 4, 5, 7, and 8.

Information about Lake Metroparks can be obtained from Lake Metroparks, Concord Woods, 11211 Spear Rd., Concord Township, OH 44077; 216-639-7275 or 800-227-7275.

Headlands Beach State Park

Headlands Beach State Park (Ch. 6) and Headlands Dunes State Nature Preserve are located in Painesville Township in Lake County, just west of Fairport Harbor. These parks on Lake Erie offer pleasant beach walking. Walking on the sand is permitted, but visitors are asked not to walk on any growing plants.

Ohio's state wide Buckeye Trail begins (or ends) in Headlands Beach State Park and is marked with two-by-six-inch blue rectangles painted on trees or posts. Information about the park can be obtained from Headlands Beach State Park, 9601 Headlands Rd., Mentor, OH 44060; 216-257-1330 or 216-881-8141.

Headlands Dunes State Nature Preserve is located at the east end of Headlands Beach (216-563-9344).

Mentor Marsh State Nature Preserve

Mentor Marsh State Nature Preserve (Ch. 6) consists of 644 acres of land owned jointly by the Ohio Department of Natural Resources and the Cleveland Museum of Natural History. It is located 3.5 miles west of Painesville on SR (State Route) 283, then 0.5 mile north on Corduroy Rd. The blue-blazed Buckeye Trail is identified here as the Zimmerman Trail. There are other short hiking trails in the preserve accessible from local roads. Information can be obtained from Mentor Marsh State Nature Preserve, 5185 Corduroy Rd., Mentor, OH 44060; 216-257-0777 or 216-563-9344.

Holden Arboretum

The Holden Arboretum (Ch. 9) is a unique 2,800-acre private preserve of natural woodlands, horticultural collections, display gardens, ponds, fields, and ravines. A daily admission fee is charged to non-members who wish to use the many resources and trails available at Holden. Membership information is available from Holden Arboretum, 9500 Sperry Rd., Kirtland, OH 44094-5172; 216-946-4400.

Geauga County

General information about Geauga County is available from Geauga County Visitors Bureau, 800-775-8687, and Geauga County Historical Society, Century Village, 216-834-4012.

Geauga Park District

The Geauga Park District consists of 13 parks and nature preserves of which 8 are open to the public. The others will be open in the future, some by permit only, however. District headquarters is at the Donald W. Meyer Nature Center in Big Creek Park, Chardon. Geauga Park District publishes a free newsletter listing guided nature walks, canoe trips, and astronomy and other programs for all ages. Chapters 10-13 describe hikes in the Geauga Park District. Information and maps can be obtained from Geauga Park District, 9160 Robinson Rd., Chardon, Ohio 44024-9148; 216-285-2222, 216-564-7131.

Punderson State Park

Punderson State Park is located about 30 miles east of Cleveland in Geauga County, near the junctions of SR 87 and SR 44. The main entrance to the park is on SR 87, one mile west of this junction. A stately tudor manor house provides guest rooms, dining rooms, and meeting rooms. The 996-acre park also has housekeeping cabins, a camping area, an outdoor swimming pool, and Punderson Lake for boating, swimming, and fishing. Hiking trails surround the golf course and the glacially formed lakes and go through the wooded hills and open fields. Information can be obtained from Punderson State Park, Box 338, 11755 Kinsman Rd., Newbury, OH 44065; 216-564-2279 or 216-564-2201.

Portage County

General information about Portage County is available from Portage County Visitors Bureau, 800-648-6342, and Portage County Historical Society, 330-296-3523.

Nelson-Kennedy Ledges State Park

Nelson-Kennedy Ledges State Park (Ch. 14) is located north of the town of Nelson on SR 282 in the northeast corner of Portage County. This small 167-acre park has interesting hiking trails that wind through caves and ancient ledges that were formed millions of years ago. Information is available from Punderson State Park, Box 338, 11755 Kinsman Rd., Newbury, OH 44065; 216-564-2279 or 216-564-2201.

Tinker's Creek State Nature Preserve

Tinker's Creek State Nature Preserve (Ch. 17) is in both Portage and Summit counties and has several short hiking trails surrounding seven ponds. Adjacent to it is Tinker's Creek State Park, containing a 10-acre man-made lake for water recreation and one short hiking trail. Information about both parks is available from Tinker's Creek State Park, 5708 Esworthy Rd., SR 5, Ravenna, OH 44266-9659; 330-562-5515 or 330-527-5118.

Eagle Creek State Nature Preserve

Eagle Creek State Nature Preserve (Ch. 18) in Nelson Township is a 441-acre park in Portage County with a bird observation blind, a boardwalk, and a system of trails. Information is available from Ohio Department of Natural Resources (see address under Hach-Otis State Nature Preserve); 330-527-5118.

West Branch State Park

West Branch State Park (Ch. 20) is near the town of Campbellsport on SR 14, east of Ravenna. It offers 5,352 land acres and 2,650 water acres for recreational enjoyment. The Buckeye Trail follows the perimeter of Kirwan Lake over rolling terrain with ever-changing views for a challenging nine-mile hike. Information about facilities in the park can be obtained by writing to: West Branch State Park, 5708 Esworthy Rd., SR 5, Ravenna, OH 44266-9659; 330-296-3239.

Summit County

General information about Summit County is available from Summit County Visitors Bureau, 330-376-4254, and Summit County Historical Society, 330-535-1120.

Cuyahoga Valley National Recreation Area

The Cuyahoga Valley National Recreation Area (CVNRA), created in 1974, is a 33,000-acre natural valley administered by the National Park

Service of the U.S. Department of the Interior. Located primarily in Summit County but with a small section in Cuyahoga County, it preserves a beautiful 22-mile corridor of pastoral green space between Cleveland and Akron. It is easily accessible to residents of both cities for active recreation, for education, for study of nature and history, and for that refreshment of body and spirit so needed by those of us who are city dwellers.

The Cuyahoga River, remnants of the Ohio & Erie Canal and its towpath, and the historic Cuyahoga Valley Scenic Railroad extend down the center of the CVNRA. Miles of trails are found throughout the CVNRA, the most popular being the 19.5-mile Ohio & Erie Canal Towpath Trail. This hard-surfaced, flat path is open to hikers, bicyclists, and joggers between Rockside Rd. in Independence and Indian Mound Trailhead just south of Ira Rd. near Akron.

Hikes in the CVNRA vary in difficulty. Those described in this guide are: Tree Farm Trail (Ch. 24); Peninsula and Deep Lock Quarry Metro Park (Ch. 25); Brandywine Gorge and Stanford Trail (Ch. 26); Lake and Cross-Country Trails in Virginia Kendall Park (Ch. 27); Salt Run Trail in Kendall Park (Ch. 28); Old Carriage Trail (Ch. 29); and Boston Mills to Peninsula (Ch. 30).

The National Park Service (NPS) maintains headquarters in the small historic town of Jaite, on Vaughn Rd. at Riverview Rd. The restored yellow buildings in Jaite have been rehabilitated by the Park Service from old homes that once belonged to Jaite Paper Mill workers. They are now used for official activities of the NPS. Their address and phone are: National Park Service, 15610 Vaughn Rd., Brecksville, OH 44141-3018; 216-526-5256

Park rangers at two visitor centers provide scheduled programs, visitor assistance, trail maps, and information about the CVNRA. Canal Visitor Center is located in an old restored house near Hillside Rd., at 7104 Canal Rd., Valley View, OH 44147; 216-524-1497 or 800-445-9667. Happy Days Visitor Center is in Virginia Kendall Park on SR 303, east of the town of Peninsula and west of SR 8; 216-650-4636 or 800-257-9477. Both centers are open from 9 a.m. to 5 p.m. daily.

Metro Parks Serving Summit County

Created in 1921, Metro Parks consists of over 6,600 acres of land with 12 developed parks, a 23-mile Bike & Hike Trail, a nature center and arboretum, and several large conservation areas. Each year, Metro Parks naturalists conduct a full series of guided walks and bike rides, nature classes, and programs for all ages. *Green Islands*, a publication free to Summit County residents ($5 to all others), lists all the activities offered by Metro Parks.

Beyond Cleveland On Foot includes easy, moderate, and strenuous hikes in all twelve Metro Parks: Cascade Valley, Cascade Locks, Firestone, Furnace Run, Munroe Falls, Seiberling Naturealm, Gorge, Sand Run, Silver Creek, Goodyear Heights, Hampton Hills, and O'Neil Woods (Chapters 31-42).

For more information about these and other trails, contact Metro Parks Serving Summit County, 975 Treaty Line Rd., Akron, OH 44313-5898; 330-865-8060.

Portage Lakes State Park

Portage Lakes State Park (Ch. 23) is near SR 93 and SR 619, close to Akron. It consists of 1,000 land acres with hiking trails and 2,520 water acres. Information is available from Portage Lakes State Park, 5031 Manchester Rd., Akron, OH 44319-3999; 330-644-2220.

Medina County

General information about Medina County is available from Medina County Convention and Visitors Bureau, 330-722-5502.

Hinckley Reservation

Hinckley Reservation is the only one of Cleveland Metroparks' 14 reservations not in Cuyahoga County. Hinckley is the site of an annual event known as the return of the buzzards (actually turkey vultures), and is dominated by 90-acre Hinckley Lake. Whipp's Ledges (Ch. 46) and the smaller Worden's Ledges (Ch. 43) are composed of ancient rock formations deposited millions of years ago. Information is available from Cleveland Metroparks, 4101 Fulton Pkwy., Cleveland, OH 44144; 216-351-6300.

Medina County Park District

Medina County Park District (330-722-9364) consists of several developed parks with short hiking trails, and others that are in transition, either with limited access or still under development.

The developed parks with hiking trails are: Hubbard Valley Park (Ch. 44), Buckeye Woods Park, Letha House Park, Plum Creek Park (Ch. 45), and River Styx Valley Park. The parks still under development or with limited access are: Allardale, Alderfer-Oenslager Park, Hidden Hollow Park, Rail Trails, Chippewa Lake Nature Areas, and Princess Ledges. For more information about these parks write or call Medina County Park District, 6364 Deerview Lane, Medina, OH 44256; 330-722-9364, 330-225-7100 ext. 9364, or 330-336-6657 ext. 9364.

Lorain County

General information about Lorain County is available from Lorain County Visitors Bureau, 216-245-5282, and Great Lakes Historical Society, Inland Seas Maritime Museum, 216-967-3467.

Lorain County Metro Parks

Lorain County Metro Parks, formed in 1957, currently consists of seven

reservations totaling over 4,600 acres. A free quarterly publication, called
Arrowhead, lists guided hikes, walks, and nature programs in the parks
and at the nature and visitor centers. *Beyond Cleveland On Foot* includes
hikes in Black River Reservation (Ch. 48), Vermilion River Reservation
(Ch. 49), Carlisle Reservation (Ch. 50), and French Creek Reservation
(Ch. 52). Information and maps are available from Lorain County Metro
Parks, 12882 Diagonal Rd., LaGrange, OH 44050; 216-458-5121, 216-246-
2010, or 800-526-7275.

Findley State Park

Findley State Park (Ch. 51), is on SR 58 near Wellington, offers hiking
trails and recreational swimming and boating on Findley Lake. Information is available from Findley State Park, 25381 SR 58, Wellington, OH
44090; 216-647-4490.

Erie County

General information about Erie County is available from Erie County
Visitors Bureau, Sandusky, OH 44870; 800-255-ERIE.

Erie MetroParks

Erie MetroParks, organized in 1968, includes six park and recreation
areas: Osborn Recreation Area, Castalia Quarry Reserve, Pelton Park, Edison Woods Reserve, The Coupling Reserve, and James H. McBride
Arboretum. Nature education programs and interpretive events are listed
in a quarterly publication called *The Leaflet*. More information about Erie
MetroParks is available from Administrative Office, Osborn Recreation
Area, 3910 East Perkins Ave., Huron, OH 44839-1059; 419-625-7783.

Kelleys Island State Park

Kelleys Island (Ch. 56 and Ch. 57), the largest U.S. island in Lake Erie, is
the location of 661-acre Kelleys Island State Park. The Glacial Grooves of
Kelleys Island are internationally famous among geologists. When the
Wisconsinan glacier entered Ohio from northern Canada about 25,000
years ago, it deeply gouged the island's limestone bedrock. The mile-thick
sheet of ice sculpted round grooves in the rock that are dramatic upon first
viewing and gain impressiveness upon further reflection. Exposed are a
set of grooves 396 feet long, 25-30 feet wide, and 15 feet deep. More information is available from Kelleys Island State Park, Kelleys Island, OH
43438; 419-746-2546.

Cuyahoga County

Cleveland Metroparks

Cleveland Metroparks, established in 1917, celebrated its 75th anniversary in 1992. The park district consists of 19,069 acres of land in five counties and is governed by a three-person board of park commissioners that

oversees the 14 reservations and connecting parkways as well as Cleveland Metroparks Zoo and RainForest (216-661-6500). The tax district for Cleveland Metroparks includes all of Cuyahoga County, and Hinckley Township in Medina County. Lake, Lorain, and Summit counties own 3,428 acres of this land.

Information, maps, and a free publication, *The Emerald Necklace*, are available from Cleveland Metroparks, 4101 Fulton Pkwy., Cleveland, OH 44144-1923; 216-351-6300 (phone line available 24 hours).

Hiking trails in Cleveland Metroparks, except for Hinckley Reservation, are not included here. Many, however, are described in the companion volume to this book, *Cleveland On Foot*.

Hach-Otis State Nature Preserve

Hach-Otis State Nature Preserve is in Willoughby Township, one mile east of Willoughby Hills. Managed by the Ohio Department of Natural Resources (ODNR), Hach-Otis has short boardwalks and trails that provide spectacular views of the Chagrin River 150 feet below. Information can be obtained by calling 216-563-9344, or by writing to: ODNR, Division of Natural Areas and Preserves, Bldg. F, Fountain Square, Columbus, OH 43224; 614-265-6453.

Hiking Clubs

Sierra Club

The Sierra Club's northeast Ohio chapter can be reached by calling 216-843-7272. This group holds regular meetings and offers hiking, canoeing, and other activities for its members. Environmental education and conservation are major interests of the Sierra Club.

Buckeye Trail Association

The Buckeye Trail (BT) is a blue-blazed 1,200-mile-long trail extending around the perimeter of the state of Ohio, from Lake Erie in the north to Cincinnati in the south and to Toledo in the west. Much of the BT is on country roads, but a large portion of it goes through city and state parks, canal towpaths, forests, woods, and public and private lands.

This Ohio footpath was put together by volunteers of the Buckeye Trail Association (BTA) who conceived the idea, planned, laid out, and blazed the routes, and today take care of maintaining the trail. The BTA sells maps and guides for many portions of the trail, holds annual and regional meetings, and publishes a quarterly newsletter called *The Trailblazer*. To obtain information or to join, write to: Buckeye Trail Association, Inc., Box 254, Worthington, Ohio 43085.

Cleveland Hiking Club

The Cleveland Hiking Club (CHC), founded in 1919, celebrated its 75th Anniversary in 1994 and is one of the largest and oldest continually operating hiking clubs in the country. The CHC offers many opportunities for large-group hiking. Selected club hikes are listed in *The Emerald Necklace*, published by Cleveland Metroparks. The club also publishes its own schedule. Six club hikes must be completed before membership is obtained. Information is available from Cleveland Hiking Club, Box 347097, Cleveland, OH 44134-7097.

Other local and national resources

After getting started with walking and hiking in northeast Ohio, you may wish to consider joining a hiking organization as you get more involved in the sport. The previous sections have listed many local organizations to write to for information and maps. In addition, the organizations listed below may offer you an opportunity to do more walking, enhance your knowledge and enjoyment of nature, participate in volunteer trail maintenance work, and, of course, enjoy the friendship and fellowship of others who love walking and hiking and the out-of-doors.

Akron Metro Parks Hiking Club, 1435 Carey Ave., Akron, OH 44314

American Hiking Society, 1015 31st St. N.W., Washington, D.C. 20007

Appalachian Mountain Club, 5 Joy St., Boston, MA 02108

Appalachian Trail Conference, Box 807, Harpers Ferry, WV 25425

Cleveland Museum of Natural History, Wade Oval, Cleveland, OH 44106; 216-231-4600

Cuyahoga Valley Trails Council, Inc., 1607 Delia Ave., Akron, OH 44320

Keystone Trails Association, Box 251, Cogan Station, PA 17728

Nature Conservancy Ohio Chapter, 1504 West First Ave., Columbus, OH 43212; 614-486-4194

North Country Trail Association, Box 311, White Cloud, MI 49349

Ottawa National Wildlife Refuge, 14000 West SR 2, Oak Harbor, OH 43449; 419-898-0014

Rails-to-Trails Conservancy Ohio Chapter, Suite 307, 36 West Gay St., Columbus, OH 43215; 614-224-8707

Wilderness Center, 9877 Alabama Ave. S.W., Box 202, Wilmot, OH 44689-0202

THE HIKES

To the attentive eye each moment of the year has its own beauty, and in the same field, it beholds, every hour, a picture which was never seen before, and which shall never be seen again.

—Ralph Waldo Emerson, *Essay on Nature*

LAKE COUNTY

Lake County, bordering on Lake Erie, is one of northeast Ohio's prime water recreation areas, with plenty of opportunities for fishing, boating, and swimming. The county's proximity to the Lake also makes it a very favorable location for fruit and vegetable farming because produce is protected from an early frost by the warm lake temperatures. Grape growing is especially successful along Lake Erie thanks to this tempering effect. The Vintage Ohio wine festival is held annually at Lake Farmpark, and one of the county's vineyards, Chalet Debonne in Madison, has won national awards.

Painesville, the county seat, was founded in 1840 and was a major port of entry to the Western Reserve by way of Fairport Harbor and the Grand River. The village was an important stop on the road between Buffalo and Cleveland during the 19th century and continued to prosper when the Cleveland, Painesville, and Ashtabula Railroad came through.

Ohio's largest natural sandy beach is in Mentor—Headlands Beach State Park, with its 125 acres of sandy shoreline. Mentor Marsh and Headlands Dunes state nature preserves are unique natural features of Lake County. Headlands Dunes is one of the last dune ecosystems along Lake Erie, and Mentor Marsh harbors a wide variety of plant and animal life (Ch. 6).

Other major attractions of Lake County include Fairport Marine Museum, Holden Arboretum (largest arboretum in the nation), Kirtland Temple, the James A. Garfield National Historical Site/Lawnfield, and Lake County History Center.

Lake Metroparks provides many recreational and educational opportunities in its 24 public parks and other facilities. Information is available from Lake Metroparks, 11211 Spear Rd., Concord Twp., OH 44077; 216-639-7275 or 800-227-7275.

Additional information about Lake County is available from Lake County Visitors Bureau, 1610 Mentor Ave., Painesville, OH 44077; 800-368-5253 or 216-951-5700.

1 INDIAN POINT PARK AND PAINE FALLS

Easy

Description: The ridgetop trail slopes downhill somewhat from east to west but is wide and easy to follow, although there are no trail blazes. Use CAUTION on any of the side trails that lead over to the cliff edge, where there are long sweeping views of the Grand River and Paine Creek below.

Directions: From I-90 take Exit 205, Vrooman Rd. Drive north on Vrooman Rd. about a mile. Watch for a right turn at the foot of the hill. Turn right (east) here onto Seeley Rd., a rough dirt road leading to the lower park entrance on the left.

Parking & restrooms: Parking areas and restrooms are available at both the lower and upper entrances.

Indian Point Park, listed on the National Register of Historic Places because of its 500-year-old Indian mounds, is one of Lake Metroparks' most geologically and historically interesting reservations. Located on Seeley Rd. in Leroy Township at the confluence of Paine Creek and the Grand River, this small park is primarily located high on a ridge overlooking both the creek and the river. The Grand River watershed drains about 40 percent of Lake County land.

A central hogback ridge of Chagrin Shale, steeply sloped and formed by erosion, separates Paine Creek from the Grand River. In 1974 the Grand River received a State Wild and Scenic River designation because of its steeply incised, 360-million-year-old Chagrin Shale walls. Multiple layers of this soft gray shale (fossilized mud) are interspersed with harder, light-colored siltstone overlaid with vertical erosion marks. Because of the high cliffs in this small park, hikers enjoy rewarding views of the river and valleys below, particularly in early spring and late autumn, when the trees have lost their leaves.

Two parallel mounds on top of the ridge and the ditches alongside it provide an interesting record of the late prehistoric settlement period called the Whittlesey Tradition. Farming people who lived along the Grand River from about 1250 to 1650 A. D. built villages high on isolated plateaus overlooking this and other river valleys.

Also on the ridge is a sheltered totem stone engraved in 1910 with the names of high school boys staying at Camp Wissalohichan, a boys' military camp.

Picnic areas, restroom, drinking water, fishing, and hiking are available in Indian Point Park.

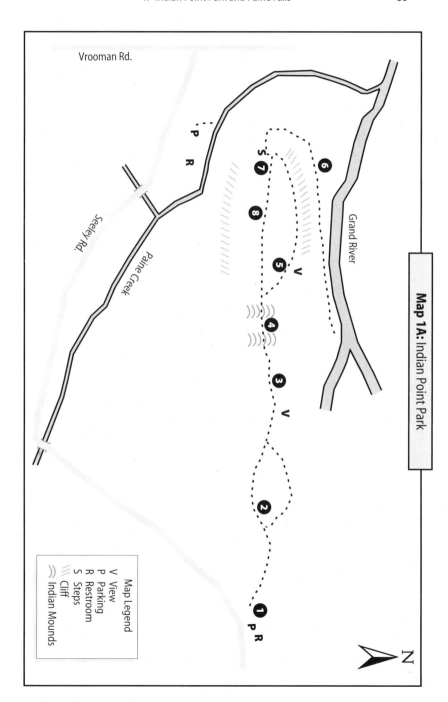

Map 1A: Indian Point Park

Map Legend
V View
P Parking
R Restroom
S Steps
)) Cliff
Indian Mounds

Option: At the lower park entrance there is a magnificent view of the Chagrin Shale cliff directly ahead. While it is possible to reach the ridgetop from here by crossing Paine Creek and ascending steps on a very steep hill, this hike begins farther east. Continue on Seeley Rd. to the upper entrance across a small bridge over a creek tributary and a larger steel bridge spanning Paine Creek (in winter this road may be impassable). Follow the road uphill to reach the upper parking and picnic area on the left.

(NOTE: If you elect to begin the hike at the first park entrance, and if the water of Paine Creek is low, follow the stream westward a short distance to find rocks that allow you to cross the stream without getting your feet wet. On the north side of the creek and at the nose of the cliff is a set of 145 wooden steps leading up to the top of the cliff. At the top, follow the trail straight ahead (east) and follow the trail descriptions below in reverse order.)

HIKE A: INDIAN POINT PARK

Distance: 1 mile
Hiking time: 1 hour

1. Begin the hike to the left (west) of the picnic tables, passing through the opening in the split rail fence. Avoid taking the trail on the right (north) and take the trail heading west. After 0.1 mile this old woods road reaches a fork.

2. Bear left (west) at this fork and continue on the main trail. Pass another trail intersection, where you will stay left on the main trail.

3. Continue walking westward through a lovely hemlock forest that graces the top of this steep hogback ridge. On the right far below is the Grand River. At 0.3 mile on the left is a bronze plaque affixed to a glacial boulder dedicated to the memory of Edna Crofoot Phelps, a member of the Crofoot family to whom this land was transferred by the Connecticut Land Company in 1802.

4. The trail crosses over the first of two parallel north-south earthworks built across the ridge of land between Paine Creek and the Grand River. These mounds are 3 to 5 feet high, 8 feet deep, and 150 feet long. On the right is an Ohio Historic Marker describing this as a prehistoric Indian fortification. However, it is currently believed that these mounds date to the Whittlesey period. Stockaded villages are known to have been built on high ridges in northeast Ohio after about 1200 A.D., and this one can be dated to before 1650. Archaeological research has revealed that the farmers of the Whittlesey Tradition were not Erie Indians, as originally thought, but in fact predate them.

These two large mounds are all that remain of north-south walls where earth had been piled high at the base of posts. The naturally steep embankments of the ridge provided a safe location for a village. Houses may have been built of saplings and bark or thatch. Corn, squash, beans, and other crops were cultivated nearby with hoes made of sticks and musselshells. Food was prepared and stored in elaborate pottery jars. The natives hunted with bows and arrows and fished with bone hooks and nets. Music was performed on flutes, drums, and rattles. The Whittlesey Tradition is thought to have been destroyed by Iroquois Indians in 1653.

5. Just beyond the historic marker, take the side trail on the right that leads along the top of the cliff for views of beautiful Grand River below on the right.

CAUTION: Stay behind the fence that has been erected to protect hikers from a steep drop over the severely eroded shale cliff edges.

At a park bench, pause for an outstanding view of the Grand River in both directions. To the northwest is a view of the confluence of Paine Creek and the Grand River.

6. Continue west along this side trail until it meets the main trail and the 145-step wooden stairs ahead.

OPTION: From this point you may descend the steps to the bottom then turn right (north) and right again (east) on a small fishing trail that parallels the Grand River. If you do this, look up at the fine Chagrin Shale cliff on the right. You will see interspersed layers of harder, fine-grained siltstone and vertical erosion marks made in the gray shale (see Appendix A). The trail soon peters out—it is primarily used by fishermen along this stretch of the river. Retrace your steps to the stairs and ascend them to the top.

7. Take the main trail going east. (Avoid the parallel side trail that you came on curving toward the northeast.) On the right at the top is a wooden platform from which to enjoy a long view of Paine Creek on the south. Continue along the main trail (east).

8. Reach a granite boulder protected under a small shelter, the Camp Wissalohichan totem stone (1910). Barely visible are a carved symbol and the names of campers who attended this military camp for high-school boys in the early 1900s.

Continue on the main trail over the two prehistoric earthworks and past the trail junctures on the left to return to the parking area.

HIKE B: PAINE FALLS PARK

Distance: 0.1 mile

Hiking time: 1/4 hour

Description: Close to Indian Point Park is Paine Falls Park, a very small scenic area along Paine Creek with a picnic shelter, restrooms, and a short loop trail to the 30-foot falls.

Directions: To reach this park from Indian Point Park, continue east on Seeley Rd. about 3/4 mile to Paine Rd. Turn right (south) on Paine Rd. and follow it about 200 feet to the park entrance on the right, where there is ample parking.
•From I-90, take Exit 205 (Vrooman Rd.) and follow Vrooman Rd. south to Carter Rd. Turn left (east) on Carter to Paine Rd. At Paine Rd. turn left (north), cross the bridge to the park entrance on the left.

1. Enter the trail west of the picnic shelter. A Historic Marker at the head of the trail commemorates Hendrick E. Paine, nephew of Edward Paine, the founder of Painesville. Hendrick Paine, born in 1789, was an early settler from East Windsor, Connecticut, and at the age of 29 built a log cabin and settled here in what was called Paine's Hollow. He built a sawmill at the brow of the falls, and soon an ashery where potash was made. A blacksmith shop, iron forge and furnace, and wagon shop followed. In 1828, Parkman Baker built a tannery nearby, and by 1840 this was a thriving industrial center of Leroy Township with many log homes and a school. Over-foresting of trees and subsequent flooding caused the demise of Paine's Hollow by 1850.

2. Take the steps to descend to a gravel trail and boardwalk for a lovely view of Paine Falls cascading over many layers of Chagrin Shale. This grayish shale is thought to have been deposited as mud and silt under an inland sea that covered Ohio about 360 million years ago. There are several tiers of very picturesque falls coursing over fossilized mud layers. Chagrin Shale is the lowermost and oldest rock unit exposed in this area (see Appendix A).

3. The loop trail continues up 61 steps to the parking area.

Patricia Morse, Naturalist, Lake Metroparks, reviewed this chapter for accuracy.

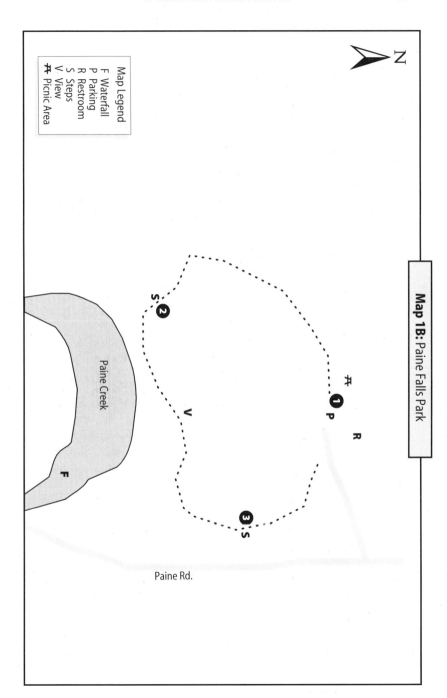

Map Legend
F Waterfall
P Parking
R Restroom
S Steps
V View
☰ Picnic Area

N

Map 1B: Paine Falls Park

Paine Creek

Paine Rd.

2 HIDDEN VALLEY PARK

Distance: 1 mile

Easy

Hiking time: 3/4 hour

Description: The one main trail in this park begins at the parking area and follows the edge of the Grand River below high Chagrin Shale cliffs. This short, pleasant walk is on a flat, well-delineated trail. Beaver may sometimes be seen swimming in the river, and there is evidence of their chisel work on trees alongside the river.

Directions: From I-90 take Exit 212 (SR 528). Take SR 528 (Madison Rd.) south, past River Rd. to Klasen Rd. Turn right on Klasen. Follow it downhill to the park entrance on the left.

Parking & restrooms: The parking area is off Klasen Rd.; restrooms are located near the picnic area.

Hidden Valley Park, situated in Lake County's Madison Township, is a small, scenic park on the Grand River offering fishing, hiking, canoeing, picnicking, a playground, playing field, and sledding hill. The park borders the beautiful Grand River below a spectacular Chagrin Shale cliff, one of the best examples in the county of exposed outcrop of this shale. Most of this grayish shale is beneath the surface of the great lake plain to the east. Interspersed in the shale is fine-grained, harder siltstone that juts out from the surface of the softer shale. Vertical erosion marks are also a feature of this exposed, 360-million-year-old cliff.

Attractive views of the wide, scenic river are visible from a riverside trail. The Grand River, considered by some to be among the finest natural streams in Ohio, was designated a State Wild and Scenic River in 1974. After rainfalls in the spring and summer, pretty waterfalls cascade over the steep Chagrin Shale cliff walls. Nearby Hogback Ridge is close enough for both parks to be easily be visited on the same day.

1. The paved trail begins at the parking lot. Follow it westward between the sledding hill and the restroom building to the split-rail fence. Follow the path westward and across a wooden bridge over a small stream.

2. About 50 feet past the bridge, pass a small trail intersection on the left. Continue straight ahead (southwest) past beautiful hemlock, sycamore, and maple trees. Sweeping views of the Grand River appear on the right.

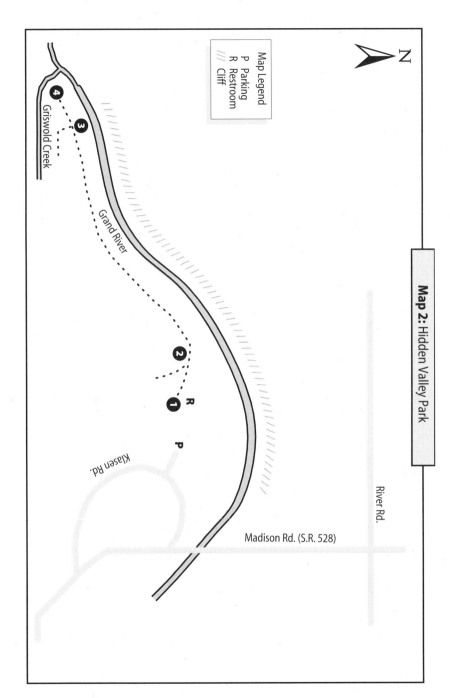

Here, find visible evidence of busy beavers at work. Like those of all rodents, the beaver's ever-growing incisor teeth are covered with a hard enamel on the front and a softer dentine on the back. As the beaver gnaws, the back wears faster than the front, thus providing an ingenious self-sharpening system. Beavers usually favor aspen, willow, and birch trees for food and whatever else they can cut down for construction of dams, ponds, and lodges.

The American beaver, an aquatic rodent with a glossy brown fur coat and paddle-shaped tail, can remain submerged for up to 15 minutes. Ordinarily, beavers build lodges, but here they may burrow into the mud alongside the river to create their living quarters. Sometimes you may see evidence of a beaver dam that these animals have built beside the river, but they are frequently washed away by the river's current.

CAUTION: Avoid touching the many stinging nettle plants that thrive along this trail in the summer and fall. The stem of this plant is densely covered with stiff, bristly, stinging hairs.

3. At about 0.4 mile, pass a trail on the left that goes uphill on soft shale steps cut into the hill.

CAUTION: Avoid taking this unimproved path as it is a steep, dangerous uphill climb over badly eroded tree roots and rocks.

Farther ahead, Griswold Creek enters the Grand River, but this confluence is on private property and cannot be reached on this trail.

4. Retrace your steps alongside the river going in the reverse direction to enjoy different views as you return to the parking area.

This chapter was reviewed by Patricia Morse, Lake Metroparks Naturalist.

Mike Dolence

3 PENITENTIARY GLEN RESERVATION

Easy

Distance: 4 miles

Hiking time: 2 hours

Description: The trails on this hike are generally flat and include both paved walkways and dirt paths. The gravel Bobolink Loop provides views of the deep gorge, and the Gorge Rim Loop affords close-up views of this natural feature. An optional walk down a 130-step stairway allows a view of a small waterfall and close-up observation of the gorge.

Directions: From I-90 take Exit 193 (SR 306). Follow SR 306 south to Kirtland-Chardon Rd. (at the foot of the hill) and turn left (southeast). Continue southeast on K-C Rd. two miles. Entrance for Penitentiary Glen Reservation is on the right. Holden Arboretum (Ch. 9) is farther ahead and can be visited by going north on Sperry Rd.

Parking & restrooms: At the nature center.

Originally established in 1980, Penitentiary Glen Reservation is a 360-acre park named for the very deep gorge that cuts through it. The gorge itself is not a part of this hike because of its ecologically sensitive fauna and rocky steepness. It may be seen only on a guided hike led by a park naturalist. Reservations may be made by calling 216-256-7275 or 800-669-9226.

In 1992, Penitentiary Glen opened a new and greatly expanded Penitentiary Glen Nature Center. It houses a large nature display room, the Don C. Strock Library, the Nature Connection gift shop, classrooms, a wildlife window, and a 150-seat auditorium. The older portion of this building was the horse barn for the Samuel Halle family, who once owned this land and maintained a summer home here. Well-marked trails, ponds, a picnic shelter, a handicapped-accessible observation deck, and an outdoor amphitheater are among other improvements made to Penitentiary Glen.

A wildlife rehabilitation center, located behind the nature center, displays injured animals that can no longer maintain themselves in the wild. There, the animals are cared for and featured in wildlife education programs. The main goal of the center is to rehabilitate and release these animals to the wild.

The Penitentiary Glen Railroad, located west of the center, is operated

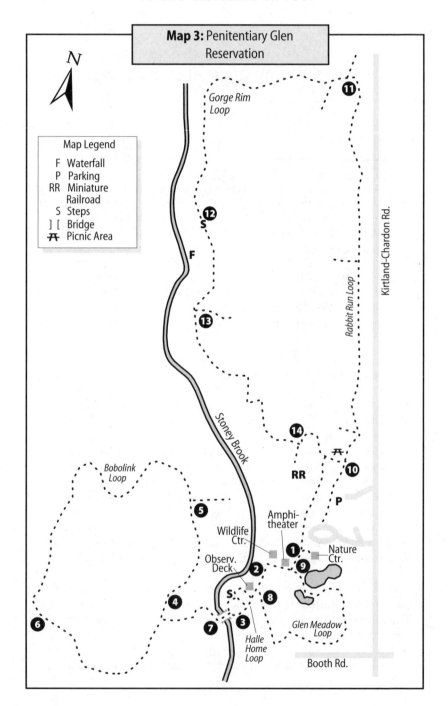

Map 3: Penitentiary Glen Reservation

N

Gorge Rim Loop

Kirtland-Chardon Rd.

Rabbit Run Loop

Map Legend
F Waterfall
P Parking
RR Miniature Railroad
S Steps
] [Bridge
Picnic Area

S

F

Stoney Brook

Bobolink Loop

RR

P

Amphi-theater

Wildlife Ctr.

Observ. Deck

Nature Ctr.

S

Glen Meadow Loop

Halle Home Loop

Booth Rd.

by the Lake Shore Live Steamers Club and offers free miniature steam railroad rides during the summer months.

An annual Ohio wine festival is held in early August at nearby Lake Farmpark, another unit of Lake Metroparks. This 235-acre science and cultural center with over 50 breeds of livestock is located on Chardon Rd. (US 6) in Kirtland. To reach Lake Farmpark from Penitentiary Glen, continue southeast on Kirtland-Chardon Rd. to Sperry Rd. Turn right (south) on Sperry Rd. to Chardon Rd. (US 6), then right (west) on US 6 to Lake Farmpark on the left (8800 Chardon Rd., Kirtland 44094). Open 9 a.m. to 5 p.m. year round, the park charges a small admission fee (216-256-2122 or 800-366-FARM).

1. Start the walk at the nature center and stop in to see the exhibits and other features of the center. Once outside, view the raptors tethered to their stands in the Wildlife Rehabilitation Center. Walk past the amphitheater on the right. Turn right on the paved Glen Meadow Loop to the Observation Deck on the right for a view of the gorge. Down below is Stoney Creek, responsible for carving this deep valley through bedrock and thus exposing layers of sedimentary shale and sandstone that were formed 360 million years ago, when this area was covered by an inland sea.

On the railing of the deck is a thoughtful quotation that reads: "Within ourselves there is a deep place at whose edge we may sit and dream."

2. Follow the loop past the Halle family's original rose garden, now a wildflower and rhododendron garden, and descend the steps ahead. Here on the embankment is the porch foundation—all that remains of the summer house that this wealthy Cleveland family enjoyed from the 1920s to 1940s. As you walk along the lower part of the Halle Home Loop, you will notice on your right the broken dam across the brook. This cement wall once held back water to form a swimming pool for the family to enjoy on hot summer days. Berea Sandstone was quarried here for construction of the property's original buildings and walkways.

3. Continue to the Bobolink Loop sign, cross the bridge, and ascend the small rise to a trail intersection.

4. Turn right onto the 1-mile gravel Bobolink Loop. Follow this path northward.

5. A path to the right leads to the gorge rim on a side trail for a scenic view. Retrace steps to the Bobolink Loop.

6. Continue on the Bobolink Loop through a beautiful meadow with tall prairie grass (in the summer and fall); the land originally was a plowed field on the Halle farm. Many birds may be heard in the meadow; groundhogs burrow in holes in the field. A large variety of wildflowers thrives in this sunny meadow in the spring, summer, and fall.

The gravel trail shortly leads into and out of the woods and loops around the field past a side trail that goes to Booth Rd. Turn right to return to the bridge, completing the loop.

7. Follow the trail back across the bridge over Stoney Brook, go up the hill and past the wildflower garden and observation deck.

8. Turn right onto the paved Glen Meadow Loop; this loop ends near the marsh and pond behind the nature center.

9. A variety of water fowl are often observed at the pond, as well as turtles, frogs, snakes, and many kinds of plants. Turn right to pass the amphitheater (on the left) and continue past the nature center (on the right). Follow the paved trail past the bulletin board and miniature railroad on the left.

10. At the trail intersection in front of the picnic shelter, turn right then left to reach Rabbit Run Loop, which becomes a wide gravel road. Avoid taking the Rabbit Run cut-off on the left and continue ahead to the sign marking a service road.

11. Bear left at the service road sign and just ahead enter the Gorge Rim Loop. This trail goes through a beautiful beech, maple, and oak forest to the rim of the gorge, then bends around to the southeast.

12. On the right at about the midpoint of the trail is a set of 130 wooden steps going down into the gorge. This side trip is worth the effort. At the bottom of the stairs is a viewing area from which to observe small, pretty Stoney Brook Falls. Tiny cascades fall over many thin layers of shale to create a picturesque view. These Chagrin Shale layers were deposited 360 million years ago at the bottom of the inland sea and have been exposed by the relentless cutting action of the stream. Stoney Brook Gorge exposes many layers of ancient rock in sequence from youngest to oldest: Berea Sandstone, viewed near the start of the hike; Bedford Formation; Cleveland Shale; and here, Chagrin Shale (see Appendix A).

13. Turn right (south) at the top of the stairs and continue along the path, bypassing the Gorge Rim shortcut trail on the left. This portion of the Gorge Rim Loop provides the best views of beautiful, deep Penitentiary Gorge. Large hemlock trees have been growing in this hospitably cool climate for many, many years. These giants, however, are occasionally uprooted by soil erosion and fall over into the gorge. Stunning moss-covered rocks and feathery ferns also enhance the beauty of this wonderfully cool, moist environment.

14. Follow Gorge Rim Loop back to Rabbit Run Loop by turning left at a "T" junction, heading north, then east to Rabbit Run Loop to return to the parking area. Children may enjoy a visit to the Penitentiary Glen Railroad for free rides, if it is open on the day of your visit.

Patricia Morse, Naturalist at Lake Metroparks, reviewed this chapter for accuracy.

4 HOGBACK RIDGE

Distance: 1 mile

Moderate

Hiking time: 1 hour

Description: The 3/4-mile Hemlock Ridge Loop begins on a wooden boardwalk and continues on a wide gravel trail high above the cliffs. The hike also includes a steep climb down (and back up) a set of 138 steps to continue the walk on the Bluebell Valley Trail to a waterfall on Mill Creek. The hike continues on the north and west sides of the Hemlock Ridge Loop. (An optional extension to this hike descends to Mill Creek on the Old Emerson Rd. Trail.)

Directions: From I-90 take Exit 212 (SR 528). Go south on SR 528 (Madison Rd.) to Griswold Rd. Turn left (east) on Griswold Rd. to Emerson Rd. Emerson leads north directly into the park.

Parking & restrooms: At the park entrance.

Lake County's Hogback Ridge, located off Madison Rd. in Madison Township, is a small park containing a 100-foot-high, semicircular hogback, or narrow ridge, between the Mill Creek on the north and Grand River on the south. This prominent ridge with steep valleys on either side is so named because it resembles the bony spine of a hog. It is thought to have been used by prehistoric Indians, although excavations in 1929 revealed few artifacts. There are no hiking trails on the hogback itself.

In the 1800s the Emerson family, for whom the park entrance road is named, operated a mill near the confluence of Mill Creek and Grand River. Old Emerson Rd. Trail is a park path that follows this old road downhill to Mill Creek. Local residents used to ford the stream to reach a continuation of the road on the opposite side. Old Emerson Rd. Trail is now used by people fishing the stream for bass, bluegill, and steelhead salmon.

The period from late March through the end of May is the best time to identify abundant spring wildflowers in Hogback Ridge. Be sure to bring along a wildflower book to enjoy this activity to its fullest when visiting the park at that time.

Picnic facilities, restroom, and drinking water are all available here. Nearby, Chalet Debonne Vineyards (7734 Doty Rd., just east of Emerson Rd.) is open year round (216-466-3485 or 800-424-9463).

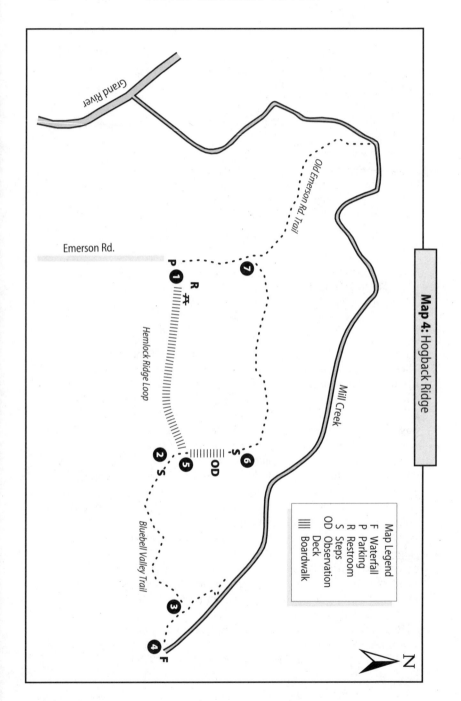

Map 4: Hogback Ridge

Grand River

Emerson Rd.

Old Emerson Rd. Trail

Hemlock Ridge Loop

Mill Creek

Bluebell Valley Trail

P ①

R

②
⑤
⑥
⑦

③
④

OD
S
S

F

Map Legend
F   Waterfall
P   Parking
R   Restroom
S   Steps
OD Observation
    Deck
|||| Boardwalk

N

1. Enter the Hemlock Ridge Loop at the southeast corner of the picnic area at the fence gates opening onto a wooden boardwalk. This path winds through a beautiful maple and beech forest to a bench that invites a pause to view the valley below. Spring wildflowers grow in abundance here, especially trillium, squirrel corn, trout lily, spring beauty, hepatica, and several kinds of violets.

2. At 0.2 mile reach a trail junction and some steps on the right. Descend the ridge on the 138 sloping timber steps to the flood plain. At the foot of the steps, the Bluebell Valley Trail (not marked with tree signs) leads directly to Mill Creek. Gorgeous bluebells thrive in this moist environment in late April and early May.

3. When you reach the bank of Mill Creek, note this point carefully, because it is here that you will make a sharp left turn to get back to the wooden steps on the return portion of the hike. (You may wish to mark it with a bit of ribbon that you can remove.)

At the creek, turn right (southeast) and follow the path closely, hugging the bank of the stream.

4. At about 0.4 mile, and just before a hill, you will see a very pretty waterfall on Mill Creek cascading over many layers of shale. It is interesting to contemplate the power of this small stream that, over millions of years, has cut through to form the ridge.

CAUTION: Do not approach closer to the falls, as there has been severe undercutting of the river bank here.

Return along the same path (to the turn described in Note #3). Turn left (west) and follow the path to the steps.

5. At the top, turn right (north) and continue on the boardwalk to the Observation Deck.

6. At the end of the boardwalk, descend several timber steps on the gravel path to continue the Hemlock Ridge Loop. In the fall or spring when the lack of leaves permits a view, Mill Creek can be seen below on the right. Continue to follow the gravel trail through the forest.

White, black, and chestnut oaks dominate the forest above this river valley. The understory is home to other wildflowers that you may spot in the spring: pipsissewa, Canada mayflower, solomon's seal, foxglove, or wild indigo.

7. At 0.9 mile meet a juncture with the Old Emerson Rd. Trail. Turn left (south) here to return on the path and up a set of steps to a picnic shelter and the parking area.

OPTION: If you elect to turn right (north) on the 0.5-mile Old Emerson Rd. Trail, you will follow the badly eroded path downhill to Mill Creek and subsequently return uphill on the same trail.

Patricia Morse, Naturalist, Lake Metroparks, reviewed this chapter for accuracy of trail descriptions.

5 HELL HOLLOW WILDERNESS AREA

Distance: Less than 1 mile

Moderate

Hiking time: 3/4 hour

Description: The main trail leads from the picnic area along a ridge and down a set of 262 very steep timber steps that descend in a switchback pattern to the creek valley below and to Paine Creek.
CAUTION: There are no marked trails in the valley, and those that are visible are not maintained by Lake Metroparks. Because this is a wilderness area, it is very easy to get lost near the creek. Therefore it is advisable to return via the steps to the upper level of the park.
The views from the top of the cliff, the ambiance of the quiet woods, and the view of Paine Creek all make a visit to Hell Hollow well worth while.

Directions: Because Leroy Center Rd. is closed west of the park, a rather roundabout route is necessary to reach Hell Hollow. From I-90 take Exit 205, Vrooman Rd. Follow Vrooman south for a half mile to Carter Rd. Turn left (east) on Carter, and follow for 2 miles to Paine Rd. and turn left (north). Head north on Paine for 1 mile to Ford Rd. and turn right. Continue east on Ford to Trask Rd. Turn right (south) at Trask to Brockway Rd. Continue south on Brockway to Leroy Center Rd. Turn right (west) on Leroy Center Rd. to the park entrance on the right.

Parking & restrooms: Just inside the park entrance.

Hell Hollow Wilderness Area is notable for its high clifftop overlooking the valley of Paine Creek. Located in Leroy Township, this 708-acre park is similar to others in Lake County in that it includes a 360-million-year-old Chagrin Shale cliff above a deep river valley. The more than 100-foot-deep ravine was carved thousands of years ago by the cutting action of Paine Creek after glaciers finally retreated from Ohio. Paine Creek flows northwest and empties into the Grand River at Indian Point Park, north of I-90 (Ch. 1).

Hell Hollow offers a picnic shelter, restrooms, drinking water, a play area, and baseball diamond.

1. The gravel trail begins at the split-rail fence north of the picnic area. Views of Paine Creek open up below on the left.
CAUTION: Please stay behind the fence to enjoy these views safely.
2. An alternate parallel trail comes in from the right to join the main

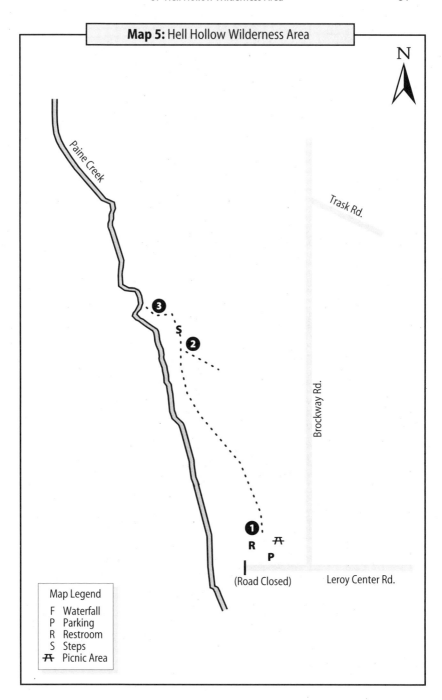

Map 5: Hell Hollow Wilderness Area

N

Paine Creek

Trask Rd.

Brockway Rd.

S

R

P

(Road Closed)

Leroy Center Rd.

Map Legend

F Waterfall
P Parking
R Restroom
S Steps
☴ Picnic Area

trail near the top of the 262 steps. Descend these steep steps to the bottom and continue ahead to the creek.

CAUTION: Do not follow the non-maintained trail, as it is easy to get lost in this semi-wilderness area.

3. Reach the creek for a pleasant view of the stream flowing over ancient shale.

Return along the creek to the timber steps, ascend to the top, and reach the picnic and parking area on the same gravel trail as before.

Patricia Morse, Naturalist, Lake Metroparks, reviewed this chapter for accuracy.

6 HEADLANDS BEACH STATE PARK AND MENTOR MARSH

Distance: 6 miles

Moderate

Hiking time: 2-1/4 hours

Description: This hike starts at Headlands Beach and follows the blue-blazed Buckeye Trail (also called the Zimmerman Trail) along a hummock on the west side of Mentor Marsh. Tall reed grass and cattails grow in the marsh alongside stumps of dead trees from a once-lush forest. Many birds, waterfowl, and other varieties of wildlife thrive in Mentor Marsh.

Directions: From SR 2 take the exit for SR 44 (north). At the end of the off-ramp, turn left (north) directly to Headlands Beach State Park.

Parking & restrooms: Park in the lot farthest to the east (P-1). Several restrooms are located along the beach.

Headlands Beach State Park, Headlands Dunes State Nature Preserve, and Mentor Marsh State Nature Preserve are all under the jurisdiction of the Ohio Department of Natural Resources (which manages Mentor Marsh jointly with the Cleveland Museum of Natural History). Many activities, guided hikes, and programs are offered by a naturalist at Mentor Marsh Nature Center, 5185 Corduroy Rd., Mentor 44060; 216-257-0777.

The four-mile-long, 750-acre Mentor Marsh, a National Natural Landmark, features exceptional diversity of plants and animals. Many birds, ducks, reptiles, amphibians, and insects thrive in this rich environment. The miles of open area contain the tall plume grass *Phragmites australis*, an invasive plant that is crowding out native species.

The wetland was formed by the Grand River, which formerly flowed through what is now Mentor Marsh and emptied into Lake Erie several miles west of here. During the 800 to 1,000 years the Grand River took to find its present outlet at Fairport Harbor, the old river channel gradually changed from swamp forest to marsh.

1. Begin the hike at the Buckeye Trail sign at the north end of parking lot P-1. Beyond the sign to the right is Headlands Dunes State Nature Preserve. This vast accumulation of sand along the Lake Erie shoreline was created by wind and water along the western side of the mouth of the Grand River. Each year the sandy shoreline builds up and extends farther out into the lake because of the existence of the breakwall at the river's mouth.

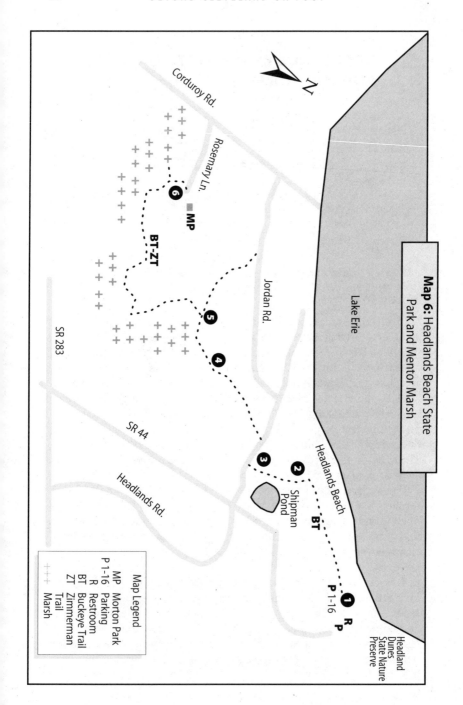

Map 6: Headlands Beach State Park and Mentor Marsh

N

Lake Erie

Corduroy Rd.

Rosemary Ln.

MP

BT-ZT

Jordan Rd.

❺

❹

SR 283

SR 44

Headlands Rd.

❸

❷
Shipman Pond

Headlands Beach

BT

❶
P 1-16
R
P

Headland Dunes State Nature Preserve

Map Legend

MP   Morton Park
P 1-16 Parking
R   Restroom
BT   Buckeye Trail
ZT   Zimmerman Trail
+++   Marsh
      Trail

This nature preserve is open to the public for research, nature study, bird watching, art, and photography, but visitors are asked to walk only on the sand and not disturb any of the rare plants growing here. Plant species found here include dune-making switchgrass and beach grass, sea rocket, and beach pea. Monarch butterflies often stop to rest here on their long migration between Canada and Mexico.

Start this hike by going west on the paved walkway, enjoying the views of Lake Erie. There are few blue blazes here, because the trail passes parking areas, picnic shelters, and the Ranger Office and First Aid Station.

2. At the parking area marked P-16, turn left (southeast) and go through the park service area at the sign "Service Only." Turn right (west) at Headlands Rd. and go uphill a short distance. Shipman Pond is hidden on the left (east).

3. On the left is the Shipman Pond parking lot and the start of the Zimmerman Trail. The trail is marked both with blue blazes of the Buckeye Trail and white blazes of the Zimmerman.

4. Enter cool woods to find a well-used trail with several wooden footbridges over wet spots. On the left are views of the marsh. You will see very large old oaks and maples along the trail, as well as numerous saplings.

5. Bear left at a trail intersection (1.6 miles). In the autumn and winter there are lovely long views of the marshlands on the left. Continue to follow the gently rolling trail another 1.5 miles to reach another intersection.

6. Just ahead is a wooden fence where the trail bears right and comes out to Morton Park, a recreation area with a playground, private pool, and restrooms.

The Buckeye Trail continues west along Rosemary Lane, but this hike returns back along the same route to Headlands Beach.

7 CHAPIN FOREST RESERVATION

Distance: 4.5 miles

Moderate

Hiking time: 2-1/2 hours

Description: This moderate hike on various well-marked, wide gravel trails includes a portion of the blue-blazed Buckeye Trail. There is a moderate hill to climb in order to reach 1,160-foot-high Gildersleeve Knob, from which there is a splendid view of Lake Erie in the distance.

Directions: From I-90, take Exit 193 (SR 306). Go south on SR 306 to US 6 (Chardon Rd.). Take Chardon Rd. west 1 mile to Hobart Rd. At Hobart turn right (north); park entrance on the right about 1/4-mile.

Parking & restrooms: Just inside the entrance road there is ample parking; restrooms are adjacent to Pine Lodge (closed unless a nature program is held there).

This very scenic 390-acre park is noted for its tall trees and ancient sandstone ledges. Chapin Forest's trees are typical northern hardwoods: oak, maple, tulip, and beech. Chestnut trees once predominated here, but only stumps remain since the blight of the 1920s. Spectacular Sharon Conglomerate sandstone ledges, similar to others found in northeast Ohio, are an outstanding feature of the park. These rock ledges were formed about 320 million years ago during the Pennsylvanian Age. They are composed of sandstone embedded with white quartz pebbles locally called "lucky stones." The probable source of these pebbles is far north, in Canada, whose streams brought them to the sandy shore of the inland ocean that once covered Ohio.

In the early 1800s, Berea Sandstone was found at what is now Quarry Pond and used to construct foundations for many local buildings, including the 1836 Kirtland Temple, a National Historic Landmark. (Open daily with free tours, the Temple is located at 9020 Chillicothe Rd. [SR 306], Kirtland, OH 44094; 216-256-3318.) Berea Sandstone was formed of sand deposited along an ancient continent's shoreline during the Devonian Age, about 360 million years ago. This sand accumulated as river deposits, delta lobes, or offshore bodies of sand.

In 1949 Frederic H. Chapin purchased the land on which this reservation is located and donated it to the state of Ohio to protect the beautiful forest from logging. During the 1950s the Ohio Division of Forestry and

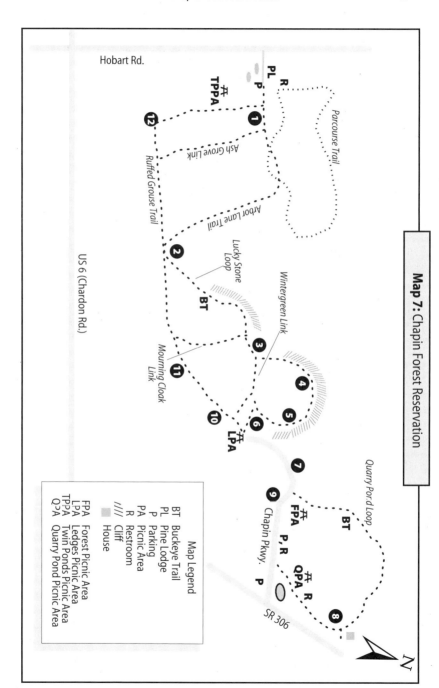

Map 7: Chapin Forest Reservation

Reclamation used this property for experimental research to determine growth and survival rates of various kinds of trees. Some of the trees near the parking area stand in straight rows, just as they were planted by the Division. Under a lease agreement with the state, Lake Metroparks now manages the reservation.

1. Begin the hike at the trail information sign marked "Arbor Lane Trail" and follow it past the ball field on the right. Pass the Ash Grove Link on the right. Where the Parcourse (fitness trail) crosses the main trail on both right and left, remain on the Arbor Lane Trail. The Parcourse again crosses the main trail, but continue straight on the Arbor Lane Trail, which is also marked with blue tree blazes for the Buckeye Trail. The trail now bends toward the right (southeast) and begins a gentle ascent.

2. At 0.3 mile meet the Ruffed Grouse Trail on the right, but continue straight ahead uphill to an intersection of the Lucky Stone Loop. Here take the left branch of the Lucky Stone Loop, also marked with blue Buckeye Trail blazes.

3. At about 0.7 mile pass Mourning Cloak Link on the right. (This is a cross-over trail to the south branch of Lucky Stone Loop.) Stay left. Much storm damage to tall oak, maple, and beech trees is evident here. Next pass Wintergreen Link on the right (another cross-over trail to Lucky Stone Loop). Stay left.

4. At 1 mile reach a trail intersection at the top of Gildersleeve Knob. A short path on the left leads to a wooden fence from which there is a splendid panoramic view of Willoughby and Lake Erie several miles away to the north. The view to the west shows the skyline of Cleveland 17 miles away. Below is an abandoned 20th-century quarry of Sharon Conglomerate.

As you look toward Lake Erie, note the relatively flat lake plain that gradually ascends to the Allegheny Plateau upon which you are standing. The transitional area between the lake plain and high area is the Portage Escarpment. This escarpment is the eroded face of the plateau overlaid with glacial deposits.

5. Return to the main trail and continue ahead (east). Avoid taking a side trail on the left marked Scenic Overlook since tall trees obscure the view from this point and there is no protective fence constructed here.

6. Continue to follow Lucky Stone Loop as it gradually descends. Take the next left turn where the trail goes steeply downhill to Ledges Picnic Area (1.3 miles).

7. Here the Buckeye Trail follows Chapin Pkwy. eastward to a trail entrance just before Forest Picnic Shelter (1.7 miles). Follow the blue blazes left on this wide gravel Quarry Pond Loop trail as it winds through a beautiful forest.

8. Just past a house on the left the Buckeye Trail leaves the main trail to go out to SR 306. Continue on the Quarry Pond Loop until it reaches Quarry Pond Picnic Shelter and restroom building. This is the site of the abandoned 19th-century Berea Sandstone quarry that supplied stones for Kirtland Temple.

9. Follow Chapin Pkwy. westward past Forest Picnic Shelter to Ledges Picnic Shelter (3.3 miles).

10. Ascend the hill above the picnic area; at the top turn left to follow the south branch of Lucky Stone Loop. Here you are on the top of the massive ledges of Sharon Conglomerate sandstone. The 320-million-year-old rock ledges were eroded by glaciers that crept in and out of here about 1.6 million years ago until retreating completely around 12,000 years ago (see Appendix A).

CAUTION: Please do not deviate from the trail or climb on any of the ledges.

11. Continue to follow Lucky Stone Loop past Wintergreen Link and Mourning Cloak Link as the trail descends to meet Arbor Lane Trail once again (3.8 miles).

12. Continue ahead to meet the Ruffed Grouse Trail on the left. Bear left here (southwest) and follow this trail through lovely woods past Ash Grove Link trail to reach Twin Ponds Picnic Shelter and the parking area.

Patricia Morse, Naturalist, Lake Metroparks, reviewed this chapter for accuracy.

8 GIRDLED ROAD RESERVATION

Distance: 6.2 miles

Strenuous

Hiking time: 3 hours

Description: This mostly north-south trail leads from Radcliffe Rd. Picnic Area north to Girdled Rd. Picnic Area and returns along the same path. From Radcliffe Rd. the hike goes through farm fields, descends to the Big Creek valley, goes through deep woods, and finally ascends two steep ridges to Girdled Rd. Park trails are unmarked until you reach the blue-blazed Buckeye Trail along Big Creek. Aylworth Creek presents a wide but shallow stream-crossing on rocks. Horseback riders also use some of these trails, so caution is advised if encountering them along the route. In such a case it is important to step to the side of the trail and remain quiet until they pass.

Directions: From I-90 take SR 44 (Exit 200) and drive south to Girdled Rd. Turn left (east) and take Girdled Rd. east until it reaches SR 608. Turn right (south) and follow SR 608 to Radcliffe Rd. Turn left on Radcliffe to the park entrance sign on the left.

Parking & restrooms: At the park entrance.

Girdled Road Reservation, located in Concord Township at the Lake-Geauga county line, is a 643-acre park offering a picnic shelter, grills, a baseball diamond, a fishing pond, and trails for hiking, horseback riding and cross-country skiing.

The blue-blazed Buckeye Trail is the main trail in this park, running north-south between Girdled Rd. and Radcliffe Rd., just east of SR 608. A scenic section of Big Creek runs through the park and is accessible from the Buckeye Trail. The primary entrance to Girdled Road Reservation is on Radcliffe Rd., on the border between Lake and Geauga Counties. Access is also available from a parking and picnic area on Girdled Rd.

The road for which the park is named was the first to be cut into Connecticut's Western Reserve and one of the first routes leading into the Northwest Territory. The name is derived from the clearing practice of Connecticut Land Company surveyors who, in 1797-98, cleared a normal 25-foot width, then "girdled" the trees on either side of the clearing to make the road 33 feet wide. Girdling consisted of cutting around the big trunks, through the bark of the tree, and into the sapwood, disrupting the tree's flow of nutrients and causing them to dry out and die. A much wider road than usual was thereby created.

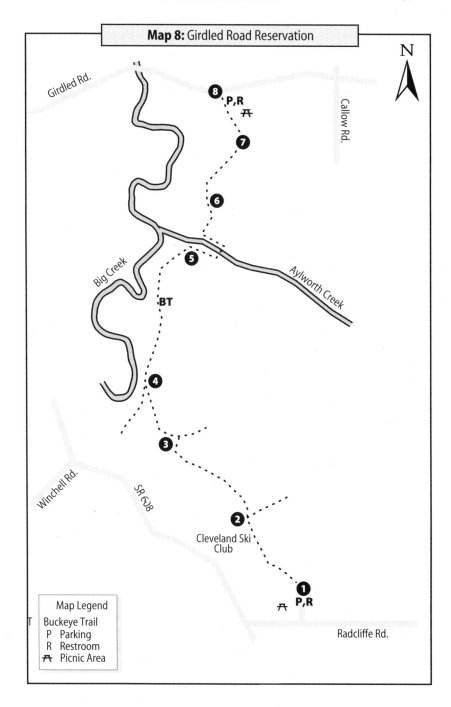

Map 8: Girdled Road Reservation

N

Girdled Rd.

Callow Rd.

8 P,R

7

6

5

Big Creek

Aylworth Creek

BT

4

3

Winchell Rd.

SR 608

2

Cleveland Ski Club

1 P,R

Radcliffe Rd.

Map Legend
Buckeye Trail
P   Parking
R   Restroom
⛺ Picnic Area

1. Start the hike at the far end of the grassy area northeast of the parking lot. The trail entrance is behind a pair of split-rail fence sections. The path cuts a swath through a grassy old farm field before entering the woods.

2. At about 0.4 mile the trail splits into a "Y" intersection. Take the left spur (the right spur is used mainly by horseback riders and, in winter, by cross-country skiers). Follow the trail northwest as it gradually descends to the creek valley.

3. Pass through fields and soon meet a trail intersection coming from the right. Stay to the left (west) as the path finishes descending the ridge to Big Creek valley.

4. At the next intersection (1.5 miles) this trail meets the blue-blazed Buckeye Trail going north and south. Here bear right (north), staying on the Buckeye Trail. Cross a muddy spot on logs. Pleasant views of Big Creek open up on the left.

Growing alongside the embankment is a common inhabitant of stream-side earth, the Scouring Rush (also called horsetail). This unusual hollow-stemmed green plant helps reduce erosion and was used by early settlers to scour pots and pans because its stems contain silica.

Unusually large glacial boulders lie in the stream. These were left behind by a retreating glacier that covered this part of Ohio around 12,000 years ago.

The path crosses a creek bed that is often dry.

5. At 2.1 miles cross wide Aylworth Creek. (NOTE: It is necessary to go upstream a few yards to cross this ordinarily shallow brook on stones.) Return to the Buckeye Trail and continue northeast as the trail now begins to go uphill.

6. (2.5 miles) About midway up the steep cliff, a large tulip tree has fallen across the Buckeye Trail, but the path continues around this obstruction and ascends to the top of the ridge.

7. Descend the hill and reach a set of wooden steps that continue downward to a small stream in a deep ravine. The path then ascends a short set of wooden steps and continues up the next hill. Stay on the Buckeye Trail until it reaches the picnic area and road.

8. At 3.2 miles reach Girdled Road Picnic Area. Here are picnic tables, restrooms, and a short circular nature trail.

Return on the Buckeye Trail, descending and ascending the wooden steps, past the fallen tulip tree, and reach Aylworth Creek again. Continue following the Buckeye Trail until it intersects with the unmarked path described in Note #4 above. Stay left here.

(NOTE: If you pass this intersection and mistakenly follow the blue-blazed trail to its end at SR 608, turn left on the road and carefully walk uphill facing traffic on this busy road. Turn left at Radcliffe Rd. and left again into the parking area.)

Continue on the trail as it ascends the hill, taking right turns as you follow the path back to the picnic area at Radcliffe Rd.

Patricia Morse, Naturalist, Lake Metroparks, reviewed this chapter for accuracy.

9 HOLDEN ARBORETUM

Distance: 5.5 miles

~~Strenuous~~

Hiking time: 3 hours

Description: This beautiful walk will take you to a variety of Holden's treasures: the deep ravine of Pierson Creek, a rolling Woodland Trail high above the creek, Buttonbush and Owl Bogs, Lotus and Corning Lakes, and Bole Woods. Pierson Creek Valley and Bole Woods are National Natural Landmarks.

Directions: From I-90 take Exit 193 for Mentor/Kirtland and SR 306. Follow SR 306 south and drive about 0.5 miles, turning left onto Kirtland-Chardon Rd. (A sign indicates SR 615). Go east about 3 miles on K-C Rd., passing Penitentiary Glen and Lake Metroparks, and follow the Holden signs to Sperry Rd. Turn left onto Sperry. Follow it to the entrance of the arboretum on the left at the Visitor Center sign.

Parking & restrooms: at the Visitor Center.

Holden Arboretum is a unique private preserve of more than 3,100 acres of natural woodlands, horticultural collections, display gardens, ponds, fields, and ravines. It also encompasses 20 miles of trails. As the largest arboretum in the United States and one of the largest in the world, Holden is among the nation's leading horticultural institutions. Holden is dedicated to collecting woody plants believed to have ornamental and scientific merit, especially for northeast Ohio.

Ideal growing conditions at Holden are provided by Lake Erie breezes that cool the air during the daytime and maintain warmer nighttime temperatures, thus decreasing daily temperature fluctuations. An extended growing season is provided by winds that blow off a relatively warmer Lake Erie to postpone the first fall freeze. In the spring, crop development is delayed by cool winds blowing over a cold lake that slows fruit blossoming until after the chance of a frost.

Many classes, tours, hikes, bird walks, and other nature activities are offered year round at the arboretum. The preserve was originally provided for through a trust of Albert Fairchild Holden, a noted mining engineer, who died in 1912. The park was initially established in 1931 on just 100 acres of land.

Because the arboretum is privately supported, it depends upon mem-

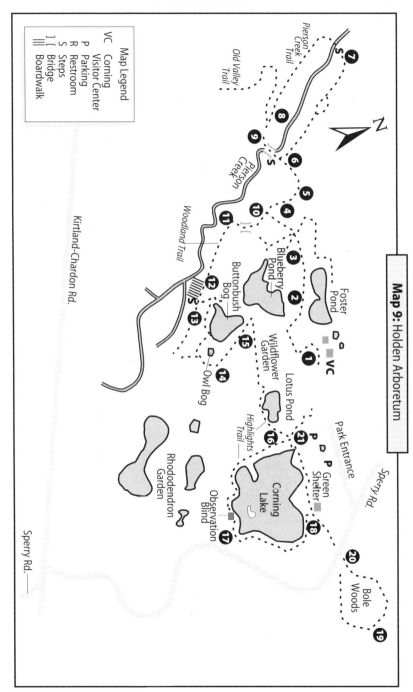

Map 9: Holden Arboretum

Map Legend

VC Corning Visitor Center
P   Parking
R   Restroom
S   Steps
Bridge
Boardwalk

Pierson Creek Trail

Old Valley Trail

Pierson Creek

Woodland Trail

Kirtland-Chardon Rd.

Blueberry Pond

Buttonbush Bog

Foster Pond

Wildflower Garden

Lotus Pond

Owl Bog

Highlights Trail

Rhododendron Garden

Park Entrance

Green Shelter

Corning Lake

Observation Blind

Sperry Rd.

Bole Woods

Sperry Rd.

VC

berships and admission fees for maintenance. Non-members who wish to use the many resources available at Holden are charged $4 a day for adults, $3 for seniors, and $2 for children 6-15 years. Admission for members and guests is free.

The Corning Visitor Center contains nature exhibits, a well-stocked library, a gift shop, and staff interpreters on duty to assist the visitor with an orientation to Holden's vast resources. Maps, brochures, trail guides, and other informative publications are available at the Visitor Center. Visits to the protected habitats of 100-foot-deep Stebbins Gulch, a National Natural Landmark, and Little Mountain may be made only with a naturalist, and frequent hikes are scheduled there. An annual plant sale is held in the spring with free admission on those days. One of the highlights of a visit to Holden is seeing its magnificent collection of flowering crab apple, lilacs, rhododendrons, and azaleas in May and June. Fishing privileges and cross-country ski touring are open to members only. Membership information is available from Holden Arboretum, 9500 Sperry Rd., Kirtland, Ohio 44094-5172; 216-946-4400.

NOTE: Allow the better part of a day for a visit to Holden Arboretum and bring a picnic lunch along, as there is no food service here. After your hike, it is wonderful to soak in the ambiance of the many cultivated gardens, ponds, and natural areas at Holden. Most of the plants and trees are fully identified for your educational benefit.

NOTE: In addition to, or instead of, this walk, you may wish to take self-guided walks to the Wildflower Garden, Rhododendron Garden, or the Boardwalk at the bottom of Pierson Ravine using free interpretive maps provided at the Visitor Center.

1. Start this walk at the Visitor Center, going west past the Thayer Building (used for classes and other gatherings) onto a gravel path. This path leads past picnic tables on the right and a Coast Redwood display (a large cross-section of a giant Califormia redwood) on the left. Turn right at the map trail sign and walk past the Pat Bole Kiosk on the left and the picnic shelter on the right, toward the Pierson Creek Trail. Steps lead down to a left turn; cross the bridge and turn right. Follow signs for the Old Valley/Woodland/Pierson Trails.

2. Foster Pond is on the right. This portion of the Woodland Trail leads to both the Pierson Creek and Old Valley trails. Stay to the left at a fork in the trail. (Please respect all fence barriers that have been erected in the park for certain trails that are closed due to soil erosion.)

3. At 0.3 mile, you will reach a trail/road intersection. Cross the road and follow the Old Valley/Pierson signs. Continue to follow the same Pierson Creek signs, enjoying these quiet woods.

4. Turn right onto the Pierson Creek/Old Valley Trail, leaving the

Woodland Trail behind. (Later in the hike you will return to this point to take the Woodland Trail.)

5. Watch for a left bend just before the fence barrier (0.6 mile). Bear left here, still going generally north toward Pierson Creek.

6. Pass by a set of stairs on the left (0.8 mile), and bear right onto a gently descending path. The trail, now marked only for Pierson Creek, winds through a beautiful beech and hemlock forest, where you will encounter tall oaks along the way. At a split in the trail, stay right; you will pass an unusually large oak tree.

7. (1.1 mile) Reach a long flight of steep wooden stairs to Pierson Creek. Here is an enchantingly cool, moist environment that changes its appearance with each season. It can be a welcome oasis on a hot summer day. Turn left at the foot of the steps, following the well-trodden path.

There are many interesting wildflowers, ferns, and clubmosses that thrive here under moist conditions. These plants enjoy an excellent habitat due not only to the water but to the fresh nutrients leaching downward from the valley walls. This valley was once much deeper and wider than it is now. It was filled in by glacial till left by this area's last retreating glacier about 12,000 years ago. Pierson Creek, flowing northward, is slowly cutting through the remaining till.

(1.2 miles) You will reach a small set of steps that go down to the stream, which you will cross on stones. Turn left and continue along the creek embankment.

8. At 1.6 miles a trail intersects from the right. (This is the Old Valley Trail loop, which, if taken, will add another 1.5 miles to the hike, ending near Buttonbush Bog.) Continue ahead.

9. Cross a wooden bridge over a side brook; just beyond is Pierson Creek. Cross the creek on stones. The trail leads up another steep wooden stairway.

At the top of the steps continue to the right on the Pierson/Old Valley Trail (2 miles). This is the same point as in Note #6, now heading generally southward.

Reach the same spot as in Note #5 above and stay on the Pierson/Old Valley Trail as it winds through the woods.

10. Turn right onto the Woodland Trail (Boardwalk). (This is the same point reached in Note #4.) Descend gradually through the forest.

11. Cross a ravine on a wooden walkway. Here the tops of many tall trees were snapped off by a fierce storm, opening up the woods to more light and new plant growth. Avoid taking any side trails.

An interpretive sign on the left explains the American beech tree fungus disease that has marred these woods.

12. On the right is a set of wooden steps that descend to the Boardwalk. If there is time, it is worthwhile to take another walk down to Pierson

Creek to learn about the flora of the valley by following several boardwalk loops. This side trip will add only another 1/4 mile to the hike. The Boardwalk provides access to 58 labeled native wildflowers, ferns, and fern allies. Peak bloom for the flowers is usually during the last week in April and the first week of May.

13. If you didn't take the Boardwalk staircase, continue on the Woodland/Old Valley Trail. Benches placed along the trail invite you to sit and listen to the peacefulness of the woods and call to mind the words of Henry David Thoreau:

> You cannot perceive beauty
> but with a serene mind.

The path gently winds southeastward. At about 2.6 miles pass the Old Valley/Highlights Trail on the right and continue ahead to Buttonbush Bog, still on the Woodland Trail. Turn right to pass Buttonbush Bog, keeping it on the left. At the north end of this bog you will see a two-level observation tower overlooking the plant-filled pond. The natural process of succession is at work here slowly transforming this pond to a bog.

14. At the end of tiny Owl Bog, turn left to pass the east sides of both bogs on the Woodland/Old Valley Trail. Owl Bog has become almost entirely filled with organic material (3 miles).

15. At the north end of Buttonbush Bog, turn right onto the gravel road. Blueberry Pond is located to the left of the trail. Alongside Blueberry Pond is a path which goes back to the Visitor Center (optional). Continue on the road going east, passing the sign to the Rhododendron Garden, which, when it is in bloom in late April and May to early July, is a magnificent sight. The fully labeled Wildflower Garden is on the left and also worth a visit. Straight ahead is Lotus Pond.

16. Stay on the road (Highlights Trail) to the right. Cross a small footbridge and continue east to cross another footbridge over the spillway outlet for Corning Lake. A sign here points toward the Observation Blind.

17. Follow a trail counterclockwise around Corning Lake, home to many waterfowl and fish. The small screened building on the edge of the lake is the Observation Blind. Private property is on the right. Continue on the grassy trail along the rim of the lake. In the spring, large yellow water lilies thrive at this end of the lake.

18. Still hugging the shore of Corning Lake on the Highlights Trail, leave the trail on a path at the far northeast end of the lake. This path leads to the Green Shelter (4 miles). This small wooden shelter was placed here by the Green Family in memory of their two sons who died in a 1965 boating accident. A sign inside reads: "Dedicated to the wondrous beauty of nature, God's great gift to mankind," and a plaque outside commemorates the two boys. You may wish to stop and sit in the shelter to enjoy a glorious view of the hills to the west. Many bluebird nesting boxes have been placed throughout the fields here.

19. Cross Sperry Rd. Just past the road barrier is the Bole Woods Trail, a one-mile forest loop through an upland beech-maple forest. These tall trees were part of a vast wilderness that extended over much of postglacial Ohio and posed a formidable barrier to early pioneers who tried to penetrate it. The maple trees were left to stand in these woods as a sugar bush to collect sap for maple syrup. Bole Woods has been designated a National Natural Landmark.

Enter a lovely deciduous forest as the path (occasionally wet in the spring) gently loops to the north. The forest floor supports abundant wildflowers in the spring: trout lilies, Dutchman's breeches, squirrel corn, toothwarts, trilliums, violets, and many others. After about half way on the trail, there is an oak on the left that is remarkable for its huge size. Many large beech trees here were felled in a storm because of shallow roots or rotted cores.

20. When you emerge from the trail, continue past the Arbor Vitae Collection to Sperry Rd., passing an enormous sugar maple tree with a bench underneath.

Walk back to the Green Shelter and follow the opposite side of Corning Lake. Pass a storage building and turn right on the walkway that borders Lotus Pond (on the left).

21. Follow this walkway back to the parking area. On the way you will pass some of Holden's magnificent horticultural collections and a lovely reflecting pool.

... my mind, set free by space and solitude and oiled by the body's easy rhythm, swings open and releases thoughts it has already formulated. Sometimes, when I have been straining too hard to impose order on an urgent press of ideas, it seems only as if my mind has slowly relaxed; and then, all at once, there is room for the ideas to fall into place in a meaningful pattern.

—Colin Fletcher, *The Complete Walker*

GEAUGA COUNTY

Geauga County, the second county to be founded in Connecticut's Western Reserve (1805), is home to Ohio's second-largest Amish settlement (after Holmes County), centered at Middlefield. Geauga County's farms are rich in soil, water, and woodlands. Dairy farming, cheese making, and maple syrup production are among the county's main agricultural activities. Several of the towns in Geauga County resemble New England villages because they were founded by eastern pioneers who were attracted to the area's beautiful rolling farmland and sugar maple forests. Chardon, the county seat—neatly laid out high on a central green—is listed on the National Register of Historic Places.

Century Village in Burton, operated by the Geauga County Historical Society, is a complex of 20 restored buildings furnished with antiques preserving the Reserve's early history. The outdoor museum is open from May through October for guided tours (216-834-4012).

One of the earliest buildings in the county is Welshfield Inn, at the junction of US 422 & SR 700. Built in the 1840s as a hotel, the structure later served as a post office and, during the Civil War, became a stop on the Underground Railroad. It is now a restaurant (216-834-4164).

The Geauga Park District provides outstanding natural areas for public recreation in 13 parks and preserves totaling 4,486 acres. Eight of these parks are open to the public: Beartown Lakes Reservation, Bessie Benner Metzenbaum Park, Big Creek Park, Headwaters Park, Eldon Russell Park, Swine Creek Reservation, Walter C. Best Preserve, and Whitlam Woods. The Rookery, a 443-acre park in Munson Township along the Chagrin River southwest of Chardon, is slated to open by the end of 1996, and West Woods, a 792-acre preserve in Russell and Newbury Townships, will open in 1997. Burton Wetlands (including White Pine Bog Forest), Becvar Preserve, and Husted Woods are not yet open to the public because of the sensitive nature of their rare foliage.

Park information is available from Geauga Park District, 9160 Robinson Rd., Chardon, OH 44024-9148; 216-285-2222; 216-564-7131.

More information about Geauga County is available from the Geauga County Chamber of Commerce and Visitors Bureau, 8228 Mayfield Rd., Chesterland, OH 44026; 800-775-8687; 216-729-6002.

10 WHITLAM WOODS

Distance: 2+ miles

Hiking time: 1+ hour

Description: The main ravine is ascended and descended on steps, but the rest of the trails here are primarily flat. Some of the paths in Whitlam Woods are wet at times, but a fine footbridge crosses the main stream. The ruins of an old sugarhouse can be seen on the Sugarbush Trail, a reminder of the maple sugaring activity for which Geauga County is well known. Tall hardwood trees in the park provide ideal reststops for birds when they flock here during migration season, and they can be easily observed in the meadow adjacent to the parking area.

Directions: From I-90 take Exit 200 to SR 44. Go south on SR 44 for 3.5 miles to Clark Rd. Turn left (east) on Clark Rd. Follow Clark to Robinson Rd. Take a right at Robinson Rd. Follow Robinson south for a short distance, then turn left (east) at Pearl Rd. Continue on Pearl to the park entrance on the left. From the town of Chardon, take North St. at the north end of the town square for 1.3 miles and turn right onto Woodin Rd. After 3/4 mile on Woodin Rd., turn left onto Robinson Rd. A sign points toward Big Creek Park. Pass this park on the left, then at Pearl Rd. turn right (east). After 3/4 mile on Pearl Rd., there will be a sign on the left for Geauga Park District and Whitlam Woods.

Parking & restrooms: Near the park entrance.

Whitlam Woods is a small park in Geauga County near Chardon that opened in 1976 and is administered by Geauga Park District. In 1959 Fred Whitlam donated money to support the use of this land for public enjoyment, creating a memorial to his parents, William and Mary Whitlam, and to other pioneers of Geauga County and the Western Reserve. This 100-acre forest is located near Big Creek Park and is bisected by two of Big Creek's tributaries, forming two major ravines. Because it is so small, Whitlam Woods can be enjoyed as a second hike after visiting Big Creek Park. A trail system has been laid out in Whitlam Woods.

1. Enter the Lookout Trail straight ahead (north) of the parking area and follow it to its end. This 0.1-mile dead-end trail overlooks ravines on either side and offers a quiet view of the forest from a sheltered bench. Return the same way and turn left (east) onto the Bridge Trail to descend on a switchback path and steps to the streambed.

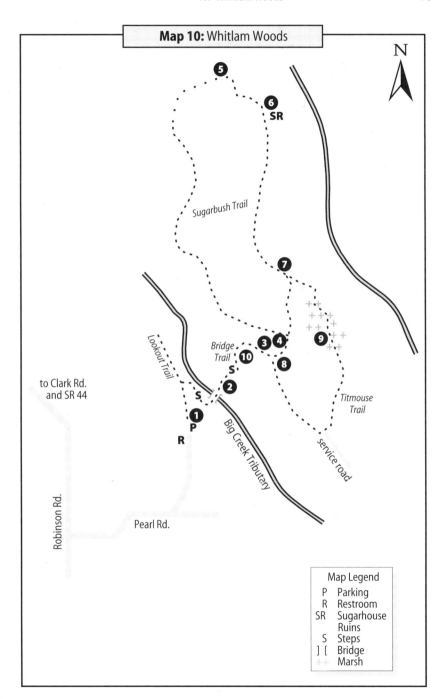

Map 10: Whitlam Woods

N

⑤

⑥ SR

Sugarbush Trail

⑦

Lookout Trail

Bridge Trail

③④

⑩

S

⑧

⑨

to Clark Rd. and SR 44

S

②

①
P

R

Big Creek Tributary

Titmouse Trail

service road

Robinson Rd.

Pearl Rd.

Map Legend
P   Parking
R   Restroom
SR Sugarhouse
    Ruins
S   Steps
] [Bridge
++ Marsh

2. Cross the stream, a tributary of Big Creek, on the sturdy footbridge and hike up the slope on a set of steps. An inviting bench for resting sits at the top on the left.

3. Bear left at the intersection of the Sugarbush Trail with the Titmouse Trail.

4. Stay left at the next intersection to continue on the Sugarbush Trail loop. Another bench invites contemplation of the woods high above the ravine on the left (west) and calls to mind John Muir's words:

> I care to live only to entice people to look at
> nature's loveliness. My own special self is nothing.

5. The trail winds through a splendid upland hardwood forest with fine, tall maples and oaks. After about a mile, it bends around to the east where, in fall and winter seasons, there is a clear view of the ravine and stream below on the left.

6. On your left, watch for an old brick chimney and hearth ruin and the ruins of a sugarhouse. All that is left of a large maple sugaring operation in this forest are the foundation, a few scraps of metal from buckets, and the evaporator. Take a brief detour to view the ruins, if you wish.

7. Once back on the main trail, continue south until you reach an intersection with a bench and signs for both the Sugarbush and Titmouse Trails. Stay right on the Sugarbush Trail.

8. At the next set of Sugarbush Trail signs, bear left, then turn left again at the sign for the Titmouse Trail on the left (southeast).

9. Enter the Titmouse Trail, pass a service road on the right, and continue through a red maple forest. Here the trail may be marshy at times.

Complete the Titmouse Trail at the same intersection reached in Note #7 (Sugarbush Trail). Turn left and follow the Sugarbush Trail southwest again to the same point reached in Notes #3 and #8 to complete the loop.

10. Continue west on the Bridge Trail. Descend the stairs, cross the footbridge, and ascend the steps and switchback path to the top of the ravine. Turn left at the top onto the Lookout Trail to return to the parking area.

This chapter was reviewed by John R. O'Meara, Director, Geauga Park District.

11 HEADWATERS PARK

Moderate

Distance: 5 miles

Hiking time: 2-3/4 hours

Description: This hike follows the Buckeye Trail initially and then a dirt and gravel road over gently rolling terrain. The way is marked for most of its length by blue Buckeye Trail blazes, two-inch by six-inch blue rectangles painted on trees in both directions. In some spots the blazes may be hard to find, especially in the wooded portion. The hike proceeds about 2-1/2 miles to US 322 and returns by the same route. Different views of the forest and lake are always a pleasant surprise when hiking the same trail in the opposite direction.

Directions: From I-271 take Exit 34 (Mayfield Rd./US 322). Go east on Mayfield/US 322 to SR 608 (Old State Rd.). At SR 608 turn right (south). On the left, just before Grandview Golf & Country Club, is the park entry road on the right. Follow the park entry drive to a small parking area on the right.

(The Grandview Golf & Country Club, a public facility, is open for both lunch and dinner during the golfing season; call 216-834-4661.)

NOTE: There is also a small parking area on US 322 before it crosses the reservoir. A second car can be dropped here in order to eliminate the return hike. A boat launch area is located here as well.

Parking & restrooms: At the parking area.

Headwaters Park, a 926-acre park surrounding East Branch Reservoir, is located on US 322 east of East Claridon in Geauga County. It is owned by the City of Akron's Water Supply Division and managed (since May 1996) by Geauga Park District. Built in 1932 and surrounded by a beautiful manmade pine forest, the reservoir was created by damming the waters of the East Branch of the Cuyahoga River to supply drinking water to Akron. The Cuyahoga rises not far from here in the woods of a dairy farm near US 6 and SR 86.

Near the south end of this popular fishing lake is a public boat launch area. Information about fishing and boating can be obtained from Geauga Park District at 9160 Robinson Rd., Chardon, OH 44024-9148; 216-285-2222 or 216-564-7131.

A pleasant 2.5-mile portion of the blue-blazed Buckeye Trail follows along a short trail and a longer dirt road on the west side of the reservoir.

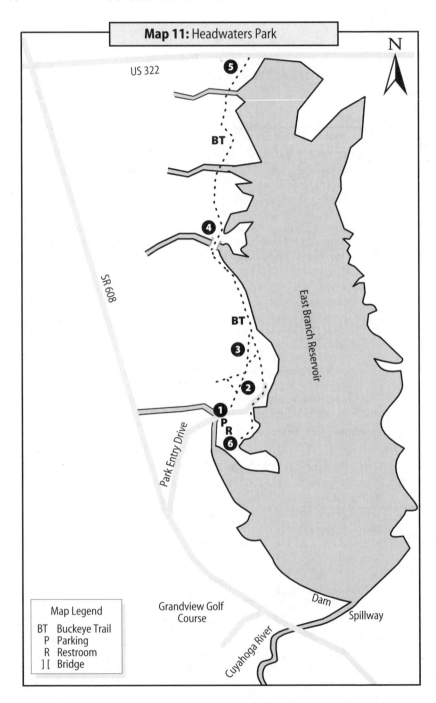

Map 11: Headwaters Park

N

US 322

SR 608

BT

❺

❹

BT

❸

❷

❶
P
R
❻

East Branch Reservoir

Park Entry Drive

Grandview Golf Course

Dam

Spillway

Cuyahoga River

Map Legend

BT   Buckeye Trail
P   Parking
R   Restroom
] [Bridge

Views of the reservoir are especially rewarding in late fall or early spring when leaves are down, but the hike is pleasant in any season. The park is open year round for hiking.

NOTE: Park plans call for opening a trail on the *east* side of the reservoir in the future. Call the above numbers for information.

1. Begin the walk on the park entry drive marked with blue Buckeye Trail blazes. On the left (west), the BT turns into the woods going northeast. Although its blue blazes may not be easy to see, the trail's entry is alongside a log railing once used for tying up horses. Follow the path through a cool pine forest. At 0.2 mile cross a stream and continue up the side of a small hill through a tall maple and oak forest.

2. At 0.3 mile there is a fork in the trail and a double blue blaze. Go to the right and emerge onto a wider, more heavily used trail.

3. At the next trail intersection, bear left. (The right fork goes downhill to the entry road.) Continue until the path drops down to the road. Turn left here. (0.5 mile)

Continue to follow the blue blazes of the Buckeye Trail along the road.

4. Cross a wooden bridge and note the unusually deep rust color of the water, an indication of the high level of iron that leaches from the rocks in the stream.

The trail enters a lovely pine forest and, after 2.5 miles, emerges onto the other parking and boat launch area at US 322.

5. Retrace your steps by turning south and following the same dirt road in the reverse direction.

6. Follow the dirt road to the reservoir. Turn off the road to walk through tall pine trees toward the water to enjoy views of the reservoir. Walk back to the parking area near the road to complete the hike.

12 BIG CREEK PARK

Distance: 4 miles (option for 2 miles)

Moderate

Hiking time: About 2 hours (option for 1 hour)

Description: The easy individual trails in this park are short, only a mile or less, but together they cover an expanse of gently rolling terrain with views of ponds and streams. Bird watching in Big Creek Park is especially rewarding during spring and fall migrations. Wildflowers are abundant in the spring. Tall maple, beech, and oak trees provide brilliant color in the fall.

Directions: From I-90 exit at SR 44 (Exit 200). Follow SR 44 south 3.5 miles to Clark Rd. Turn left (east) on Clark to Robinson Rd. Turn right on Robinson to the park entrance on the right.
From Chardon, take North St. at the north end of the village square 1.3 miles to Woodin Rd. Turn right (east) on Woodin Rd. and left (north) on Robinson Rd. The entrance to Big Creek Park is about 1.5 miles up the road on the left. At the entrance, take a left turn to the Aspen Grove parking area.

Parking & restrooms: At the Meyer Center and adjacent Aspen Grove.

Big Creek Park, one of the largest of Geauga Park District's 13 natural preserves, is located just north of the town of Chardon. It contains 642 acres of woodland through which Big Creek and its tributaries flow. This park is very near Whitlam Woods and can be hiked in conjunction with a visit to that park (Ch. 10).

A new nature center, named for the district's first park director, Donald W. Meyer, contains nature exhibits, classrooms, a small library, and a bird feeding area. Park personnel are available to assist the visitor with information, maps, and literature about the district's natural areas (216-286-9504). Fishing, primitive camping, picnic shelters, and a system of trails for both hiking and horseback riding are among the facilities offered in Big Creek Park. A section of the blue-blazed Buckeye Trail passes through the area and is identified by two-inch by six-inch blue rectangular markings placed at intervals on trees.

1. Start at the hike on the blue-blazed Buckeye Trail near the small shelter, sundial, and flagpole at the west end of the Aspen Grove parking area. This trail is also identified as the Trillium Trail and is marked with white

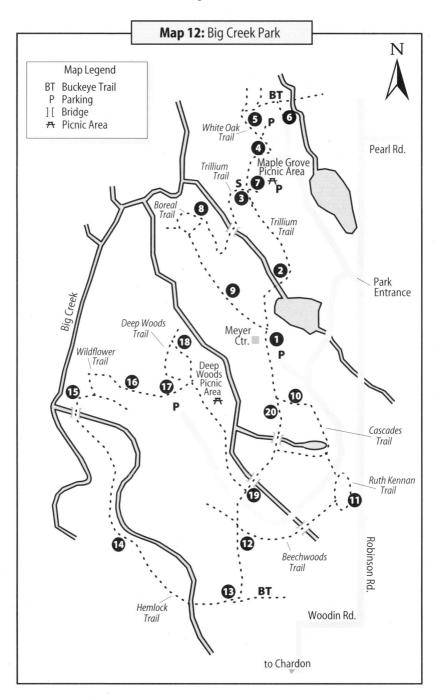

Map 12: Big Creek Park

N

Map Legend
BT Buckeye Trail
P   Parking
][Bridge
⊼   Picnic Area

White Oak
Trail

BT

⑤ P ⑥

④

Trillium
Trail

Maple Grove
Picnic Area

S ⑦ ⊼ P

③

Boreal
Trail

⑧

Trillium
Trail

②

⑨

Deep Woods
Trail

⑱

Meyer
Ctr.

①

P

Wildflower
Trail

Deep
Woods
Picnic
Area

⑯ ⑰ ⊼

P

⑩

⑮

⑳

Cascades
Trail

Big Creek

Ruth Kennan
Trail

⑲

⑪

⑭

⑫

Beechwoods
Trail

Robinson Rd.

⑬ BT

Hemlock
Trail

Woodin Rd.

Pearl Rd.

Park
Entrance

to Chardon

trillium flower signs. Enter the trail to the right going north and very soon pass Chestnut Pond on the right.

2. At the pond the trail, still the Buckeye/Trillium Trail, bears left and overlooks a stream on the left.

3. At a park bench, bear right and continue to follow the Buckeye/Trillium Trail. Pass restrooms and the Maple Grove parking area. At 0.4 mile, reach a set of wooden steps going down to a ravine. Bypass these steps and leave the Trillium Trail here. Continue on the Buckeye Trail to the right. Pass the picnic shelter and picnic grove and turn right to exit at the Maple Grove Picnic Area and parking area.

4. Just off the parking lot is a sign for the White Oak Trail, identified with an oak leaf. This 0.3-mile loop trail is a favorite cross-country skiing trail, as it follows gently undulating land at the far north end of the park.

At the first trail intersection, stay left to remain on the White Oak Trail. Continue on the White Oak Trail, passing a park bench on the right and through a beautiful stand of white oak and other hardwood trees.

5. At the next trail junction, the White Oak Trail turns sharply to the right where a cross-country skiing sign has been posted high on a tree. Cross a small wooden bridge, pass a spur of the Buckeye Trail which goes east pout of the park. Pass picnic tables and shelters to reach the campground parking area.

6. At the campground, follow the gravel road south to an asphalt-paved road, which leads back to the Maple Grove Picnic Area and parking.

7. At the west end of the parking area, pass the White Oak Trail entrance again. At the blue Buckeye Trail blaze, turn right to go past the Maple Grove shelter. Behind the shelter enter the Trillium Trail again and descend the wooden steps that were bypassed earlier in Note #3. The steps lead down to a boardwalk and bridge over a tributary of Big Creek, and up the opposite side of a broad ravine.

8. Soon there will be a sign for the Boreal Trail on the right. The 0.1-mile Boreal Trail loops to the top of a ridge and affords a fine view northwest across the valley as well as a view of Big Creek below. At an intersection where an unmarked trail goes downhill to the creek, stay to the left to continue on the Boreal Trail until it intersects with the Trillium Trail again.

9. Turn right to follow the Trillium Trail south until you reach the Meyer Center. The Donald W. Meyer Center, opened in 1991, is the administrative center for Geauga Park District. It is also used for nature classes and programs, and there is a small wildlife viewing area. The center is open 8:30 a.m.-5 p.m. weekdays, and 10 a.m.-6 p.m. on weekends.

NOTE: This marks the 2-mile or midpoint on this hike; the hike may be ended here or continued for another 2 miles.

10. On the southwest side of the parking area is a sign for the paved

Cascade Trail. Enter the trail here, pass the Beechwoods Trail sign (marked with a leaf symbol), and continue south. This is also the Buckeye Trail and is another fine cross-country skiing trail. At the next sign for Beechwoods Trail, turn left to go through a stand of beech trees of all sizes and cross the paved Cascade Trail to the park entry road.

11. Cross the park road to the paved, all-purpose Ruth Kennan Trail, commemorating a naturalist and teacher. This path loops through the woods and meets the Beechwoods Trail. Turn left on the Beechwoods Trail and continue walking in a southwest direction. After a few yards there will be cross-country ski signs on trees.

Cross two small wooden bridges.

12. Reach a trail intersection with the Hemlock Trail, marked with a tree symbol, and turn left (south) on the Hemlock Trail.

13. Pass a service road on the left where the Buckeye Trail exits the park. A park bench also on the left invites a rest to enjoy the pleasant woodland scenery.

14. At about the 3-mile point, the trail goes through a lovely hemlock forest, passes a ravine on the left, and reaches another view of Big Creek.

15. Descend a hill and cross a branch of Big Creek on a wooden bridge, then ascend another hill. At the top, turn left (north) to enter the Wildflower Trail. This pretty trail, symbolized by a cluster of three small flowers, is particularly enjoyable in April and May when many spring wildflowers are in bloom.

16. Descend a set of steps, cross a wooden bridge, and continue up the rise of land to the Deep Woods picnic and parking area (3.5 miles).

17. Just to the left of the picnic tables is the entrance to Deep Woods Trail. This 0.3-mile loop takes the hiker through a lovely wooded area and, again, is a popular cross-country skiing trail.

18. At the trail junction sign, turn right to continue the loop and return to the Deep Woods picnic shelter.

19. Continue alongside the paved park road south, turning left (north) off the road onto the Beechwoods Trail/Buckeye Trail. Cross a small bridge, then pass a trail intersection where the Beechwoods Trail goes off to the right (east).

20. Continue north on the Buckeye Trail, crossing a stream and the paved Cascade Trail just before reaching the Meyer Center parking lot.

This chapter was reviewed by John R. O'Meara, Director, Geauga Park District.

13 SWINE CREEK RESERVATION

Distance: 3.5 miles

Moderate

Hiking time: 1-1/2 to 2 hours

Description: This park contains several small tributaries that flow southeast to Swine Creek. Many marked trails in the hardwood forest lead up and down ravines that were formed by these streams, providing a varied terrain for hikers and skiers. At times, horseback and wagon riders will use some of the trails, so hikers should use caution, particularly when on the Gray Fox and Wagon Trails.

Directions: From I-271, take Exit 29 (Chagrin Blvd.). Follow Chagrin east until SR 87 splits off as Pinetree Rd. Take SR 87 east through the town of Middlefield. About 2 miles past the town and past SR 528, reach Hayes Rd. Take a right (south) on Hayes Rd. and continue south for 1.5 miles. Just past Bridge Rd., watch for the entrance to Swine Creek on the right. Enter on the park road and take an immediate left. (The road to the right leads to Lake Side Picnic Area, a sugarhouse, and a departure point for wagon/sleigh rides.) Follow the park road south, past a parking area on the right to another parking area at the end of the road. On the right is a large pond crossed by a bridge leading to the log cabin education center, Swine Creek Lodge.

Parking & restrooms: Parking is at the end of the park road; restrooms are behind the education center.

Swine Creek Reservation, located southeast of Middlefield, was once part of a private 1,200-acre hunting preserve belonging to Windsor Ford of Mesopotamia. In 1981 this 331-acre reservation became a public park. The property contains a small log hunting lodge now used as an education center. Swine Creek Lodge is open to the public on winter Sunday afternoons and for special events. Near Woods Edge Picnic Area is a sugarhouse, where the process of making maple syrup can be observed on weekends in March. Horse-drawn wagon and sleigh rides are offered to the public seasonally in Swine Creek Reservation. Call 216-286-9504 for event times.

Fishing (with a license) can be enjoyed in Lodge and Killdeer Ponds; hiking and cross-country skiing take place on a network of well-marked trails. Because Swine Creek Reservation is in the heart of Amish country, one can see many neat Amish dairy farms and homes without electricity

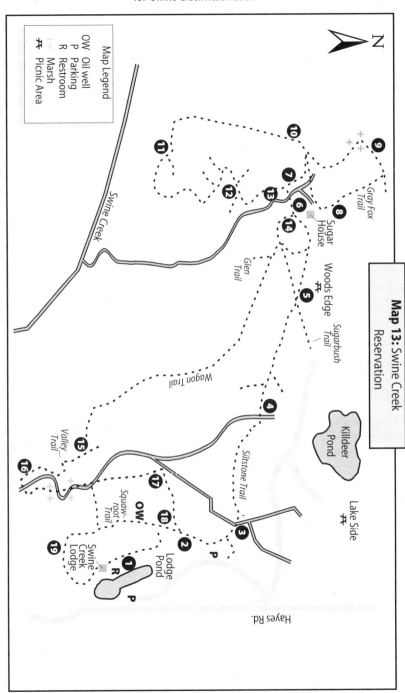

Map Legend

OW Oil well
P   Parking
R   Restroom
＋   Marsh
⊼   Picnic Area

N

Map 13: Swine Creek Reservation

Swine Creek

Gray Fox Trail

Sugar House

Glen Trail

Woods Edge

Sugarbush Trail

Wagon Trail

Valley Trail

Siltstone Trail

Killdeer Pond

Lake Side
⊼

Squaw-root Trail

OW

Swine Creek Lodge

Lodge Pond

P

R

P

Hayes Rd.

while driving to this park. Use caution on the roads as there are many slow-traveling horse-drawn buggies on the streets. A visit to some of the Amish shops and restaurants in the villages, particularly Middlefield, will enhance your visit to this part of Geauga County.

1. From the lodge and restroom buildings go north on a path that leads to Squawroot Trail. At the intersection, turn right on the north loop of the Squawroot Trail and pass an active, fenced-in oil well pump on the left.

2. At the next intersection, stay on the Squawroot Trail, to the right. The stream below on the left is a tributary of Swine Creek.

3. Bear left (west) onto the left branch of the Siltstone Trail. Cross the creek on rocks, taking care not to slip on these mossy stones. The trail leads to the right and uphill.

4. Continue along this easy trail until you reach another small tributary that flows down to Swine Creek. At the top of the small rise meet the gravel Wagon Trail and bear right (0.5 mile). Pass the north branch of the Silt-stone Trail on the right.

5. Cross the paved path (Sugarbush Trail) where a sign indicates that this path leads to the Gray Fox Trail. Woods Edge Picnic Area, with drinking fountain and restrooms, is off to the right. Follow the path to the sugarhouse, open weekends in March if there is sufficient sap to boil for maple syrup. Continue on the Sugarbush Trail loop.

6. Just off the path enter the Gray Fox/Glen Trail on the right. Enter a lovely forest of tall hardwood trees, a very pleasant environment for walking, especially in fall foliage season.

7. Cross another tributary of Swine Creek and immediately go to the right uphill on the Gray Fox Trail. (Another section of the Gray Fox Trail also goes to the left.) At the next intersection, turn right, still on the Gray Fox Trail. Cross the same stream again.

8. At 0.9 mile reach an open meadow with a view to the north across a field to a large white Amish farm on Bridge Rd. Walk along the west edge of the meadow where bluebird boxes have been placed. This is also the Meadowlark Trail used by horsemen and cross-country skiers.

9. Bear left at an intersection of the Meadowlark and Gray Fox trails, staying left on the latter trail going south.

The field may be wet and swampy during some seasons, as a stream rises here and wends its way down to Swine Creek. Beautiful wildflowers bloom in this field in late spring and summer. The trail reenters the woods.

10. Bear right at the next intersection, where a sign points toward a continuation of Gray Fox Trail. Cross-country ski signs are posted high up on trees along the trail. The trail passes along the western edge of the reservation, which is fenced with with barbed wire on the right.

11. At the next intersection, bear right to stay on the Gray Fox Trail. Below on the right is a deep ravine. Slowly the trail winds east, then north through a beautiful beech-maple-oak forest with tangled grape vines scattered throughout.

12. Stay on the marked Gray Fox Trail, avoiding intersecting sap-collecting trails used by the sap sled and wagon for maple syrup-making demonstrations.

13. Continue north on the Gray Fox Trail (avoiding all side trails) to the same intersection described in Note #7, and turn right to go uphill to the gravel road (Wagon Trail) just south of the sugarhouse (2 miles).

14. Turn right on the gravel Wagon Trail heading southeast. Pass the Glen Trail on the right where it goes down some steps into the ravine.

15. Follow the Wagon Trail south to its intersection with the Valley Trail (2.5 miles). At the bench, turn right and follow the Valley Trail as it gradually descends to the stream valley.

16. Cross a brook close to Swine Creek Rd. The Valley Trail now closely follows the stream on the left and soon crosses wet areas where the stream has changed its course. Pass a trail on the right.

17. At about the 3.1-mile point on the hike, the Valley Trail meets the Squawroot Trail on the right. Turn right here and climb uphill.

18. At the top of the hill turn right at the Squawroot sign. Ahead you will see the same oil well passed in Note #1. Still on the Squawroot Trail, keep the oil well below on the right and continue south past a stand of tall hemlocks on the left that appear to have been planted as a windbreak for the lodge.

19. Continue on the circular Squawroot Trail as it curves around below the evergreen trees and leads you back (north) to the lodge, pond, and parking area.

This chapter was reviewed by John R. O'Meara, Director, Geauga Park District.

I believe a leaf of grass is no less than the journey-work of the stars.
—Walt Whitman, *Leaves of Grass*

PORTAGE COUNTY

Portage County contains 11 state nature preserves, more than any other county in Ohio. It also offers 25 miles of the Upper Cuyahoga River, one of the state's 10 designated scenic rivers. These unusual natural areas are protected, preserved, monitored, and managed by the Ohio Department of Natural Resources (ODNR).

Only four of Portage County's nature preserves are open to the public, however. These are: Tinker's Creek State Nature Preserve (Ch. 17), Eagle Creek State Nature Preserve (Ch. 18), Frame Lake/Herrick Fen, and Marsh Wetlands. The rest, including Gott Fen, Triangle Lake Bog, Kent Bog, Tummonds Preserve, Evans Beck Memorial, Flatiron Lake Bog, and Mantua Bog, are open only by permit because of their extremely fragile nature.

Information about any of these preserves can be obtained from ODNR, 1889 Fountain Square Ct., Columbus, OH 43224; 614-265-6453.

The bogs and fens (low, swampy areas) in Portage County were formed by the melting of large chunks of ice left behind by the last glacier that covered Ohio about 12,000 years ago. As the glacier retreated, these huge ice blocks settled into the soft ground and made depressions in the soil where boreal plants, shrubs, and trees took hold. These plants, native to more northern temperate zones, still grow in the bogs and fens of Portage County, making ecosystems which are unique for this region. Because these areas are so ecologically fragile, they are protected from general public use and are open primarily for research, education, and low-impact activities such as nature study and appreciation, bird watching, guided hiking, and photography. These unspoiled natural areas are living museums that provide habitats for many rare and unusual plants and animals.

Portage County Park District (330-274-2746) offers hiking in Towners Woods on Ravenna Rd. east of SR 43 in Franklin Township. Major state parks in Portage County are Nelson-Kennedy Ledges State Park (Ch. 14) and West Branch State Park (Ch. 20). Aurora Sanctuary (Ch. 15) is maintained by the Audubon Society; Mogodore Reservoir (Ch. 19) is maintained by Akron's city water district.

Portage County is also home to some very different attractions, including the following: Sea World of Ohio, Geauga Lake Amusement Park, Aurora Farms Factory Outlets, Kent State University's Fashion Museum, and the Portage County Historical Society. Additional information about Portage County is available from the Convention and Visitors Bureau: 173 S. Chillicothe Rd., Aurora, OH 44202; 800-648-6342 or 216-562-3373.

14 NELSON-KENNEDY LEDGES STATE PARK

Easy

Distance: 1.7 miles

Hiking time: 1-1/4 hours

Description: This hike requires climbing up and down over rocks and ledges. One opening through a narrow passage may require crawling on hands and knees, and another, squeezing through a tight passage (not recommended for the claustrophobic). These spots can be bypassed by an alternate route. All of the trails are marked with blazes (either a hiker sign or a painted circle in one of four colors: yellow, white, red, and blue). The main features of the park are identified by additional signs. Note the barriers that have been put up for areas closed to hikers due to dangerous conditions.
Picnic tables are conveniently located in the forest to the east and north of the parking area.

Directions: Follow US 422 past the town of Parkman to SR 282, then south 2 miles to Nelson-Kennedy Ledges State Park.

Parking & restrooms: At the park entrance on the east side of SR 282. (The ledges are on the west side of SR 282.)

Nelson-Kennedy Ledges State Park is located in Portage County at the watershed between the Mississippi River to the south and the St. Lawrence River to the north. The drive to this park from Cleveland takes you through some beautiful Ohio farmland. Although the park is small, its extensive exposed ledge formations of Sharon Conglomerate sandstone are spectacular. Generations of children have enjoyed scrambling in and around these amazing rock formations.

About 320 million years ago, during the Pennsylvanian Age of the Paleozoic Era—about the time when amphibians developed—the land that is now Ohio was under a shallow inland sea. Quartz, originally from Canada, washed downstream to the edge of the sea and rolled around the ocean sand to eventually form a conglomerate rock of sand and quartz called Sharon Conglomerate. Embedded within Sharon Conglomerate are the abundant small, shiny, quartz pebbles locally called "lucky stones." These pebbles, worn smooth by the ancient action of the water and waves, have in places fallen out of the rock to create what appears to be a pock-marked ledge. As the sandy floor of the ocean was compressed into extremely hard sandstone rocks and the earth shifted, these ledges were

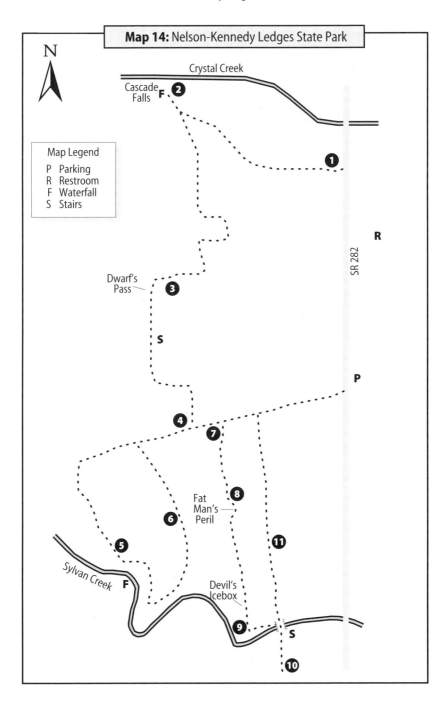

Map 14: Nelson-Kennedy Ledges State Park

exposed. They have been carved by the action of an ancient river flowing to the sea and by the advance and retreat of glaciers covering this part of Ohio thousands of years ago. Erosion of these prehistoric ledges proceeds very slowly still. Cracks, fissures, and caves were formed in the ledges by the settling of the sandstone over softer layers of underlying rocks of the Cuyahoga Formation (see Appendix A).

(The Nelson Ledges are in this section of the park; those designated as the Kennedy Ledges are in an undeveloped area off Fenstermaker Rd., just east of here.)

1. Start the hike by crossing SR 282 at the north end of the parking area. You will see a large sign identifying park trails.

2. Follow the yellow hiker signs going north to Cascade Falls, a beautiful tall waterfall, below which are huge slabs of rock wall that have fallen into the creek. Gold Hunter's Cave is a large overhanging rock that can also be viewed from the boardwalk. The water flowing through here is Crystal Creek, which has formed a deep recess through the rocks. It flows eastward, eventually to enter the St. Lawrence River.

3. Turn back to the yellow trail and follow it south through dark passageways and over boardwalks to Dwarf's Pass (0.2 mile).

Note the Sharon Conglomerate sandstone rock and quartz pebbles that form these remarkable ledges (see Appendix A). Climb the wooden stairs to the top of the shelf and continue on the yellow trail straight ahead.

4. Reach a junction directly opposite the parking area. The red, white, and blue trails begin and end here. Take the white trail on the right as it loops southwest above the ledges.

5. On the white trail at about 0.6 mile, reach Sylvan Creek, an outlet stream of Quarry Lake, and bear left (east). Here a very deep ravine has been carved by the stream, which flows toward the Ohio River and eventually reaches the Mississippi.

CAUTION: Use extreme care here not to get too close to the edge. It is a long way down!

6. Continue on the white trail as it loops northward back to the intersection of the white and red trails (0.7 mile).

7. At the junction of the white and red trails, turn to the right (east). Below, painted on the rock wall is a red arrow pointing toward a narrow, rocky entrance. Turn downhill here to follow the red trail south. This is the most challenging of all the park trails.

CAUTION: For those who do not like tight places, it is best to avoid the red trail entirely and take the blue trail instead. It lies to the east of the red trail and parallel to SR 282; it can be reached by going east to the main entrance trail.

The red trail is well marked as it snakes up and down deep inside the ledges and past Sharon Conglomerate walls. At one point you will see long tree roots cascading down the sandstone walls on the left, an astonishing natural adaptation.

8. The trail reaches a narrow squeeze called Fat Man's Peril under the rocks, then rises. At the top turn left, then right (south), and follow the red marks down over some large boulders. Here in the spring and summer are some lovely moss-covered rocks with small ferns growing over them.

9. Devil's Icebox (0.9 mile) is a cool, deep natural cave through which Sylvan Creek runs. Go inside, stepping on small stones over the water, to enjoy the cool air that remains at this temperature all year round.

10. Cross the stream and cross a wooden bridge going south. A pale blue hiker sign identifies this path as the blue trail. Follow it up some stairs and continue southward until the path reaches a dead end.

11. Turn around and return on the blue trail. It parallels SR 282 below on the right and takes you back to the main entrance trail and a pedestrian crossing to the parking area.

15 AURORA SANCTUARY

Easy

Distance: 2.4 miles

Hiking time: 1-1/4 hours

Description: This loop hike is initially on a wide, mulched trail but soon narrows down to an easily followed path. Because there are very few trail signs, and the red-painted tree blazes are sometimes only barely visible, it can be somewhat difficult to follow the hiking loop without using the trail descriptions below. There are also several side trails in addition to the main trail. Despite considerable growth on either side of the trail, the path is usually evident. All the stream crossings in the sanctuary are on wooden boardwalks or bridges.

Directions: From I-271 take Exit 27 at US 422 east (Solon). Continue east on US 422 to the SR 91 exit in Solon. Drive south on SR 91 to just past the underpass, then turn left (southeast) onto SR 43. Follow SR 43 to Aurora. Continue past the SR 82 intersection to SR 306 (Chillicothe Rd.) in Aurora. On the right is the tall, white Church of Aurora and just opposite it, East Pioneer Trail Rd. Turn left (east) on E. Pioneer Trail and follow it about 1.5 miles. At about 0.3 mile beyond N. Page Rd. (on the right) is a small sign for Aurora Sanctuary parking area.
From Akron take I-76 east to SR 43, then SR 43 north through Kent and Streetsboro to E. Pioneer Trail Rd. Turn right (east) just before the gazebo in the center of town and follow E. Pioneer Trail about 1.5 miles to the Aurora Sanctuary parking area on the right. The parking lot is about 0.3 miles east of N. Page Rd.

Parking & restrooms: Park in the small gravel parking lot on the south side of E. Pioneer Trail Rd. There are no restrooms here.

The Aurora Sanctuary is a 162-acre wildlife sanctuary located east of the town of Aurora on East Pioneer Trail Rd. The park is owned and maintained by the Audubon Society of Greater Cleveland and its cadre of volunteers. Recent improvements added by the Audubon Society include new wooden footbridges and boardwalks over marshes and formerly impassable areas. Future plans call for new numbered signs and an accompanying guidebook.

The Audubon Sanctuary contains two lovely ponds that are very attractive to waterfowl and especially rewarding to human visitors, too, during bird migration seasons. The Aurora Branch of the Chagrin River flows

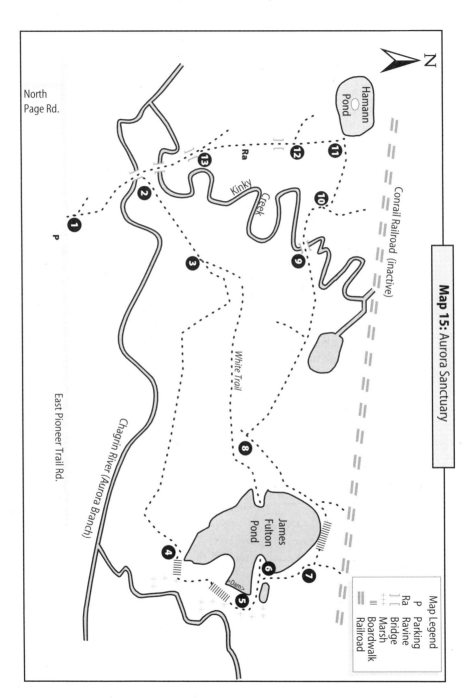

Map 15: Aurora Sanctuary

North
Page Rd.

East Pioneer Trail Rd.

Chagrin River (Aurora Branch)

Kinky Creek

White Trail

Ra

Conrail Railroad (inactive)

Hamann Pond

James Fulton Pond

Dam

P

N

Map Legend
P   Parking
Ra   Ravine
] [Bridge
+   Marsh
||| Boardwalk
▨   Railroad

past the southern boundary of the sanctuary and is fed by many small tributaries, including Kinky Creek.

NOTE: In the spring this sanctuary tends to become very wet and muddy and requires waterproof footware.

If, after this hike, you plan to take the two-mile loop hike around Sunny Lake (Ch. 16), take Page Rd. south about one mile to Mennonite Rd., then turn left (east) to Sunny Lake Park on the left. Boating and fishing are available in this lake.

1. The entrance to the sanctuary is on the north side of the road west of the parking lot. Walk about 150 yards along the south side of E. Pioneer Trail Rd.

CAUTION: Cross E. Pioneer Trail Rd. carefully as fast-moving traffic to the east comes up over the hill suddenly.

Cross a small footbridge to an opening in the hedgerow to reach the entrance to the trail. Follow the wide, mulched trail north, going past a path on the left. The trail gradually descends and narrows to a path that crosses a wooden bridge over the Aurora Branch of the Chagrin River.

2. At about 0.2 mile (from the parking lot), watch carefully for a trail on the right. Here there is a sign marked "Wildlife Sanctuary" posted on a tree and a large bulletin board. Turn right at this trail intersection. This point marks the beginning and end of the loop through the sanctuary.

3. The trail leads uphill on a set of wooden steps through a thick beech-maple forest. At 0.3 mile bypass another trail junction marked "White Trail." (This trail goes to the west side of James Fulton Pond to a bench named in memory of Myrtle Astracan, Audubon Society member and supporter of Aurora Sanctuary.)

Continue ahead (east). Some of the trees are marked with red paint to indicate this is also the Red Trail.

4. At about 0.7 mile reach the south corner of James Fulton Pond, named for a long time member of the Audubon Society and Chairman of the Aurora Sanctuary Committee. Go left a few steps for a long view of this large, plant-filled pond. Often there is a variety of waterbirds and ducks on the pond. A sign on the right indicates this path is the Carl F. Hamann Trail, named for a former mayor of Aurora and benefactor of Aurora Sanctuary.

The trail follows the south shore of the pond and crosses several wooden boardwalks above wet and marshy land and the pond's outlet stream.

5. Next ascend a hill on a pallet stairway with a rope handrail, then turn left. Stay to the right to reach a bench (named for Gordon Walker, another supporter of Aurora Sanctuary) overlooking the pond. It is a joy to view this pond during migration for the many birds and ducks that congregate here. During the spring and summer great blue herons can usually be seen fishing here.

6. On the left, just before the bench, is a short path leading out to a point where a pair of beaver lodges exist on either side of the peninsula. To have two beaver families living here is an unusual occurrence. Ordinarily, only one pair of beavers will occupy a wildlife pond at a time. It is evident that the beavers worked together industriously on these lodges and on the dam to the southeast.

Return to the Hamann Trail. On the right is a beaver drag, a small ditch connecting Fulton Pond with a small pond on the right. This drag allows beavers to move (drag) branches and logs to use for food and building materials.

Continue north around the pond through dense overgrowth.

7. At about 1.0 mile pass a trail spur on the right and continue on the main trail going northwest across another wooden boardwalk. At the end of the boardwalk, the path goes uphill and bends around to the south. Avoid taking the trail at the top of the hill, as it goes out to the Conrail tracks (currently inactive).

8. At 1.2 miles reach a trail sign for the Hamann Trail pointing to the west.

NOTE: Be sure to take this right turn (west) on the Hamann Trail because the path ahead just goes around in a circle.

Continue on the Hamann Trail, overgrown and grassy, another 0.1 mile. Next the trail bears right (northwest) at an open area and passes a trail on the left. Enter a cool beech-maple forest (1.3 miles).

9. Soon the path descends on a wider trail to reach Kinky Creek. Cross the stream on a new bridge.

10. At 1.5 miles is another trail junction and another Hamann Trail sign pointing to the west. Follow the trail to the left (west). The trail on the right (north) goes out to the railroad tracks.

11. At about 1.6 miles reach an open field. Straight ahead is small, plant-filled Hamann Pond. Turn left (south) and follow a path through a field of tall grass. Scattered through the field are old posted bluebird boxes.

12. After another 0.2 mile, reenter the woods where the trail jogs right then left to a double stairway and bridge over a ditch. This southeast-northwest ditch, running diagonally through the sanctuary, is an old railroad right-of-way for the Clinton Airline, named for New York Governor DeWitt Clinton in 1852. This railroad was to run from New York to Missouri but was never completed because of high costs and the Depression of 1856. Only the partially dug ditch remains here.

The trail now goes south on a hogback ridge above a ravine with Kinky Creek below on the left.

13. The path descends and crosses a small wooden bridge over a tributary, then a larger wooden bridge over Kinky Creek.

At 2.0 miles reach the same junction as in Note #2 above to complete the loop. Continue ahead (south), crossing the same wooden footbridge over Aurora Branch. The path gently ascends and exits to E. Pioneer Trail Rd.

This chapter was reviewed by Daniel H. Melcher, President of the Audubon Society of Greater Cleveland and Chairman of the Aurora Sanctuary Committee. Information about the Society is available by calling 216-861-5093.

16 SUNNY LAKE PARK

Distance: 2 miles

Hiking time: 1 hour

Description: The flat trail around Sunny Lake is partly asphalt-paved, partly a dirt footpath, and partly a non-vehicle gravel road. There are many nice views of the lake on this easy loop hike.

Directions: From I-271 take Exit 27, US 422 east to Solon. Exit at SR 91 south to the center of Solon. Just past the underpass in Solon, turn left (east) onto SR 43. Follow SR 43 southeast past SR 82 to SR 306 (Chillicothe Rd.) in the center of Aurora. Turn right (south) on Chillicothe Rd. (this is still SR 43); go about 1.5 miles to Mennonite Rd. Turn left (east) on Mennonite Rd. to Sunny Lake Park on the left, just past Page Rd.
From Akron take I-76 east to SR 43 north. Follow SR 43 through Kent and Streetsboro to Mennonite Rd., about 2 miles north of the I-80 underpass. Turn right (east) on Mennonite Rd. Continue about 1 mile to Sunny Lake Park on the left.

Parking & restrooms: Park just inside the entrance; restrooms are in the brick building.

Sunny Lake Park in Aurora is a unit of that city's Department of Parks and Recreation. It is a popular lake for fishing and boating, but swimming is not permitted. Picnic shelters, a children's playing area, a sand volleyball court, and a boat rental concession are located near the entrance to the park off Mennonite Rd. There is one hiking trail that encircles the perimeter of the lake. The park is accessible from April 1 to early October.

1. Start east of the parking lot by crossing the green-painted footbridge over the lake intake stream. Cross the gravel parking area to the asphalt-paved trail to circle Sunny Lake in a counterclockwise direction. The paved trail ends at about 0.3 mile and a grassy path skirting the edge of the lake begins. At 0.5 mile cross a wooden bridge over a stream.

2. Stay left at a fork in the trail (0.6 mile).

3. Stay left again when another trail comes in from the right. The main trail is marked with white rectangular blazes nailed to trees.

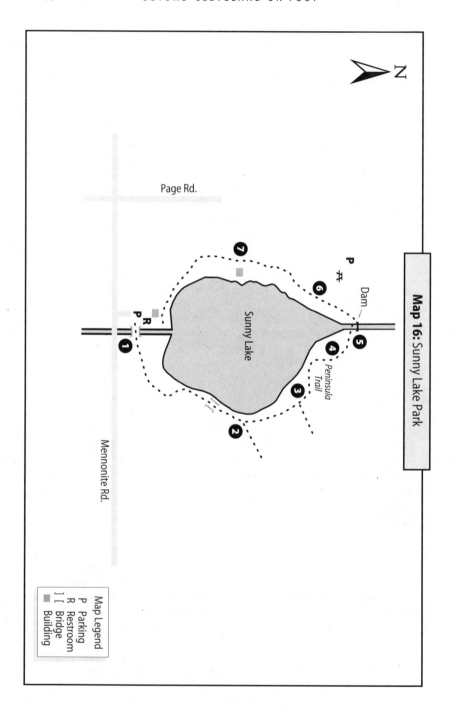

Map 16: Sunny Lake Park

4. An abandoned cabin to the right of the trail is near an open picnic spot at the lake's edge. The path ascends a slope and at 1.0 mile a sign indicates that this is the Peninsula Trail.

5. Cross a mowed field (under a power line) to the dam at the north end of the lake.

6. The trail continues now on an old gravel road past the Page Rd. parking and picnic area on the right (1.3 miles).

7. Continue on the old gravel road (closed to traffic) past a small building, benches, and picnic tables on the left, overlooking the tranquil lake. Finish the loop at the boat rental building and parking area.

17 TINKER'S CREEK STATE NATURE PRESERVE

Easy

Distance: 2 miles

Hiking time: 1-1/4 hours

Description: The three flat trails are well delineated and use high ground and boardwalks to take the hiker to each of the seven ponds in the preserve and to an observation platform for a beautiful view of the creek and marsh.

Directions: From I-480 exit at SR 91 in Twinsburg. Drive south on SR 91 for 1.3 miles to Old Mill Rd. and turn left (east). Cross over I-480 as Old Mill Rd. becomes Davis Rd. in Portage Co. and continue east. At 0.7 mile past Ravenna Rd., cross the railroad tracks and reach the parking area for the preserve on the left.
From Akron take I-76 east to SR 43. Take SR 43 north past Streetsboro to Frost Rd. Turn left on Frost to Aurora-Hudson Rd. Turn right on Aurora Hudson, then take a left on Davis Rd. The preserve parking lot is on the right just before Ravenna Rd.

Parking & restrooms: Park in the small parking lot on the north side of Davis Rd. Restrooms are on the trail at the intersection of Seven Ponds and South Point Trails.

Tinker's Creek State Nature Preserve, a 786-acre marsh and swamp forest named for the creek flowing through the marsh, is located close to the Portage-Summit county line near Twinsburg. Tinker's Creek is a long, irregular river that rises in northern Portage County and flows across a plateau of bays, swamps, and marshes. It then courses northwest through Summit County to Bedford Reservation in Cuyahoga County and finally empties into the Cuyahoga River in Cuyahoga Valley National Recreation Area.

In earlier times, the area around these wetlands was a source of great fear to pioneers and early settlers because there were rumors of sink holes and quicksand. In the late 1800s the New York, Chicago, & St. Louis Railroad built a line through the western edge of what is now the preserve and constructed an embankment that created even more swampland and marsh than was there originally.

Dedicated as a scenic nature preserve in 1974 by the Ohio Department of Natural Resources, this delightful park is about three-quarters marsh-

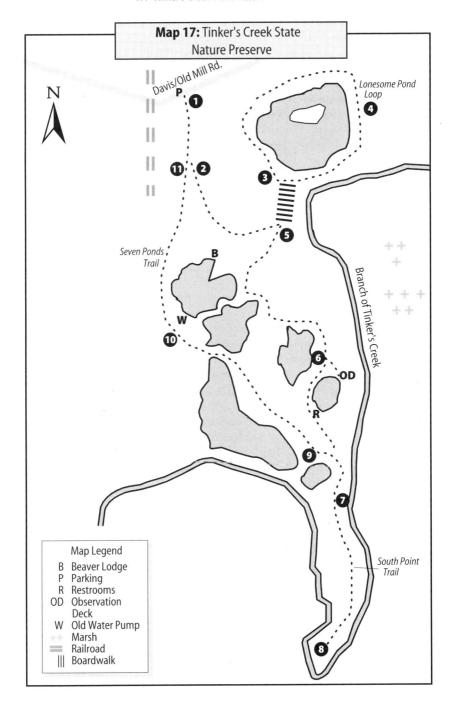

Map 17: Tinker's Creek State Nature Preserve

land with cattail, willow, buttonbush, alder, and other moisture-loving plants and trees. In the small forest are dogwood, maple, oak, pine, aspen, and wild cherry trees. Seven spring-fed ponds dot the forested land and a provide habitat for beaver, ducks, Canada geese, great blue herons, fox, deer, reptiles, and amphibians.

The park is open only during daylight hours, and visitors are asked to remain on the trails in this watery nature preserve. It is wise to bring insect repellent if you visit the park in the summer. Watch carefully for poison ivy, which is abundant. Binoculars and bird, tree, and wildflower guidebooks are quite useful here. In the spring, visit Tinker's Creek to enjoy birds and spring wildflowers; in the fall, to see migrating birds and colorful tree foliage.

1. Cross Davis Rd. from the parking area to the trail entrance adjacent to the railroad tracks and follow the path south.

2. Enter a stand of white pines, and upon reaching a trail junction turn left (east) where a sign indicates Seven Ponds Trail. (This trail also continues straight ahead.)

3. At the boardwalk turn left again (north) to walk along a hummock on the 0.5-mile Lonesome Pond Loop to the first of the seven ponds. Here there is much evidence of beaver activity; look for chisel work on trees and stumps. These prominent tooth marks are created by the beaver's ever-growing front teeth that have a hard tooth enamel in front and a softer dentine in back. As the beaver gnaws, a self-sharpening system is created.

4. Lonesome Pond Loop encircles this pretty spring-fed lake, which contains exceptionally clear water. There may be more signs of beaver activity as you circle the pond clockwise. Beaver may build dams, create ponds, and erect large beaver lodges out of aspen, willow, or birch trees, which they then use for food. Here there can be evidence of an active beaver colony. A partially filled-in marsh on the left near the end of the loop is a fine spot to look for birds and waterfowl.

Return on the boardwalk to the Seven Ponds Trail junction.

5. Go left (south) at this junction and continue following the trail south on and off boardwalks to pass the second, third, and fourth ponds on the right. On the left is the marsh and a south-flowing branch of Tinker's Creek.

6. Just beyond the fourth pond, a short path leads past a fifth pond to an observation deck on the left from which more waterfowl and other wildlife may be observed in the river and marsh. Canadian geese often congregate here to feed on fish and other aquatic organisms. Return to the main trail.

7. Continue south to the sixth pond and a trail intersection. Restrooms are located near this junction. Bear left onto the South Point Trail.

8. This hummock of land extends through an oak forest to another wide view of the swamp and marshlands at the end. Here the creek widens and begins to flow northward.

9. Return along South Point Trail to the trail junction. Back on the main trail, turn left. You will pass the sixth pond and the seventh pond on the left. Continue straight (north) toward Davis Rd. and the parking lot. Halfway back, on the right, is the opposite side of the third pond passed earlier. Farther along on the right is the second pond, also passed earlier.

10. Between the third and second ponds is an old, non-functioning water pump. Here look for a very large beaver lodge at the north end of the second pond. There might also be beaver swimming and busily working in this pond, engaged in dam building or wood harvesting.

11. Continue north to the end of the trail on Davis Rd.

18 EAGLE CREEK STATE NATURE PRESERVE

Distance: 4.7 miles

Moderate

Hiking time: 3 hours, for leisurely enjoyment.

Description: The terrain is easy to walk but wet and muddy in some places, making waterproof boots useful. There are two loop trails: the 1.5-mile Clubmoss Trail loop and the 2.5-mile Beaver Run Trail, including the short Beech Ridge Trail loop. Because of the unusual flora and fauna here, it is instructive to have binoculars and bird, fern, wildflower, and tree identification books along on the hike.

Directions: Follow US 422 to Bainbridge; exit onto SR 306 (south) to Aurora. Take a left (east) onto SR 82 to Garrettsville. In Garretsville, take Center Rd. (Twp. 293) northeast for 2 miles to Hopkins Rd. Turn south on Hopkins. Park entrance is about 1 mile on the right.
From Akron, take SR 8 north to SR 303, then 303 east to SR 88. Follow SR 88 (at Freedom/Drakesburg) northeast to Garrettsville. In Garrettsville take Center Rd. (Twp. 293) about two miles northeast to Hopkins Rd. Turn south on Hopkins about one mile to the park entrance on the right.

Parking & restrooms: There is a small parking area at the park entrance; no restrooms are available here.

Eagle Creek State Nature Preserve is in Nelson Township near Garrettsville. This 441-acre preserve opened in 1974 and is owned and managed by the Ohio Department of Natural Resources. With terrain ranging from marshland to woodland forest, the park supports a variety of trees, especially cucumber magnolia, yellow birch, and swamp-loving buttonbush. Wildlife such as beaver, fox, and deer live in this park. A bird observation blind enables visitors to identify waterfowl and many kinds of songbirds, especially during the migration season. Eagle Creek itself meanders through a floodplain from north to south and eventually enters the Mahoning River east of here. Within the preserve are cranberry bogs, swamps, marshes, and beaver ponds. Boardwalks and trails allow close-up study of many wildflowers, moisture-loving ferns (such as the royal, cinnamon, and ostrich), and the insectivorous sundew and pitcher plant.

Because its many marshes are a great breeding ground for mosquitoes, this park is best enjoyed in the spring or fall. Insect repellant is essential for summer hikes. The park is open only during daylight hours; dogs, picnicking, alcoholic beverages, and camping are not permitted.

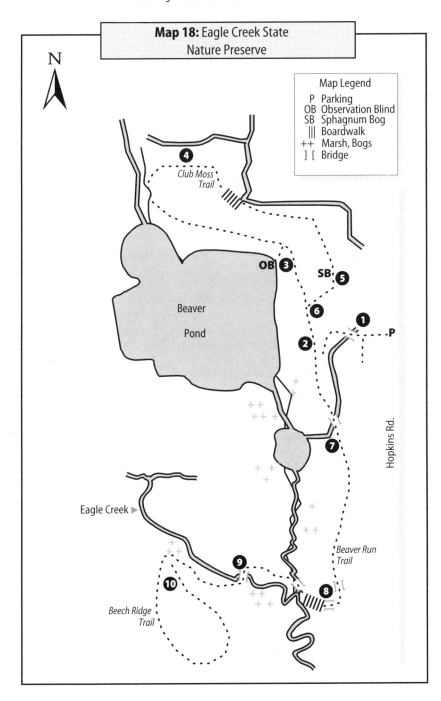

Map 18: Eagle Creek State Nature Preserve

N

Map Legend
P Parking
OB Observation Blind
SB Sphagnum Bog
||| Boardwalk
++ Marsh, Bogs
] [Bridge

Club Moss Trail

Beaver Pond

OB 3

SB 5

6

1

P

2

4

7

Hopkins Rd.

Eagle Creek

Beaver Run Trail

9

10

8

Beech Ridge Trail

1. Start the walk from the parking area, heading west across a grassy field. Pass a trail marked "Amphitheater" and continue straight ahead to the nature trails. After entering the woods, cross a small bridge over a stream. Note the buttonbush swamp on the left. The buttonbush shrub can be identified in the summer by its spherical cluster of small, fragrant white flowers.

2. At 0.2 mile reach a trail intersection, and turn right (north) onto the Clubmoss Trail. The pathway bends north, passes a bog and small pond, and meets the end of the trail loop on the right (0.5 mile).

3. Continue straight ahead on the Clubmoss Trail going toward Beaver Pond. On the right is a small stand of clubmoss, which looks like tiny, erect, dark green evergreen trees.

Reach the path on the left leading down to the bird observation blind. Pause here to enjoy the variety of wildlife on this picturesque beaver pond. You may notice the shy swamp sparrow feeding in the mud along the water's edge.

Leave the blind and return to the Clubmoss Trail, turning left at the inter-section to continue on the loop as it winds gently around the northeast.

4. Follow the trail around the loop through a forest of cottonwood trees, some of which have been felled by storms and aging. The ruins of old farm foundations and the remnants of an old sugarhouse are on either side of the trail along this stretch of the pathway. As the trail curves east-ward, you will pass small ponds and cross a boardwalk to an open field where the path begins to turn south.

5. At about 0.9 mile a sign on the right identifies the Sphagnum Bog; a short boardwalk leads into this interesting bog. Cranberry bushes and the carnivorous pitcher plant and sundew thrive here. The latter two ensnare small insects for their nourishment—the sundew with its sticky leaf hairs and the pitcher plant by holding water in its hollow-shaped leaves.

6. Return to the trail and complete the loop. Turn left (south) at the trail intersection and follow the path until it meets the trail junction described in Note #2. Begin the Beaver Run Trail by continuing south.

7. Cross a footbridge and follow the Beaver Run Trail up and down above the edge of a stream and the marshlands of Eagle Creek on the right (west).

8. After the trail bends west, cross two wooden bridges and a wooden boardwalk over marshy land before reaching a bridge over a side stream that enters Eagle Creek. The path may be wet and marshy along here as it leads westward.

9. Cross Eagle Creek on a long bridge and follow the route on higher ground now. The path goes uphill to start the Beech Ridge Trail loop.

10. Follow the Beech Ridge Trail looping counter-clockwise. Here in this forest of many beech trees, look for the yellow birch tree, with yellow-ish-to-bronze peeling bark, and the cucumber magnolia (cucumbertree) with its springtime yellowish-green blossoms. In the fall, the large tulip-shaped leaves of this deciduous tree turn bright yellow.

Some of the spring wildflowers you may see along this trail are blood root, trillium, cut-leaved toothwort, spring beauty, trout lily, purple, white, and yellow violets, squirrel corn, and Dutchman's breeches.

Complete the loop and retrace your steps along the trail. Cross the bridge over Eagle Creek and the other bridges to the same trail junction described in Note #2. Turn east (right) to return to the parking area.

19 MOGODORE RESERVOIR

Distance: 3 miles

Strenuous

Hiking time: 1-1/2 hours

Description: The Buckeye Trail is clearly marked with two-inch-by-six-inch blue blazes painted on trees and posts and occasionally with a blue arrow on a post. The terrain is generally flat with several bridged stream crossings. There are many pleasant views of the water on this hike; they are especially rewarding in early spring or late fall when the leaves are down.

Directions: Follow I-480 east until it becomes SR 14 at the I-80 interchange. Continue to Streetsboro and turn south on SR 43. Follow SR 43 through Twin Lakes, Kent, and Brimfield. When 3.3 miles south of I-76, watch for a small sign on the left for Mogodore Reservoir. Turn left into the park at the bait and tackle store.
From I-76 east (in Akron), take SR 43 south 3.3 miles to the park entrance on the left.
(To reach the campground at Mogodore Park, continue south on SR 43 to Randolph Rd., turn right and go 1 mile on Randolph Rd. Turn right at Lansinger Rd., left on Ticknor, and right to the camp office check-in building.)

Parking & restrooms: Park adjacent to the small administration building. Primitive restrooms are near the entrance to the park and on the Buckeye Trail about 0.1 mile from the parking area.

Mogodore Reservoir, just east of Akron, was created by impounding water of the Little Cuyahoga River to form a beautiful lake. The City of Akron Water Supply Reservoir System administers the park surrounding the reservoir, owns the buildings and boat concession, manages the campground and beach, and sells fishing and hunting permits. Nearby Mogodore Park, located 1 mile west of SR 43, offers camping, swimming, and picnicking.

Mogodore Reservoir contains 19 miles of shoreline and about 1,000 acres of water surface. On this hike you will follow the blue-blazed Buckeye Trail on the north side of the reservoir, east of SR 43. (The Buckeye Trail also follows the north edge of the reservoir west of SR 43.)

Mogodore Reservoir is a prime location for fishing, boating, and canoeing during most of the year, and for waterfowl hunting in November.

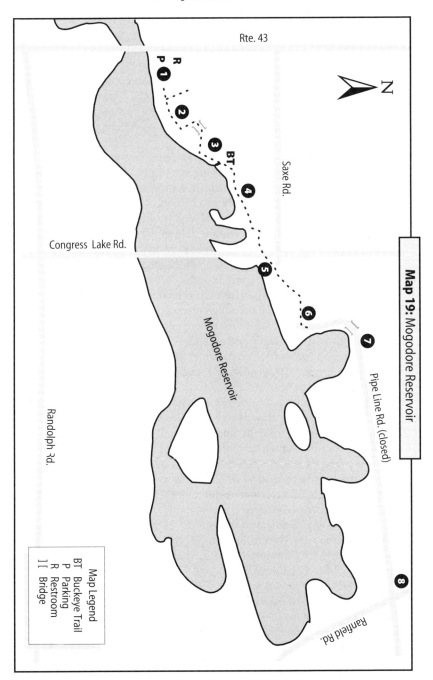

Map 19: Mogodore Reservoir

Map Legend
BT Buckeye Trail
P   Parking
R   Restroom
][Bridge

No hiking or fishing is permitted during the November hunting season. Check with the park office for information (330-628-2672) or write to: Superintendent, Mogodore Reservoir, 2578 SR 43, Mogodore, OH 44260.

1. Start the hike behind the gate in the northeast corner of the parking lot. The Buckeye Trail (BT) leads past an old trailer camp on an asphalt-paved trail. Leave the paved trail to go east (right) on a woods path. The BT quickly makes a sharp left turn (at a blue arrow) and goes up a small slope.

2. The path bends left and crosses a bridge over a small stream. (Note that a double blue blaze on a tree indicates a turn in the trail; the upper blaze indicates the direction of the turn, right or left.)

3. Continue heading generally east through a lovely forest of red and white oaks, beeches, and maples. Mogodore Reservoir is on the right (south). Canada geese are a common sight in the reservoir; they congregate in large groups to feed on fish and insects in the water. Occasionally a great blue heron may be seen wading in the shallow water searching for fish, frogs, or other aquatic animals.

The trail veers slightly away from the reservoir, then goes uphill onto an embankment overlooking the water, providing long, scenic views of the lake. Next the trail descends to the water's edge. After passing a fallen tree, the path heads in a generally northeast direction. On the left is a wire fence marking private property, beyond which are houses on Saxe Rd.

4. Cross another stream on small logs and continue on the BT along the reservoir. The path now veers away from the water. Cross another small stream on logs and reach Congress Lake Rd. at 1.2 miles.

5. Cross the road and reenter the BT directly opposite. The trail turns toward the reservoir initially and then bends away. Still following BT blazes, watch for several trees blown down across the rail.

6. Reach Pipe Line Rd. at 1.5 miles. This is an open two-lane, grass-and-cinder road now closed to vehicles. Follow it eastward as it bends to the north away from the reservoir. Avoid taking any of the grassy trails leading off both sides of the road.

7. Cross a small bridge and continue to follow the road as it turns eastward and is bordered by tall, handsome pines.

Continue to the gate at Ranfield Rd. where this hike ends. (The BT continues northward on Ranfield Rd.)

8. Reverse your direction to follow Pipe Line Rd. westward to the point where it enters the woods (Note #6). Watch carefully for blue blazes on the return path to follow the trail overlooking the reservoir, and enjoy long views in the opposite direction.

20 WEST BRANCH STATE PARK

Distance: 9 miles

Strenuous

Hiking time: 4-1/2 hours

Description: Somewhat strenuous due to its length and its traverse of rolling hills. About 10 percent of this hike is on roads.

Directions: From I-271 take I-480 east/SR 14. Follow SR 14 east toward Ravenna, passing SR 44 and SR 88 to SR 5 east. Continue east on SR 5 to Rock Spring Rd. and turn right (south). West Branch State Park is on the right about 1 mile.

Parking & restrooms: At the boat launch area off Rock Springs Rd.

Managed by the Ohio Department of Natural Resources, West Branch State Park surrounds West Branch Reservoir near Campbellsport. This beautiful loop hike on the Buckeye Trail traverses gently rolling terrain that was carved by the advance of Ohio's last glacier. In 1966, the U.S. Corps of Engineers created the reservoir by damming up the Mahoning River for flood control as well as recreation. From along Knapp Rd., remnants of the canal and railroad that once ran alongside the Mahoning River can be seen sticking up above the water out in the middle of the reservoir.

This hike features many scenic views of the reservoir and offers a day's outing or an opportunity to camp in the nearby state park campground and enjoy fishing, picnicking, and swimming.

1. Start the hike from the boat launch and parking area by going north on the well-worn path of the blue-blazed Buckeye Trail. Follow the stream and a trail marker on the right. At 0.2 mile enter a cool pine forest, and at about 0.4 mile cross a small wooden bridge.

At about 0.5 mile a Buckeye Trail sign indicates the trail turns left, where in season lovely wildflowers festoon this stretch of the trail.

2. Views of the reservoir appear, and soon the trail crosses an inlet and small bridge (1.4 miles), then a power line (1.5 miles). Follow the blue blazes and avoid taking any side trails that cross the main trail.

3. At about 1.7 miles the trail becomes a steep, downhill dirt path, then turns into a wet area that may be flooded at times. Beavers have been busy in this part of the reservoir, and evidence of their industrious work is often

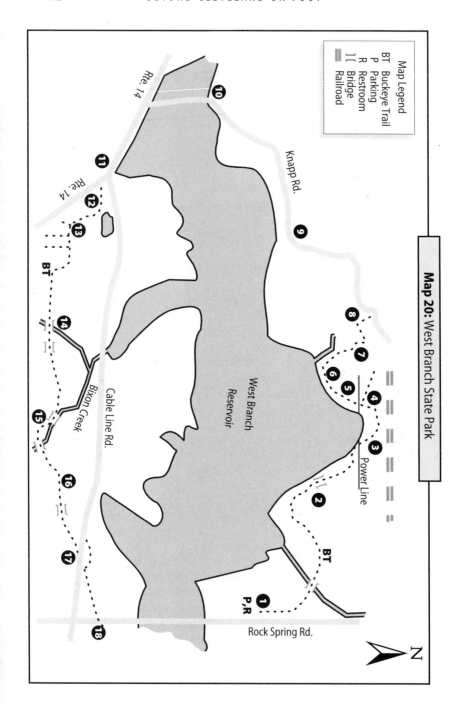

Map 20: West Branch State Park

visible. The blue blazes may be difficult to follow in this section. The trail goes to the right, uphill.

4. Ascend the slope of black cinders to the top of a culvert, crossing it carefully over the stream below.

CAUTION: Do not go onto the railroad tracks as this is an active railway and trains pass here periodically.

5. At about 2.1 miles the trail bears left, encounters the power line again, and then widens into a woods road (2.2 miles). Stay left toward the reservoir and views of the water.

6. Pass two shelters belonging to the University of Akron Outing Club. From the second one the trail goes downhill, east of the shelter. Here the trail may be blocked by a large beech tree. On the left, Note a huge beaver dam and beaver house. At times, these fascinating creatures can be seen swimming in the pond they have created from the inlet.

7. At about 2.6 miles the trail becomes a woods road again and turns left, veers away from the reservoir, and travels through an overgrown field.

8. The trail takes another left turn toward the reservoir at 3 miles, and at 3.3 miles emerges onto Knapp Rd. Here you may view the old canal and railroad remnants extending out into the reservoir at its west end.

9. Leave the Buckeye Trail behind for about 1.5 miles and follow the white blazes placed on utility poles along Knapp Rd.

10. Go south past the boat launch area, cross the bridge over the reservoir, and bear left onto the berm of SR 14.

CAUTION: Because of fast traffic on this highway, walk in single file facing the cars.

11. On SR 14, just past Cable Line Rd., look for the blue Buckeye Trail blazes on the left marking the trail entrance. There is a large pile of gravel at the entrance to the woods (4 miles). Take an immediate left (southeast) and continue following the blue blazes.

12. The trail reaches a meadow and passes a pond. At about 5 miles the trail enters a cedar and pine forest. Bear left at a woods road.

13. Cross a small brook, turn left when the trail opens up into a wider path, turn left again at a Buckeye Trail post and cross another brook.

14. At the next trail intersection (6 miles), continue straight ahead in a generally easterly direction on the Buckeye Trail. Cross several brooks and streams before ascending a small hill.

15. At about 7 miles the trail crosses a small ravine and stream, then a wider stream, Bixon Creek. Recross Bixon Creek on a log bridge (7.4 miles).

16. The trail passes an open cornfield on the left and a crosses another small brook (8 miles).

17. Reach a dirt road (Cable Line Rd.) and cross it diagonally left to the Buckeye Trail entrance at the edge of the woods.

18. At Rock Spring Rd. turn left (north). Follow the road across the bridge to return to the starting point at the boat launch area.

To see a world in a grain of sand
And Heaven in a wildflower
To hold infinity in the palm of your hand
And eternity in an hour.
—William Blake

SUMMIT COUNTY

Summit County is dominated by the city of Akron, which grew with the establishment of the Ohio & Erie Canal across the summit of land between the Tuscarawas and Cuyahoga Rivers (Ch. 32). Hundreds of industries sprang up along the canal as boats traveled in both directions through the locks that connected Cleveland with Portsmouth. Later milling and manufacturing helped the city grow—eventually it became a major rubber producing center.

In the early days, Indians carried their canoes overland from one navigable point to another ("portaged") across this summit of land on an eight-mile course called Portage Path. The string of lakes nearby named for this path are the Portage Lakes (Ch. 23). The canoe portage was necessary to connect the south-flowing Tuscarawas River and the north-flowing Cuyahoga River. Later this area became an important settlers' trading post. Until 1785, the path served as the western boundary of the United States.

Within Summit County is the major portion of the 33,000-acre Cuyahoga Valley National Recreation Area, which preserves 22 miles of green space between Cleveland and Akron. Hale Farm and Village Museum, located within the CVNRA, is a re-creation of a typical 19th-century Western Reserve village using buildings and furnishings from all over northeast Ohio (800-589-9703). Many of the Metro Parks Serving Summit County are also within this pastoral corridor.

Metro Parks Serving Summit County consists of more then 6,600 acres of land including 11 developed parks, the F.A. Seiberling Naturealm, a 23-mile Bike & Hike Trail and several large conservation areas. Selected hikes in these parks are described in Chs. 31-42. A monthly newsletter, *Green Islands*, is available free to Summit County residents or for five dollars per year to all others. To order the newsletter or to obtain information about Metro Parks, write to: Metro Parks Serving Summit County, 975 Treaty Line Rd., Akron, OH 44313-5898, or call 330-867-5511.

Additional information about Summit County is available from Akron/Summit Convention & Visitors Bureau, 77 E. Mill St., Akron, OH 44308; 330-374-8900 or 800-245-4254.

21 HUDSON VILLAGE AND WESTERN RESERVE ACADEMY

Distance: 2 miles

Easy

Walking time: 1-1/2 hours

Description: Hikes A and B are easy, pleasant walks through historic Hudson Village and the campus of Western Reserve Academy. Either or both can be taken. They are almost entirely on sidewalks and will introduce the visitor to beautifully restored 19th-century homes and public buildings and provide an introduction to the town's historical past.

Directions: From I-480 take Exit 37 in Twinsburg. Take SR 91 south 4 miles to Hudson. Pass Western Reserve Academy on the left just before entering the town on North Main St. (SR 91).
From Akron, take SR 8 north to Streetsboro Rd. (SR 303). Turn right (east) on Streetsboro Rd. into Hudson. Turn left (north) onto SR 91.

Parking & restrooms: Just before the clocktower, turn west into the Municipal Parking Lot behind the row of business buildings on North Main St.; restrooms are at the library or in any public restaurant.

Hudson Village has been mentioned as one of the top 100 historic places in the U. S. because so many of its residences and other structures are listed on the National Register of Historic Buildings and Homes. Many buildings on the campus of nearby Western Reserve Academy (originally Western Reserve College) also boast this prestigious listing. Hudson Village is reminiscent of a small Connecticut town because of its architecture and neat village green containing a bandstand and clocktower. This "New England look" is not surprising. The first settler here was David Hudson (1761-1836) of Goshen, Connecticut, who arrived in 1799 to view land in the Connecticut Western Reserve that he and four others had purchased, sight unseen, for $8,000.

Hudson had traveled upland with a small party through New York State to Lakes Ontario and Erie, then to Cleveland and the Cuyahoga River. Heading south on the Cuyahoga to Brandywine Creek, he found he could go no farther and so continued on foot, using surveyor's tools to find his five-mile-square parcel of land, identified only as Township four, Range 10.

After returning from a trip home to retrieve his family and bring other settlers, he and his men began to cut an axe-width road in from the Cuyahoga River to Hudson (as the settlement became known in 1802), over

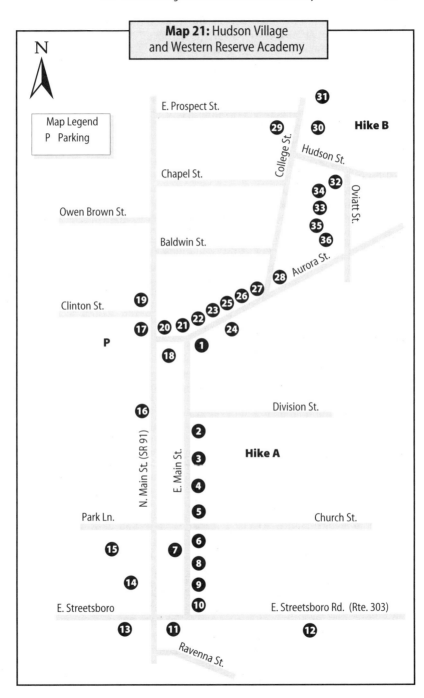

Map 21: Hudson Village and Western Reserve Academy

N

Map Legend
P Parking

E. Prospect St.

Chapel St.

Owen Brown St.

Baldwin St.

Clinton St.

P

College St.

Hudson St.

Oviatt St.

Hike B

Aurora St.

Division St.

N. Main St. (SR 91)

E. Main St.

Hike A

Park Ln.

Church St.

E. Streetsboro

E. Streetsboro Rd. (Rte. 303)

Ravenna St.

which the settlers came. This path became Hudson Rd. and evidence of its beginnings can still be seen in a wide track near the Stanford Trail in the Cuyahoga Valley National Recreation Area (Ch. 26). David Hudson's descendants lived in the Hudson family home at 318 North Main St. until 1967.

The first settlers were sturdy New Englanders who built homes, shops, a church, schoolhouse and other buildings in Hudson, reproducing the Connecticut landscape with which they were so familiar. They modeled the campus of Western Reserve College (1826) after Connecticut's Yale College, constructing brick buildings connected by walkways that criss-cross a central green.

Western Reserve College moved to Cleveland in 1882 because of economic problems and became Adelbert College; its name was later changed to Western Reserve University, and, in 1967, Case Western Reserve University, when it merged with Case Institute of Technology.

Western Reserve College's empty buildings were subsequently occupied by Western Reserve Academy, which, up to that time, had been only a department of the school. The academy struggled along and even closed for a few years until a wealthy industrialist and former pupil, James W. Ellsworth, restored the buildings and reopened the school in 1916. Through Ellsworth's wide-ranging efforts and his substantial endowment, the academy became, and still is, one of the finest independent, co-educational college preparatory schools in the nation. In the summer, a music school, Encore School for Strings, occupies the campus and offers many free concerts given by outstanding young musical artists.

HIKE A. HUDSON VILLAGE

1. From the parking lot, cross N. Main St. at Aurora St. and go northeast to the Hudson Library and Historical Society at 22 Aurora St. (216-653-6658).

The library building on the corner of E. Main and Aurora streets was originally constructed in 1834 by Frederick Baldwin, whose daughter, Caroline Baldwin Babcock (1841-1921), founded the Library and Historical Society in 1910. She and James W. Ellsworth wanted to create a library to preserve the town's important books and papers.

At first the library was part of the newly reopened Western Reserve Academy. From 1919 to 1924 it was housed in Hayden Hall on the academy campus at the corner of Aurora and College streets.

Soon the library board purchased the building at the corner of E. Main and Aurora streets, known as the Frederick Baldwin House where Caroline Baldwin had spent her early childhood years. The house was renovated and opened in 1925 as the Hudson Library and Historical Society. In 1954 a new east wing was added and in 1963 another major expansion took place. The most recent interior renovation occurred in 1995.

The library has a reputation for possessing an excellent collection of books and manuscripts. It is a major research center for scholars studying the life and times of one of Hudson's best-known citizens, abolitionist John Brown (1800-1859).

2. Turn south on East Main St. crossing Division St. At 41 E. Main is the former Edgar B. Ellsworth Store, built in 1841 and now a dental office. Ellsworth's son, James, worked in this store as a child.

James W. Ellsworth (1849-1925) acquired great wealth in Chicago as a major coal dealer and distributor. His contributions to Hudson are numerous. He provided the resources for street paving, the planing of elms, new power and water plants, a sewer system, a telephone system, renovation of homes and land, and shored-up banking and school systems. The clocktower was one of Ellsworth's final philanthropic gifts to the community. Upon his death in 1925 he left most of his wealth to Western Reserve Academy, which he had restored and reopened in 1916.

3. At 35 E. Main St. is the 1889 A. W. Lockhart House. Lockhart was a local saloon keeper whose tavern across the green on Main St. caught fire in April 1892 and caused the entire business block to burn, leaving no early buildings remaining on the west side of Main St.

4. Next is The Town-Shields House at 33 E. Main. Inside the Queen Anne—style facade of this structure is a Greek Revival house built in 1824 by Dr. Israel Town. The Queen Anne facade, built in 1890 by the Shields family, wraps around the original home. (The attic roof of the earlier building remains.)

5. Just before Church St., at 27 E. Main St., is the 1879 Hudson Town Hall. It housed the Fire Department in 1896. The First Congregational Church, founded by David Hudson in 1802, was originally located on this site. The building now serves as office space for the city of Hudson.

6. The building identified as a funeral home at 19 E. Main St. is the Town-Neibel House, Dr. Israel Town's 1836 home. It was remodeled in 1877 by the Neibel family.

7. On the green to the right (west) of here is the site of Hudson's original 1802 schoolhouse.

8. Sebastian Miller, an important Main St. merchant, built his 1878 home at 13 E. Main St. in the popular Italian Revival style.

9. Capt. Heman Oviatt was an early pioneer who built this house at 7 E. Main St. in 1825. It later became the parsonage for the First Congregational Church and, still later, the rectory for old St. Mary's Church next door.

10. St. Mary's Church (1860) originally stood at Oviatt and Maple streets three blocks east of here. In 1888 the building was moved to this location and greatly expanded. St. Mary's parish left in 1970 to build a new church, and now this beautiful old landmark is occupied by Temple Beth Shalom and the Spiritual Life Society, who both share worship space.

11. At 5 E. Main St., on the southeast corner of Main St. (SR 91) and E. Streetsboro St. (SR 303), is an imposing white three-story structure. It was originally the Free Congregational Church, built in 1841 by abolitionist Owen Brown, father of famed abolitionist John Brown. The old church has been raised up over new first-floor construction and has been expanded to house offices.

Owen Brown (1771-1856), a member of a prominent New England family, settled in Hudson in 1805. Of Owen's 17 children, John is by far the best known. The entire Brown family was strongly antislavery and all were active in the Underground Railway movement to help runaway slaves gain freedom in Canada. The family lived in a wooden home at 9 Aurora St. (where the Brewster Mansion now stands).

There is a memorial plaque for John Brown in the park between E. Streetsboro and Ravenna streets, near the spot where he made one of his last Hudson speeches before going to Harpers Ferry, Virginia. His fiery antislavery rhetoric culminated in a raid on the Federal Arsenal there in 1859. Brown was hanged in December of that year, an event that helped instigate the Civil War.

12. To the east of this park is the Inn at Turner's Mill (36 E. Streetsboro), a restaurant and historic landmark. It was built in 1852 as a steam mill by Edgar B. Ellsworth (see Note #4) and Henry N. Day. Originally, it was known as the Hudson Planing and Lumber Co., but by 1873 it became the Hudson Mill Co. and later, Turner's Mill. This landmark structure has been beautifully restored from top to bottom—from the third floor where shakers originally removed husks from the grain to the first floor where grinding took place.

13. Turn back (west) across the green to SR 91 and SR 303 (N. Main and E. Streetsboro streets). Cross SR 91 to see the small Boy Scouts of America Cabin built by Troop 321 in 1931 (not open to the public) and Hudson's World War I Monument (1917-18).

14. Cross SR 303 (E. Streetsboro St.) and walk north to another open Green. In the center of this green space is a small plaque placed by the Hudson Library and Historical Society and the First Congregational Church to mark the site of the first Thanksgiving service in Hudson.

15. Toward the rear (west) of the green at 36 N. Main St. is the Greek Revival—style Augustus Baldwin House built in 1825.

16. At the south end of the green is the 1976 Hudson Bandstand, built to celebrate our country's bicentennial. Continue walking north on N. Main St. past interesting shops and businesses.

On April 28, 1892, all the original buildings in this block—from Park Lane to Clinton St.—were destroyed in a disastrous fire, which began where 84 N. Main St. now stands. The present stores were constructed after that date.

17. Continue north to 160-164 N. Main St. and Saywell's Drug Store, built in 1913. Its old-fashioned soda fountain is a Hudson tradition.

18. Hudson's landmark Clocktower was built on the town green in 1912 by James W. Ellsworth as his gift to the community of his birth. The still-functioning, gravity-run clock is the original one made by the E. Howard Clock Company. The tower also served as a public water fountain. Note the watering trough for horses on the north side and fountains for people and small animals on the west side. A marker on the south side of the clocktower notes that it was a gift from James W. Ellsworth, and that Percy Dresser, Town Marshal, faithfully wound the weights and chimes from 1935 to 1950.

19. On the northwest corner of Clinton and N. Main streets (178 N. Main) is the 1833 Walter Wright Store, now Hudson General Store. This building and all those in this block north to Owen Brown St. escaped the 1892 fire and date from the 1830s to the 1850s. This store is typical of the old wooden buildings that formerly lined all of the west side of N. Main St.

20. Cross N. Main St. and go east on Aurora St. On the corner at 5 Aurora St. is the old Brewster Store, now First National Bank of Ohio. Next to it is the Brewster Mansion at 9 Aurora St., presently containing shops and offices. Anson Brewster (1807-1864), a native of Connecticut and direct descendant of the Mayflower's William Brewster, came here in 1825 and opened his brick, Federal-style store in Hudson in 1839.

In 1853 he built the mansion next door on the site of Owen Brown's old wooden home (Note #11), which had burned to the ground in 1842. The mansion is the only stone Gothic Revival building left standing in the Western Reserve.

21. Next, to the east, is Christ Church Episcopal Chapel (1930), which was constructed when the original 1846 Gothic-style sanctuary was torn down. It occupies the same foundation as the original church.

22. The 1834 Isham-Beebe House at 21 Aurora St. is Christ Church Episcopal's Guild Hall. Warren Isham was an early Hudson newspaper publisher. The Beebes became owners of the house when Anson Brewster's daughter, Ellen, married D. Duncan Beebe, who entered his father-in-law's store and later became sole proprietor of the business. "Brewster Row," as it was then called, extended along Aurora St. from the family store to the Beebe House.

23. The new, enlarged Christ Church Episcopal, completed and opened on Christmas Eve, 1994, connects with the rest of the church's buildings.

24. East of the library, at 30 Aurora St., is the 1826 Whedon-Farwell

House. This structure was originally built in Greek Revival style, but an 1870 renovation made it look more like a Victorian home.

25. At 37 Aurora St. is the 1847 Brick Academy. At one time it housed women students who were taught by Western Reserve Academy professors—in their free time, because women were not then permitted on the all-male campus.

26. Next along beautiful Aurora St. is First Congregational Church of Hudson. A plaque affixed to the side of the original building describes its long history.

HIKE B. WESTERN RESERVE ACADEMY

27. Continue walking northeast on Aurora St. to College St. and turn left (north). On this corner is Hayden Hall (1870), the original home of the Hudson Library. Six grand pillars front this imposing building surrounded by beautiful gardens. Once a cheese warehouse, then a community center, this building later became the school's fine arts center. Presently it houses the music department, containing studios, a recital hall, and practice rooms.

28. On the northwest corner of Aurora and College streets is Loomis Observatory, established and built by Professor Elias Loomis in 1838. It is the oldest observatory on its original foundations in the United States. Loomis, a Professor of Mathematics and Philosophy, was one of America's preeminent 19th-century astronomers. The observatory has been restored several times but still contains its original telescope, transit, astronomical clock, and chair.

Continue north on College St. past lovely old homes. On the right are Seymour Hall, the Chapel, and four-story North Hall. Between Baldwin and Chapel streets are faculty homes.

29. Pass the playing fields and Hudson St. to Ellsworth Hall on the southwest corner of College and E. Prospect streets. Built in 1922, this structure was named for the school's major benefactor, James W. Ellsworth (Note #2). It contains a dormitory, dining room, student center, publications office, radio station, laundry, and meeting rooms.

30. On the east side of College St., opposite Prospect St., is the four-story Athenaeum (1843), a girls' dormitory and the largest of the college's original buildings. At first it was the natural science building, becoming a dormitory in 1917. Its name came from a literary society once housed there. Ohio's first Phi Beta Kappa chapter received its charter in this building in 1847.

31. Beyond the Athenaeum is Bicknell Athletic Complex, originally built in 1920 with subsequent additions. In 1930, a swimming pool was added, and then a gymnasium in 1951. In 1983, renovations added a new swimming pool and diving well, squash courts, indoor tennis courts, and a wrestling room.

32. On College St., backtrack to Hudson St. and go east past faculty homes. At Oviatt St. turn right (south). More faculty homes are on the left (east) side of the street. On the right (west) side of Oviatt is Harlan Wood House (1953), a boys' dormitory named for a former teacher, dean, and headmaster.

To the south of Wood House is Knight Fine Arts Center (1986), a major teaching and performance facility. It houses 400-seat auditorium with a full stage and classrooms for drama, dance, art, stagecraft, publications, and photography, as well as the Moos Gallery.

33. Just past Knight Fine Arts Center and before Aurora St., enter the campus on the drive off Oviatt St. and walk toward the Chapel, the focal point of Brick Row.

The Chapel, built in 1836, is now the site of school meetings, concerts, and lectures. In the summer, Encore School for Strings holds its recitals here. The building has undergone many renovations and improvements over the years. A new Holtkamp organ was installed in 1966 and the third tier of the steeple was replaced in 1989.

34. North of the Chapel is North Hall (1837), a girls' dormitory and one of the original college buildings. Despite a major restoration in 1986, it has undergone the fewest changes of any of the old buildings.

35. South of the Chapel is Seymour Hall, containing administrative offices and classrooms. It was built in 1913 on the sites of Middle College (1826) and South College (1830).

36. At the end of the green is Wilson Hall (1963), containing the academy's library, classrooms, laboratories, and a 100-seat lecture hall.

Continue southwest on the sidewalk past the Loomis Observatory and again reach Aurora St. Continue southwest on Aurora St. to N. Main St. and the parking area.

Mr. Thomas L. Vince, Librarian and Curator, the Hudson Library and Historical Society, contributed valuable suggestions and reviewed this chapter for historical accuracy.

22 HUDSON SPRINGS PARK AND BICENTENNIAL WOODS

Distance: 3 miles

Easy

Hiking time: 1-1/2 hours

Description: The 1.8-mile Lake Trail in Hudson Springs Park follows the north shoreline of the lake and continues through the woods along its southern edge to return to the starting point. The wide path is surfaced with fine gravel, and the terrain is mostly flat or gently rolling.
The 0.5-mile Bicentennial Woods trail is also surfaced and winds up an easy slope to Victoria Pkwy., returning on the same path.

Directions: Follow I-271 south to Exit 21 for I-480 east. Go east on I-480 to Exit 37, SR 91 (south). Continue 4 miles on SR. 91 south to Hudson Village. Just past the town green, turn left (east) onto SR 303. Go 2 miles to Stow Rd. Turn left (north) on Stow Rd. and continue about 1 mile to the park entrance on the right.
From Akron, take SR 8 north to SR 303. Turn right (east) on SR 303 into Hudson. Continue east on SR 303 to Stow Rd. north to the park entrance on the right.

Parking & restrooms: At the parking area inside the entrance.

Hudson Springs Park lies three miles northeast of Hudson Village adjacent to the Ohio Turnpike. This 260-acre park, owned and operated by Hudson's Park Commission, offers boating and fishing, for bass and bluegill, in its 50-acre keyhole-shaped lake. Other facilities in the park include picnic tables with grills, two picnic pavilions, a children's playground area, a playing meadow, and a hiking trail that surrounds the lake. Among the wildlife inhabiting the lake, woods, and fields of Hudson Springs Park are ducks, geese, fox, beaver, muskrat, and deer.

Bicentennial Woods is a small, 33-acre parcel of land directly opposite (west of) Hudson Springs Park. It was acquired in 1970 by some of Hudson's private citizens and organizations for the enjoyment of all the town's residents. Children from local schools frequently use Bicentennial Woods for nature and environmental studies.

1. At the Lake Trail sign, enter the trail to hike clockwise around the water on a wide, gravel walkway that starts toward the east. Pass a playground on the left and begin to see views of the beautiful lake ahead on the right. Picnic pavilions and a boat launch area are situated near the shore-

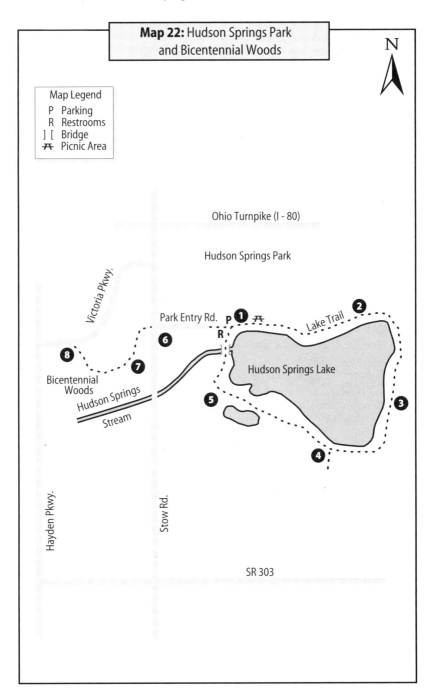

Map 22: Hudson Springs Park and Bicentennial Woods

N

Map Legend
P   Parking
R   Restrooms
] [Bridge
π   Picnic Area

Ohio Turnpike (I - 80)

Hudson Springs Park

Victoria Pkwy.

Park Entry Rd. P ❶ π

R

Lake Trail

❷

❻

❽

❼

Bicentennial
Woods

Hudson Springs

Stream

Hudson Springs Lake

❺

❸

❹

Hayden Pkwy.

Stow Rd.

SR 303

line. Early spring and late fall, when the leaves are down, are fine times to enjoy lake views from here.

The trail is also used by bicyclists—use CAUTION when encountering them.

2. At 0.7 mile pass a bird observation deck on the left. The path now rises and winds away from the lake at its far east (dammed) end. The trail passes through a young beech-maple forest.

3. A bench on the left at 1 mile invites a restful pause for pleasant enjoyment of the woods. The path now winds south through woods as it veers away from the lake and gently rises uphill.

4. A dirt trail joins from the left (1.2 miles), but continue northwest on the gravel trail. Deer may be spotted in this park in the morning or late afternoon. Here many springs rise and flow down to the lake, giving it and the park their name.

The path now winds west past several more park benches and goes down to lake level.

5. Continue past a small pond on the left (1.7 miles), cross a wooden bridge over Hudson Springs stream, and follow the gravel path uphill past the boat launch and picnic pavilion to return to the parking area.

6. Turn left on the park entry road and follow it to Stow Rd.

CAUTION: There is fast traffic here—cross carefully!

Directly opposite the park entrance is the unmarked trailhead for Bicentennial Woods.

7. Enter the path, going west initially, then south on the wide gravel trail. Below on the left is Hudson Springs stream.

8. Follow the trail uphill through a beautiful hardwood forest for 0.5 mile. At the end of the path are private homes and property on Victoria Pkwy. On a public green is a plaque commemorating the purchase of the woods in 1970 by Hudson citizens and businesses in time for our nation's bicentennial celebration.

Retrace your steps along the path to return to the parking area in Hudson Springs Park.

23 PORTAGE LAKES STATE PARK

Distance: 4 miles

Hiking time: 2 hours

Description: This easy hike is on a flat trail that skirts the shorelines of Turkeyfoot Lake and Latham Bay and crosses several picnic areas. There are beautiful views of the lake and its boats at several vantage points along Turkeyfoot Beach. Boating, camping, fishing, and hunting regulation information may be obtained from the Park Office at 5031 Manchester Rd., Akron, OH 44319; 330-644-2220.

Directions: In Akron, follow I-76/I-77 or I-277/US 224 to S. Main St. Head south on S. Main St. to SR 619 (Turkeyfoot Lake Rd.). Turn right (west) on SR 619 to Manchester Rd. Turn left (south) on Manchester for 1 mile. The park entrance is on the left (east).
From Cleveland, take I-77 south to I-76 east. Exit at South Main St., heading south, then follow the directions above.

Parking & restrooms: After entering the park, pass the road to the Park Office and continue to the first parking lot on the right (Big Oaks Picnic Area). Restrooms are near the parking area.

Portage Lakes State Park, located south of Akron, is on high land from which many lakes flow either north to Lake Erie or south to the Ohio River. Boating, swimming, camping, and fishing are the main attractions of this state park, but there are several miles of scenic hiking trails in its developed portion. Because this recreation area contains 2,520 acres of water to 1,000 acres of land, many kinds of waterfowl, shorebirds, and mammals nest in the marshes throughout the year. At various times you may spot mallard and other ducks, Canada geese, herons, deer, skunks, raccoons, hawks, owls, and many species of songbirds.

The topography of the park was created after the last glacier retreated from Ohio about 12,000 years ago. Large chunks of ice broke off the glacier, settled into depressions, melted, and formed kettle lakes—the bogs and marshes located here are aged kettle lakes.

Indians and early settlers carried their canoes overland ("portaged") on an eight-mile course called Portage Path. The name was also given to the nearby lakes. The Portage Path connected the headwaters of the south-flowing Tuscarawas River with the north-flowing Cuyahoga River. Later this area became an important settlers' trading post, and the path served

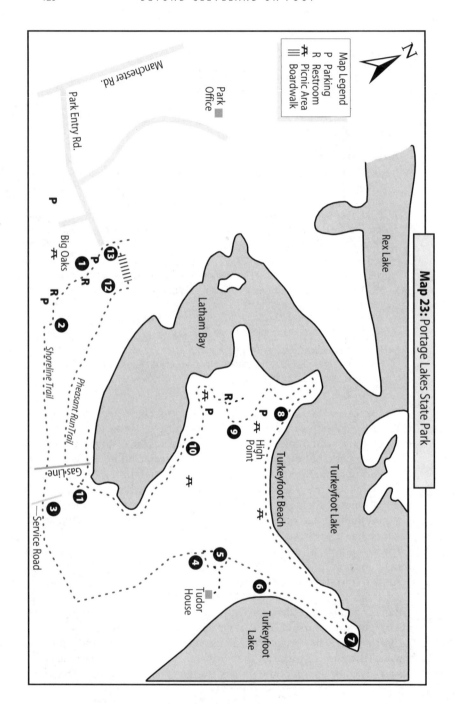

Map 23: Portage Lakes State Park

Map Legend
P Parking
R Restroom
⚲ Picnic Area
▦ Boardwalk

Park Office

Manchester Rd.

Park Entry Rd.

Big Oaks

Shoreline Trail

Pheasant Run Trail

Gas Line

— Service Road

Latham Bay

High Point

Turkeyfoot Beach

Turkeyfoot Lake

Rex Lake

Tudor House

Turkeyfoot Lake

as the western boundary of the U.S. until 1785. (Call 330-644-2220 for information about the park.)

1. Begin the hike by heading southeast through the parking lot to the sign for the Shoreline Trail. Enter the trail to the left (southeast) of the restroom building.

2. After 0.2 mile reach another parking lot and turn left (east). Continue through the parking lot to the trail entrance at the signpost with a yellow arrow. The path follows the south border of the park through a white pine forest and past backyards of private homes.

3. Continue eastward and at 0.6 mile pass an exposed gas line, then a park service road. Although the trail twists and turns, the pathway is distinct.

4. At 1.3 miles, reach tall iron post gates marking the entrance to the Tudor House property, Franklin Park Civic Center. At the "Y" fork, turn right toward Tudor House. (Another road leads southeast to Mason Manor, a nursing home.)

The asphalt road leads to Tudor House, a facility used for business meetings and private parties, and for a daily senior lunch program. It is open by appointment only (330-644-1728).

5. Return on the same asphalt road to the trail on the right, just before the sign indicating additional parking. The trail entrance is again posted with a yellow arrow. On the left is a huge parking lot used in the summer for visitors to Turkeyfoot Beach.

6. At a "T" intersection, with the lake directly ahead, turn left (north). (The trail to the right dead ends at the lake.) Reach Turkeyfoot Beach. Now the trail follows the northeast edge of Turkeyfoot Lake, parallel to a dirt road on the left.

7. Reach Mosquito Point, the end of the peninsula (2 miles). Here are wide-open views of boating activity on Turkeyfoot Lake. To the east is Samoa Bay; directly north is a golf course. This peninsula, once an island, was filled in about 40 years ago to provide easy access to the point.

Turn left (west) and follow the opposite side of the peninsula back to the beach.

8. Cross Turkeyfoot Beach and enter the trail at the far northwest end of the sandy beach. Pass a trail on the left that goes to a parking lot; continue straight ahead (north).

As you approach Latham Bay, watch for a sharp left turn where the arrow sign points uphill. (The path ahead goes to the bay and circles uphill.) Turn left at the top of the hill to the parking lot for High Point Picnic Area.

9. Follow the arrow posts to the south end of the parking lot. Continue on the paved road to the trail entrance off the road on the right (2.8 miles). A sign at the trail entrance reads "Emergency and Authorized Vehicles Only."

At the concrete restroom, stay to the left to follow the trail heading southwest. Latham Bay is on the right. At about the 3-mile point, the trail turns left (east) to the road and parking lot.

10. Follow the road past the parking lot on the left. Turn right (south) at the sign for Shoreline Trail.

11. At the next trail junction (3.5 miles), turn left (southeast), still remaining on the (yellow) Shoreline Trail. (This is also the red Pheasant Run Trail.) Pass the same gas line and continue west.

12. The trail takes a sharp right turn (northwest), enters a new-growth forest, then crosses a boardwalk.

13. Pass a trail juncture on the right and turn left (south), staying on the yellow Shoreline Trail, which leads out to the Big Oaks Picnic Area and the parking area.

24 TREE FARM TRAIL

Distance: 3 miles

Easy

Hiking time: 1-1/2 hours

Description: This is an easy loop trail for hikers and cross-country skiers. The terrain is undulating and, in addition to the beautiful evergreen trees, offers open fields and stands of hardwood trees. Wildflowers, birds, deer, and other wildlife can be enjoyed here. In the spring this trail can be muddy in spots.

Directions: From I-271, take Exit 12 to SR 303 east. Just past the exit ramp, turn right (south) on Major Rd. (Be alert.) Pass Oak Hill Rd. on the right and continue on Major Rd. to the sign for Horseshoe Pond on the left.

Parking & restrooms: At Horseshoe Pond.

The Tree Farm Trail, one of the shorter trails in the Cuyahoga Valley National Recreation Area (CVNRA), is located on Major Rd. off Riverview Rd., not far from the village of Peninsula. This lovely trail with many evergreen trees once belonged to the Robert Bishop family, which maintained a large cut-your-own Christmas tree farm. Today, a member of the Bishop family still continues to operate a tree farm on adjacent private property.

Because of its gently rolling terrain, the wide Tree Farm Trail is especially popular with cross-country skiers. For hikers it is a pleasurable trail because of its variety and unexpected evergreen tree tunnels. Horseshoe Pond, a favorite fishing pond stocked by the CVNRA, is located at the beginning of the trail.

1. Enter the trail east of the parking area at the pond sign. Start north and take the left branch of the loop to head in a clockwise direction. Cross the embankment at the east end of the pond and note from this vantage point its distinct horseshoe shape. At the end of the dam turn right to enter the woods on one of the wide tree-farm roads. Small, pretty spruce trees line this path. Soon the trail curves left (north) through a mixed hardwood forest.

2. After about a mile the trail curves right (east) and reaches a field. Cross this land to reach a view of much of the Cuyahoga Valley to the east. Below are symmetrical rows of attractive Christmas trees.

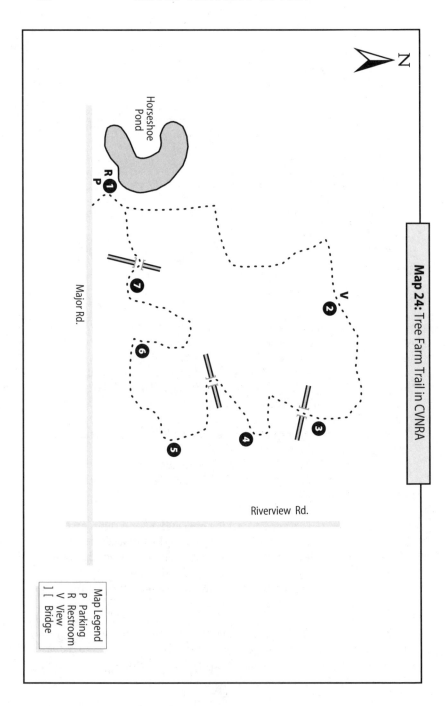

Map 24: Tree Farm Trail in CVNRA

3. The trail now descends the hill and crosses an old farm road. Continue through the scrubby brush and reach a small bridge over a stream crossing.

4. Continue following the gentle ups and downs of the trail through pine, spruce, and hemlock trees and scrubby shrubbery. Delightful evergreen tunnels meet your path every so often.

5. After crossing another small brook, you will hear cars on Riverview Rd. to the left (east) and, further on to the left (south), on Major Rd. Reach a log bench at the top of an incline that invites you to rest.

6. The trail follows the contours of the land on wide farm lanes as it curves north away from the road. Near an open field the path turns right, descends, and turns left to enter a stand of pine trees.

7. Bear right at the next open area, cross a wooden bridge, then reach the end of the loop where you started at the parking area.

25 PENINSULA AND DEEP LOCK QUARRY METRO PARK

Distance: 2.8 miles

Easy

Hiking time: 1-1/2 hours

Description: The Canal Towpath Trail is generally flat and is exceptionally scenic as it follows the shore of the Cuyahoga River. Within the Metro Park is a moderately steep hill to climb to see the quarry itself and an optional set of steps to climb down into the quarry for a clearer view.

Directions: From I-271, take Exit 12 for SR 303. Drive east on SR 303 to Peninsula. In Peninsula, follow the signs to Lock 29 Trailhead. Turn north on Locust St. (at the Peninsula United Methodist Church) and go 1 block north, then 1 block east. Cross the railroad tracks of the Cuyahoga Valley Scenic Railroad to enter the Lock 29 Trailhead.

Parking & restrooms: Located at Lock 29 Trailhead.

Peninsula and Deep Lock Quarry Metro Park are both within the Cuyahoga Valley National Recreation Area (CVNRA) and provide visitors with interesting history pertaining to the Ohio & Erie Canal. This park is managed by Metro Parks Serving Summit County.

Constructed between 1825 and 1832, the 309-mile Ohio & Erie Canal extended from Cleveland and Lake Erie to Portsmouth and the Ohio River. A disastrous flood in 1913 destroyed much of the canal and hastened the end of an interesting era of transportation. Cascade Locks Metro Park also preserves significant canal history (Ch. 32).

The hike begins in Peninsula, at Lock 29 Trailhead. Here you will find an expansive view of a waterfall on the Cuyahoga River. This waterfall flows over a dam that was built to power an 1823 gristmill on the west side of the river near Lock 29. A newly constructed parking area now provides easy access to the lock and the Canal Towpath Trail.

At Lock 29 the CVNRA has erected an information kiosk, interpretive signs, and a viewing deck from which to study the old lock. It is at this point that the Ohio & Erie Canal made its crossing on an aqueduct, from the west to the east side of the Cuyahoga River (now replaced by an arched footbridge).

Before starting the walk, you may wish to explore Peninsula and its interesting shops housed in old Victorian buildings. The small town of Peninsula was a very busy canal port from the 1820s onward, with hotels,

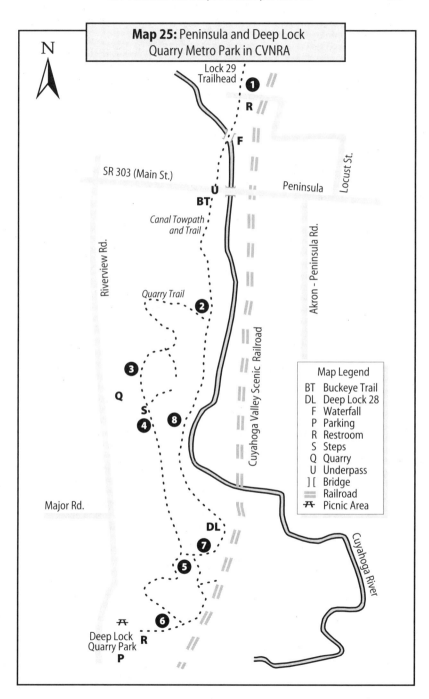

Map 25: Peninsula and Deep Lock Quarry Metro Park in CVNRA

N

Lock 29
Trailhead ❶

R

F

SR 303 (Main St.)

Peninsula

Locust St.

U
BT

*Canal Towpath
and Trail*

Riverview Rd.

Akron - Peninsula Rd.

Quarry Trail

❷

❸

Q

S

❹   ❽

Cuyahoga Valley Scenic Railroad

Map Legend
BT Buckeye Trail
DL Deep Lock 28
F Waterfall
P Parking
R Restroom
S Steps
Q Quarry
U Underpass
] [Bridge
▦ Railroad
🛆 Picnic Area

Major Rd.

DL

❼

❺

Cuyahoga River

🛆   ❻

Deep Lock   R
Quarry Park
P

bars, boatyards, mills, beautiful homes, and a full complement of shops and stores. When the railroad came through this valley in 1880, Peninsula's importance as a commercial center quickly diminished. It is now a quiet town whose greatest fame lies in its past.

The interesting Fox House (c.1880) just above the river at 1664 W. Main St. (SR 303) and Riverview Rd. was restored by the CVNRA in 1985. The house stands at the site of what was one of Peninsula's busiest boatyards. It is easy to imagine what an active canal port this village must have been in its heyday!

Peninsula is listed on the National Register of Historic Places. For more information about its history, visit the Peninsula Library and Historical Society at 6105 Riverview Rd. just south of SR 303.

The offices of the Cuyahoga Valley Scenic Railroad (CVSR) are located near Lock 29 Trailhead, in a building near the railroad tracks. The CVSR operates many train trips throughout the year through the CVNRA from Independence near Cleveland to Hale Farm and Village, and to Quaker Square in Akron (800-468-4070).

Deep Lock Quarry Metro Park is just south of Peninsula on the Canal Towpath Trail and adjacent to both the Cuyahoga River and the Cuyahoga Valley Scenic Railroad. Both the river and railroad carried Berea Sandstone excavated from the quarry. Huge blocks of stone were used to make locks and bridges, and for other canal construction as well as for homes and public buildings.

The deepest lock along the entire length of the canal is found within this park. Normally locks were dug to a 10-foot depth, but here Lock 28 reaches 17 feet—it's the "deep lock" for which this park was named. The Canal Towpath Trail follows the original towpath of the Ohio & Erie Canal. This path is also part of the statewide 1,200-mile-long Buckeye Trail.

1. Start the hike at Lock 29 Trailhead. Climb the steps to the top of the viewing deck and turn left (south) to begin the Canal Towpath Trail. An interpretive sign describes the former eastward bend of the Cuyahoga River that once isolated the town on a "peninsula" of land. At a later time the river was dammed and a new channel cut through to give the river its present course, eliminating the peninsula.

The trail crosses under Main St. (SR 303) and continues south along an attractive stretch of the river. Bicyclists also use this trail and may whiz by at great speed. It is usual for hikers to stay to the right.

The Canal Towpath Trail is also marked as the "A" trail, and the Buckeye Trail (BT) intersects with it. Here you may see wildlife such as great blue herons, mallard ducks, turtles, woodpeckers, and other birds. In the spring there are many wildflowers here to identify, and there are many specimens of the state tree, the Ohio Buckeye, whose five leaflets differentiate it from the horse chestnut's seven leaflets. The Ohio Buckeye tree has a tall, white, upright cluster of blossoms and a shiny brown seed that resembles a buck's eye.

The canal is to the right (west) of the trail and in some places is overgrown with brush and trees. The towpath—once used by mules pulling canal boats—was always located between the canal and the river so it would act as a barrier, keeping the two streams of water apart. It also often situated away from a hillside to avoid having mudslides block either it or the canal.

2. At about 0.5 mile the trail reaches Deep Lock Quarry Metro Park where a sign points to the quarry. Take this trail to the right to make a zigzag ascent of a steep hill to the quarry. At the next sign continue straight ahead (westward) to the quarry rim.

3. Opened in 1829, the quarry was an important source of Berea Sandstone (see Appendix A), used for many types of construction: canal locks and bridges; home foundations; millstones; railroad bridges and roadbeds; shelters, steps, and bridges in Cleveland and Akron parks; harbor structures in Cleveland; and other uses in many local buildings. Akron's Ferdinand Schumacher, a part-owner of the quarry in 1879, used millstones from it for milling oats at his well-known factory, which later became the famous Quaker Oats Company. Early settlers also used this sandstone for fashioning grindstones, pulpstones, and hulling stones to process the food crops they harvested, and to sharpen their scythes and knives.

To extract the slabs, workmen at the quarry cut large blocks of solid rock by drilling, wedging, channeling, and blasting. Looking at the quarry now, more than 100 years later, one can imagine the vast activity that took place here. Although this dangerous work was slow when blocks were cut by hand, by the 1880s machines were employed in the quarrying process. Channeling devices were used to cut openings about three inches wide in the solid stone, from which smaller blocks were then wedged or blasted out. Some of the channel marks are still visible in the rocks.

The Quarry Trail follows the top of the pit for a short distance, then leaves the quarry going south down steep, slippery stone steps. Use CAUTION during wet or snowy weather or if fallen leaves cover these steps (1 mile).

4. At the foot of the steps continue to the left (south) following the main trail. The quarry can be explored at this point but is now virtually a swamp. Two plants rarely found in Cleveland-area parks do enjoy this wet environment: the narrow-leaved cattail and the rose pink. The narrow-leaved cattail not only has narrower leaves than the common cattail, but its upper and lower spike parts are separated by a distinct gap. Rose pink or bitterbloom blooms in the summer and early fall and has small pink flowers with five petals.

5. At the next trail intersection, take the spur to the right (west), which goes uphill on a woods path lined with discarded sandstone blocks left by the quarrying operation.

6. The loop path ends on the main trail. Turn right and head up the slope to the picnic area. Here are primitive restrooms, picnic tables, and a parking lot for Deep Lock Quarry Park (1.5 miles).

7. From the picnic area return on the same Quarry Trail to the second trail intersection on the right. Turn right (east) at this junction going down toward Deep Lock 28. Along the trail are several large millstones abandoned by mill workers; perhaps these were not suitable for grinding because of cracks or other defects. It is thought that the small mounds of earth along the trail may have been left by workmen scraping dirt from underneath stones removed from the quarry. An interpretive sign indicates that some of the large sandstones scattered throughout the woods are not only millstones, but spalls (fragments) and foundations of old buildings. Another sign points out that a railroad once ran along this path carrying flatcars loaded with millstones from the hill above.

Just ahead lies Lock 28 alongside the Canal Towpath. At 17 feet, it is the deepest of the 42 locks built between Cleveland and Akron and is in remarkably good condition after more than 170 years. A bronze historic marker is located on its inner side.

Constructing the canal was painful, backbreaking, and dangerous work. Many men (and boys) of the Western Reserve, augmented by German and Irish immigrants, lost their lives in the process. They died either from the treacherous digging job itself—in all seasons and in all kinds of weather—or from rapidly spreading "canal fever" (malaria). Canal workers suffered the additional hardships of poor working conditions and poor pay.

During the early and mid-19th century, the lock system on the 309-mile-long Ohio & Erie Canal was vitally important to navigation between Lake Erie and the Ohio River, as well as ports in the southern and eastern U. S. Because the high point of land in Akron was 395 feet above that of Lake Erie, 44 locks (later reduced to 42) were necessary to raise and lower boats traveling between these two cities.

Visible on Lock 28 are the remains of some of the iron work used to open and close the wickets in the water gates at each end of the lock. Holes in the tops of the walls held mooring posts to tie up boats as they were being raised or lowered inside the lock. The square openings down in the walls were internal culverts used to drain water out of the lock when the gates were closed.

8. Follow the Canal Towpath Trail north along the river to return to Peninsula and Lock 29 where the hike began.

26 BRANDYWINE GORGE AND STANFORD TRAIL

Distance: 1-1/2 miles for Brandywine Gorge; 2 miles to Averill Pond (Option 1); 4.5 miles to the Stanford House Hostel (Option 2)

Hiking time: 1 hour+ for Brandywine Gorge; 1-1/2 hours for Option 1; 3 hours for Option 2

Description: There are two options (see Note #5) on this hike, offering alternatives for extending the walk. After viewing scenic Brandywine Falls, the hike begins on the Brandywine Gorge Trail near the Inn. The path goes downhill above Brandywine Creek (on the north side of the gorge) to a creek crossing on large sandstone blocks.
NOTE: In late winter and early spring, or after a heavy rainfall, the stream becomes too high to cross on these blocks. If such is the case, there is no alternative but to return uphill on the same trail. You may call the CVNRA (216-526-5256) for information about this creek crossing.
The hike continues on the south side of Brandywine Gorge with moderately steep up and down climbs on the well-marked trail. Option 1 continues south to Averill Pond and Option 2 continues even farther south to the 30-bed Stanford House Hostel. There are several moderately sized hills to climb on all three hikes.

Directions: From I-77 take Exit 149 for SR 82 (east). Follow SR 82 east to Riverview Rd. Take Riverview south to Vaughn Rd. in Jaite (CVNRA Headquarters). Turn left (east) on Vaughn/Highland Rd. to Brandywine Rd. (blinking light). Turn right (south) on Brandywine Rd. to just past the Inn at Brandywine Falls (on the right). Cross the bridge and turn right onto Stanford Rd. The entrance to Brandywine Falls parking area is just past the exit road, on the left.
• From Akron, take I-77 north to SR 21 north (Cleveland Massillon Rd.). Cross over the Ohio Turnpike (I-80) and turn right (east) on Snowville Rd. At Riverview Rd. turn left (north) one block to Jaite. Turn right (east) on Vaughn/Highland Rd. and follow it east past Brandywine Ski Resort/Dover Lake Water Park to Brandywine Rd. (blinking light), then follow the directions above.
NOTE: Stanford Rd. is permanently closed to vehicles between the Brandywine Falls parking area and Stanford House Hostel.

Parking & restrooms: At the Brandywine Falls parking area.

Brandywine Falls is a lovely scenic spot in Sagamore Hills at the east rim of the Cuyahoga Valley National Recreation Area (CVNRA). A series of

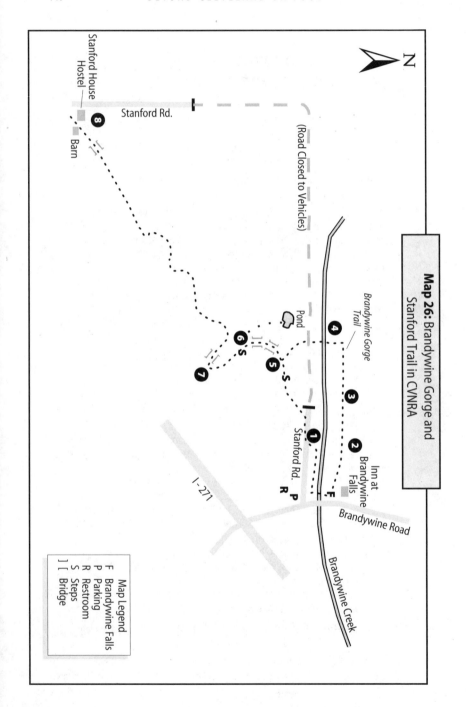

N

Stanford House
Hostel

Stanford Rd.

8

Barn

(Road Closed to Vehicles)

Pond

Brandywine Gorge Trail

6 S

7

5

S

4

3

Map 26: Brandywine Gorge and Stanford Trail in CVNRA

1

Stanford Rd.

2

Inn at Brandywine Falls

R P

F

I-271

Brandywine Road

Brandywine Creek

Map Legend
F Brandywine Falls
P Parking
R Restroom
S Steps
] [Bridge

wooden walkways, stairs, and a viewing platform enable visitors to enjoy the scenery of the beautiful 65-foot-high waterfall of Brandywine Creek. The foundation of an old gristmill that was used later for a 1920 electric shop is at the east end of the walkway. Brandywine was once a town of a dozen households with the mill employing 20 workers. Today very little remains of the old village, which reached its zenith in 1852.

History records that George Wallace, a New England entrepreneur, saw the potential of creating an industrial village at this spot by harnessing the water power of the falls. He first built a sawmill on the north side of the creek in 1814, followed a year later by a gristmill on the south side that produced flour and cornmeal. A profitable whiskey distillery was built a half-mile north of the sawmill, and a few years later Wallace opened a woolen mill, school, post office, and village store. The construction of the Ohio & Erie Canal, and the subsequent growth of railroads, contributed to the demise of this once-thriving village. Business went to larger commercial centers with better transportation.

In 1848 George's son, James Wallace, built a farmhouse on the north side of the falls, now restored as the Inn at Brandywine Falls. Open year round, it is now operated by Mr. and Mrs. George Foy as a bed and breakfast. The six-bedroom main building and annex is on the National Register of Historic Places and is open to the public ONLY by prior arrangement (216-467-1812 or 216-650-4965).

1. Begin the walk by crossing Stanford Rd. from the Brandywine Falls parking area to the walkway entrance. Walk down the steps to the lower viewing area, enjoying vistas of the waterfall along the way. The platform at the foot of the stairway is a popular place for wedding ceremonies and is closed to the public when services are being held here.

NOTE: The stairs to the waterfall are closed in the winter because of icy conditions. Call 216-526-5256 for information.

The waterfall cascades over eroded shale of varying degrees of hardness. The shale is composed of mud and silt laid down in successive layers by an ancient sea that once covered what is now Ohio. At the top of the falls is 360-million-year-old, erosion-resistant Berea Sandstone capping the older gray Bedford Formation (shale) beneath it (see Appendix A). In the stream farther down, large blocks of Berea Sandstone have fallen from above, having broken off at fracture lines. These boulders will eventually move downstream, just as the lip of the waterfall, over millions of years, will gradually move upstream.

Walk back up the same wooden steps, turning left at the top to follow the walkway to its far eastern end. Signs along the way point out interesting historical features. A different view of the falls appears at the ruins of the gristmill/electric shop.

Readily evident are potholes in the sandstone caused by swirling sand and water, and grooves worn in the rock from the water's swift flow. The groove that extends all across the top once diverted water to the old grist-mill and its water wheel. Downstream are small waterfalls and rapids where the force of the water constantly eats away at the Bedford Formation (shale) as the creek flows downward to the Cuyahoga River west of here.

2. Walk eastward down the steps to another, smaller parking area and cross the bridge over Brandywine Creek to its north side.

CAUTION: Crossing the creek on rocks is forbidden as they are slippery and extremely dangerous.

On the north side are different views of Brandywine Falls. Picnic tables and park benches invite a pause to admire the picturesque scene.

Follow the path along the fence to the trail entrance marked with a sign at the far west end of the lawn. The Brandywine Gorge Trail descends 3/4 mile to the creek crossing below. This wide, smooth trail was built by volunteers from the Cuyahoga Valley Trails Council and CVNRA personnel. The path follows an old road that originally went down to the Cuyahoga River from Brandywine Rd.

Brandywine Creek is visible below on the left. In the spring and summer a variety of wildflowers thrive in this cool, moist gorge.

CAUTION: Stay back from the cliff, because constant erosion loosens soil along the edge.

3. As you continue down, note the ancient sedimentary rock layers on the boulders along the north side of the trail. These silt and sandstone layers were laid down by the same inland sea that covered much of this area. Water ripple marks, alternating ridges and troughs, are prominent in the Berea Sandstone. They are evident on some of the rocks that have slumped from above. Cross bedding is also evident in some of the sandstone blocks. It is characterized by sedimentary layers that run at an angle to normal horizontal bedding. They indicate the direction of water currents at the time the sandy layers were deposited. (see Appendix A).

Many old maple, oak, beech, and tupelo trees have grown magnificently tall in this favorable environment.

Just after the log steps near the foot of the gorge, turn left (south) on a short spur to the edge of the stream for a lovely photo spot with a long view of the creek. After the next set of short, upward log steps, a left (south) turn leads to a log bench and another view of the water.

4. At about 0.6 mile the trail crosses Brandywine Creek on large sandstone blocks quarried from this area.

CAUTION: If the water is too high or if the blocks have been washed askew following a flood, do not cross. As noted above, the only alternative is to retrace your steps to the top of the gorge on the same Brandywine

Gorge Trail. After returning to the parking area, you may descend on the Stanford Trail to Averill Pond or Stanford House Hostel (Options 1 or 2).

After crossing the creek, continue on the trail until it emerges onto Stanford Rd. After crossing the road, the trail continues and joins the Stanford Trail going south.

5. At this trail junction, if you are not taking options 1 or 2, turn left and follow the Stanford Trail uphill. You will shortly climb a set of wood steps cut into the embankment and continue steeply uphill. When the trail emerges onto Stanford Rd., continue east for about 1/4 mile to the parking area (1.5 miles).

At #5 there is also an opportunity to extend the hike by taking either of the options below.

Option 1: To continue the hike by another half-mile to Averill Pond, continue on the Stanford Trail toward the right (southwest), crossing two bridges as the trail follows the up-and-down contours of the land.

6. Turn right at the next trail sign to visit the small Averill Pond, a scenic wilderness spot. Note that this trail is wider than the others. It is the old Hudson Rd. that New England pioneers followed on their way to land they purchased in the Connecticut Western Reserve. David Hudson pioneered this route to the settlement that subsequently bore his name and became the town of Hudson in 1802 (Ch. 21).

To return to the hike's starting point, retrace your steps on the Stanford Trail going uphill and following posted signs to the Brandywine Falls parking area (2 miles).

Option 2: To continue to the Stanford House Hostel, follow the Stanford Trail south.

7. The trail crosses a bridge, goes up and down ridges, and eventually crosses a larger bridge.

Follow the path to the end until it changes to an open grassy trail. A large barn on the Stanford property appears ahead. Take the path toward the barn (southeast). (The path to the right is part of a loop trail around the farm property.)

8. Follow the path along the driveway. The old Stanford House (1843) was restored and opened in 1986 by the National Park Service and the Northeast Ohio Council of American Youth Hostels. This 30-bed hostel is closed during the day but is open from 7-9 a.m. and 5-10 p.m. to accommodate hikers, bicyclists, skiers, and the general public. There is a kitchen to allow guests to prepare their own meals. Very little parking is available at the hostel. For information call 216-467-8711.

To return to the car, retrace your steps along the well-marked Stanford Trail and follow signs to the Brandywine Falls parking area.

27 VIRGINIA KENDALL PARK: KENDALL LAKE AND CROSS-COUNTRY TRAIL

Distance: 3.5 miles

Moderate

Hiking time: 2+ hours

Description: This hike begins at the Kendall Lake Shelter, where there are picnic facilities and a fishing dock. The hike starts by encircling the lake on the 1-mile Lake Trail, then loops southeast and northwest on the 2.5-mile Cross-Country Trail, marked with skier symbols posted on trees. The latter trail is a fine, wide hiking trail through woods of tall pines, oaks, and hemlocks, following the contours of the land. It reaches a broad meadow, crosses Salt Run on a bridge, and, at the end, descends a long, open hill— all of which provide hikers with great variety and enjoyment. You may even catch a glimpse of wild turkey or deer roaming through the upland forest.

Directions: From I-271 exit at SR 303 (Exit 12). Follow SR 303 east to the town of Peninsula. After crossing the Cuyahoga River bridge, turn right (south) onto Akron Peninsula Rd.; follow it about 2-1/2 miles to Truxell Rd.(A "Camp Manatoc" sign is at this intersection.) Turn left (east) onto Truxell Rd. and follow it uphill to the Kendall Lake parking area on the right. From Akron take Akron Peninsula Rd. north to Truxell Rd. and turn right on Truxell Rd. to Kendall Lake (or follow directions from I-271 above).

Parking & restrooms: At Kendall Lake parking area.

Virginia Kendall Park is noted for its spectacular Ritchie Ledges,* composed of Sharon Conglomerate sandstone, and its beautiful hardwood forest with abundant wildlife. This park was established with 420 acres of farm and forest land that had served as a country retreat for Clevelander Hayward Kendall. He deeded this magnificent spot to the city of Akron in 1929 in memory of his mother, Virginia Kendall. Originally administered by the Akron Metropolitan Park District, it is now part of the Cuyahoga Valley National Recreation Area (CVNRA). It was the first park incorporated into CVNRA after its creation in 1974 by an act of Congress. Several of its shelters and other buildings were constructed in the 1930s by the Civilian Conservation Corps.

Salt Run stream and its several tributaries course through the area of this hike (and of another Kendall Park hike described in Ch. 28). The Cross-Country Trail is not only a pleasant hiking trail but also a popular ski trail. Kendall Lake Winter Sports Shelter is open seasonally with infor-

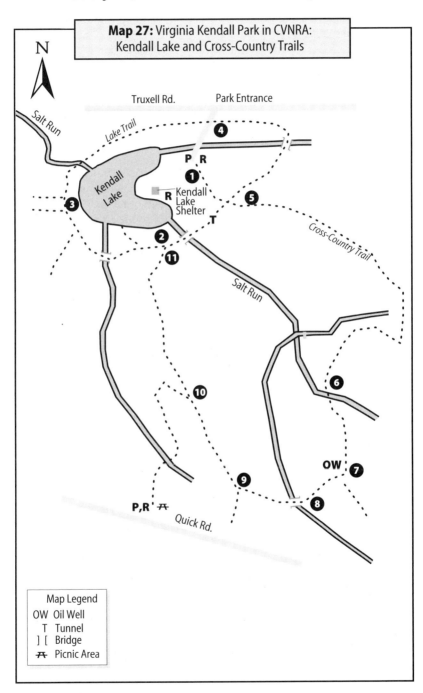

Map 27: Virginia Kendall Park in CVNRA: Kendall Lake and Cross-Country Trails

N

Truxell Rd.   Park Entrance

Salt Run

Lake Trail

Kendall Lake

Kendall Lake Shelter

Cross-Country Trail

Salt Run

Quick Rd.

OW

Map Legend
OW Oil Well
 T   Tunnel
] [Bridge
🪑 Picnic Area

mation available about skiing, snowshoeing, sledding, and tubing (650-4636 or 800-257-9477).

NOTE: A 4.5-mile hike to Ritchie Ledges is described in *Cleveland On Foot*, Second Edition (1995), Ch. 36, p. 222. (see Bibliography.)

1. Enter the trail from the parking lot at the southwest corner near the large trailhead sign. Follow the Lake and Cross-Country trails partway uphill on the left. Turn right on this open slope (about midway uphill) to pass through the tunnel (on the right) under a toboggan hill, still following Lake Trail signs.

2. Cross Salt Run stream on a bridge and continue straight ahead. At the next intersection, where the Cross-Country Trail goes to the south (left), continue ahead on the Lake Trail at the edge of Kendall Lake, where you may see ducks, Canada geese, or herons. Cross the corner of an open sledding hill at the top of which is a new building for winter sports. The trail soon reaches an earthen dam impounding Salt Run stream to create pretty Kendall Lake.

3. As you cross the dam, you will see on the left trail intersections for Salt Run Trail. Continue on the Lake Trail to the opposite side of the lake, keeping Truxell Rd. on the left and the lake on the right.

4. Cross the park entrance road and continue eastward along an elevated gravel path. CAUTION: Stay on the trail through this former swamp. Cross a tributary of Salt Run on a bridge, then climb some steps up to a pine forest. Soon you will reach the same open slope near where the hike started (Note #1).

5. Turn left (east) to enter the wide Cross-Country Trail and pass through another pine forest. A little farther along note the many sweet-gum and tulip trees, and huge old white oaks. You may also see some of the foundations of former Kendall Farm buildings.

6. The gently rolling trail eventually reaches an exposed meadow that is bordered by a split-rail fence on the right and a single picnic table on the left. Cross a small stream.

7. At a trail intersection, stay to the right (west). (The path straight ahead leads out to SR 8). An inactive oil well pump is in the field on the right, at the end of an abandoned access road.

8. Continue westward now on the path cut through the meadow. At the far end of the field, reenter the woods, following the wire fence on the left, and descend steeply to a bridge over Salt Run.

9. Ascend a hill and reach another trail intersection. Here take the main trail as it bends sharp right (north). Avoid taking the service road on the left that goes out to Quick Rd.

10. At another trail intersection, where there is a trail bench and a left turn going to Pine Hollow parking area on Quick Rd., bear right (north) to stay on the Cross-Country Trail marked "Loop." Continue down a beautiful open meadow of Kendall Hill until this trail reaches Kendall Lake Trail again.

11. Turn right onto the Lake Trail and follow it back to Kendall Shelter by going through the tunnel and turning left down the slope to the parking lot (3.5 miles).

28 VIRGINIA KENDALL PARK: SALT RUN TRAIL

Distance: 5 miles

Strenuous

Hiking time: 2-1/2 to 3 hours

Directions: From I-271 take Exit 12 for SR 303. Follow SR 303 east to Peninsula. After crossing the Cuyahoga River bridge, turn right (south) onto Akron-Peninsula Rd.; follow it about 2-1/2 miles to Truxell Rd. (A "Camp Manatoc" sign is at this intersection.) Turn left (east) onto Truxell and follow it uphill to the Kendall Lake parking area on the right. From Akron take Akron-Peninsula Rd. north to Truxell Rd. and turn right on Truxell to Kendall Lake, or follow directions from I-271 above.

Parking & restrooms: At Kendall Lake parking area.

Virginia Kendall Park is noted for its spectacular Ritchie Ledges, its beautiful hardwood forests, and abundant wildlife.

This park was established with 420 acres of farm and forest land that had served as a country retreat for Clevelander Hayward Kendall. He deeded this magnificent spot to the city of Akron in 1929 in memory of his mother, Virginia Kendall. Originally administered by Akron Metropolitan Park District, it is now part of Cuyahoga Valley National Recreation Area (CVNRA). It was the first park incorporated into CVNRA after it was established in 1974 by an act of Congress. Salt Run stream and its several tributaries course through the park. Several of its shelters and other buildings were constructed in the 1930s by the Civilian Conservation Corps.

In the winter Kendall Lake Winter Sports Shelter, located off Truxell Rd., offers sledding, tubing, cross-country skiing, and snowshoeing. For information about opening hours call 216-650-4636 or 800-257-9477.

1. Start the hike at the Kendall Shelter parking area and take the Lake/Cross-Country Trail at the southwest corner of the lot near the trailhead sign. Follow the Lake Trail part way up the hill on the left to its intersection with the Cross-Country Trail. About midway uphill, turn right and go through the tunnel under the former toboggan hill.

2. Cross the bridge over Salt Run stream. Go straight at the next intersection, where the Cross-Country Trail turns to the left.

3. Follow the shore of Kendall Lake, crossing the corner of a meadow and then re-entering the woods on the right to reach the dam.

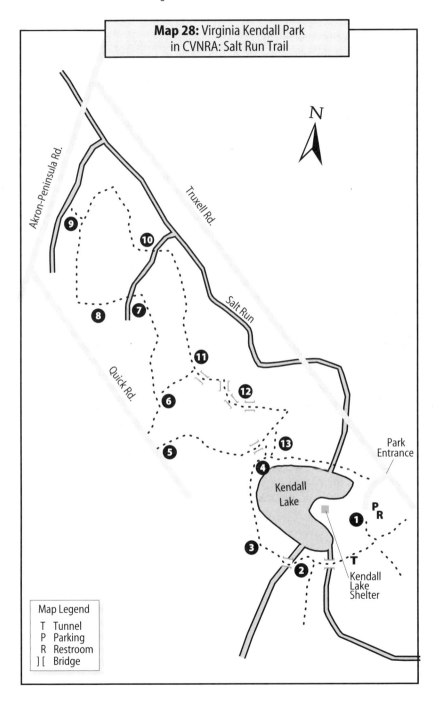

Map 28: Virginia Kendall Park
in CVNRA: Salt Run Trail

N

Akron-Peninsula Rd.

Truxell Rd.

Salt Run

Quick Rd.

9

10

8

7

11

12

6

5

13

4

Kendall
Lake

Park
Entrance

1

P
R

3

2

T

Kendall
Lake
Shelter

Map Legend

T   Tunnel
P   Parking
R   Restroom
] [Bridge

4. About midway across the earthen dam that impounds Salt Run stream to form Kendall Lake, take the first left turn at the Salt Run sign. Follow the trail westward in a clockwise direction. The path soon descends to cross a small bridge over the stream.

5. The trail continues in a generally west direction and emerges onto Quick Rd. Follow the road only a short distance until it re-enters the woods on the right (north).

6. Reach the shortcut trail going off to the right. (If you elect to return to the starting point now, you may take this shortcut trail, then follow Notes #11-13.)

7. Continue ahead. The trail passes a wooden bench, descends, then ascends to White Oak Spring, where what is left of a natural spring appears at the base of a white oak.

8. Pass another bench and descend a steep hill as the trail bends around to the north on a section of old East River Rd. The cars you hear on the left are on Akron-Peninsula Rd.

9. Stay on the Salt Run Trail at the next trail intersection, where a path comes in from the left off A-P Rd. to join the trail you are on.

10. The trail bends toward the east and crosses a Salt Run tributary. Here the ground can get muddy at times, but in the spring the moisture nurtures lovely wildflowers, ferns, and mosses.

11. After descending a hill, you will reach the north end of the shortcut trail. Descend a steep slope and cross a bridge. Here you are in a beautiful, cool hemlock forest. There is some evidence of old mudslides in the ravine caused by unstable soil.

12. Cross three bridges in succession and continue past some magnificent hemlocks. A little farther along, enter a pine forest.

13. Near the end of the loop, the trail bears right and then left to rejoin the Lake Trail. Turn left (east) on the Lake Trail and enjoy beautiful views of the lake with its waterbirds, mallards, and Canadian geese. Continue up a small hill, then down, until the path returns to the Kendall Lake parking area at the park entrance road.

29 OLD CARRIAGE TRAIL

Distance: 5.7 miles

Strenuous

Hiking time: 3 hours

Description: This trail is gravel-improved for bicycles, but after reaching the top of a steep hill, cyclists turn off onto Holzhauer Rd. to gain access to the 23-mile Bike & Hike Trail. The remainder of the Old Carriage Trail is a fine hike on a wooded footpath through a magnificent forest. It winds up and down ravines, over the three handsome steel truss bridges, and finally descends to the flat Canal Towpath again.

Directions: From I-77 take Exit 149 for SR 82 (Chippewa Rd.). Go east on SR 82, then take a right (south) on Riverview Rd. Follow it to Vaughn Rd., the location of CVNRA headquarters in the former community of Jaite. Turn left (east) on Vaughn Rd. (which becomes Highland Rd.). Go about 1 mile to Red Lock Trailhead on the left (north).
From Akron, take I-77 north to the exit for SR 21 north (Cleveland-Massillon Rd.). Continue over the Ohio Turnpike (I-80) and turn right (east) on Snowville Rd. At Riverview Rd., turn left (north) one block to the Jaite complex (CVNRA headquarters). Turn right (east) on Vaughn/Highland Rd. about 1 mile to Red Lock Trailhead, on the left (north).

Parking & restrooms: At Red Lock Trailhead.

When the Cuyahoga Valley National Recreation Area (CVNRA) purchased land in this valley in 1974, some old trails already existed. Early settlers, who depended upon the Cuyahoga River for transportation, created pathways down to the river from the hills where their farms were located. Some of the old trails became roads when settlers used them to carry their farm produce down to the Ohio & Erie Canal. Holzhauer Rd., near the top of the Old Carriage Trail, was once connected to a loading dock near Old Red Lock, just off Highland Rd.

Later, a wealthy Cleveland drug store merchant and botanist, Wentworth G. Marshall, purchased this land, built a summer home, and created an extensive network of carriage trails on some of the old roads to better enjoy his beautiful wooded acreage. In the late 1980s the CVNRA built the present Old Carriage Trail using some of Marshall's original carriage roads. In order not to encroach on Greenwood Village private property, the CVNRA built three beautiful steel truss bridges along this trail. The first two are 150 feet long and the third one measures 160 feet.

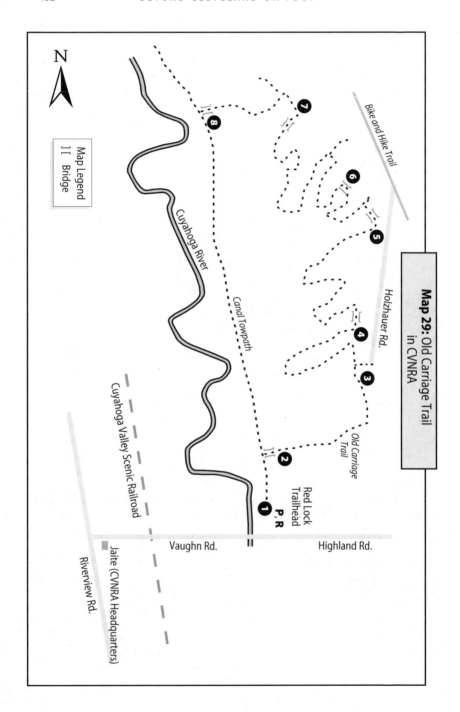

N

Map Legend
⟙⟛ Bridge

Cuyahoga River

Canal Towpath

Bike and Hike Trail

Map 29: Old Carriage Trail in CVNRA

Holzhauer Rd.

Old Carriage Trail

Red Lock Trailhead

P, R

Cuyahoga Valley Scenic Railroad

Vaughn Rd.

Highland Rd.

Jaite (CVNRA Headquarters)

Riverview Rd.

1. Begin the hike at Red Lock Trailhead. The trail starts near a large signboard. Just past the entrance to the path are the ruins of the old lock for which the trailhead was named. Red Lock was one of 42 locks on the old Ohio & Erie Canal that allowed canal boats to be lifted and lowered as they traveled between the high plateau of Akron to Cleveland, 395 feet lower in elevation. The Canal Towpath Trail is the path mules took as they pulled boats along the canal when this section opened in 1827. The overgrown canal is on the right; the Cuyahoga River is far to the left; and the towpath is underfoot. A description of the canal boats and lock system and a demonstration of a working lock are shown at the Canal Visitor Center, 7104 Canal Rd., (just south of Rockside Rd.), Valley View, OH 44147; 216-524-1497.

Follow the Towpath Trail about 3/4 mile to an intersection and bridge over the canal on the right.

2. Turn right (east) here and ascend the 150-foot hill on the Old Carriage Trail.

3. The trail flattens out at the top and curves around to the north. At an intersection on the right, bicyclists exit out to Holzhauer Rd. and the Bike & Hike Trail. Stay left on the Old Carriage Trail as it winds its way up and down long finger-like ridges. These hills were formed by Ohio's last glacier that retreated about 12,000 years ago. Melting water etched these deep ravines as it found its path down to the river valley below.

4. At about 2.1 miles, cross Rocky Run Bridge above Rocky Run (stream). Continue ahead, enjoying the peaceful forest.

5. At 2.7 miles is the second steel truss bridge, Twin Oaks Bridge, named for the oaks at its north end. A well-marked short trail bypass on the right has been cut through to avoid a wet area ahead. Farther on, another trail comes in on the right, but continue to the left on the Old Carriage Trail.

6. After another 0.2 mile the third bridge, Hemlock Bridge, crosses a lovely hemlock ravine. Here the trail bends very close to the backyards of homes in the Greenwood Village development. Stay to the left at another trail intersection.

7. Another short bridge is crossed before encountering an uphill trail on the right. Stay to the left on the Old Carriage Trail. At this point (4 miles) the trail begins to descend to the river valley.

8. Cross a bridge over the canal to the Canal Towpath Trail and turn left (south) to return along the path to Red Lock Trailhead. Pretty views of the river and marshlands are found along here, where many water birds feed and nest.

30 BOSTON MILLS TO PENINSULA

Distance: 8 miles $\boxed{\text{Strenuous}}$

Walking time: 3-1/2 hours

Description: Although noisy at the beginning and end from nearby interstate traffic, this long walk is well worth the effort. You will climb up and down hills, hike through a cool pine forest, and cross the valley of Boston Run on the first part of the hike. At mid-point you will have an opportunity to visit the historic town of Peninsula and new Lock 29 Trailhead. The return section of the hike goes along the flat canal Towpath Trail with views of the Cuyahoga River and wildlife along the way.

Directions: From I-77 (south) take Miller Rd. east to SR 21. Follow SR 21 south to Snowville Rd., and Snowville Rd. east to Riverview Rd. Follow Riverview Rd. south to Boston Mills Ski Resort. Turn east on Boston Mills Rd., crossing the Cuyahoga Valley Scenic Railroad tracks and the Cuyahoga River bridge past the old town of Boston Mills. The Boston Trailhead parking area is on the right at the trailhead sign.
From Akron take I-77 north to I-271 northeast (toward Erie, PA). Exit from I-271 at SR 303 east, and continue east to Riverview Rd., just before the town of Peninsula. Follow Riverview Rd. north to Boston Mills Rd., then follow the directions above.

Parking & restrooms: At Boston Trailhead and Lock 29 Trailhead.

The Cuyahoga Valley National Recreation Area (CVNRA) preserves a 22-mile green space between Cleveland and Akron, and its visitor centers contain a repository of the early history of the Western Reserve of Connecticut. The old town of Boston Mills was once a thriving community of boatyards, shops, a tavern, and a hotel that almost disappeared in a great flood in 1913.

The 1836 Boston Store alongside the canal on Boston Mills Rd., just west of the Boston Trailhead parking lot, has been the site of an archeological dig recently. Artifacts have been recovered from this site that, beginning in 1827, served canal boats plying up and down the Ohio & Erie Canal. A small museum depicting 19th-century canal life and boat building is planned for this old store.

On this hike you will visit the old towns of Boston Mills and Peninsula, enjoy walking in deep woods on the Buckeye Trail, see remnants of locks on the old Ohio & Erie Canal, and view the scenic Cuyahoga River on the Canal Towpath Trail.

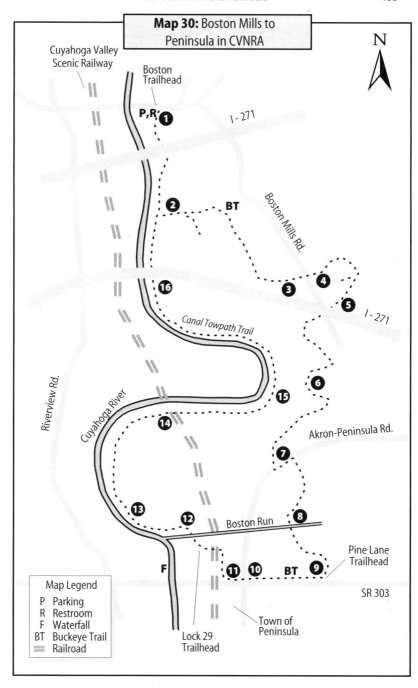

Map 30: Boston Mills to Peninsula in CVNRA

N

Cuyahoga Valley Scenic Railway

Boston Trailhead

P, R 1

I-271

2   BT   Boston Mills Rd.

3   4

5   I-271

16

Canal Towpath Trail

6

15

14   Cuyahoga River

Akron-Peninsula Rd.

7

Riverview Rd.

13   12   Boston Run   8

Pine Lane Trailhead

11 10   BT   9

F   SR 303

Map Legend
P   Parking
R   Restroom
F   Waterfall
BT   Buckeye Trail
≡   Railroad

Lock 29 Trailhead

Town of Peninsula

1. Begin on the blue-blazed Buckeye Trail (BT) at the Boston Trailhead going south, keeping the Cuyahoga River on the right. (Use CAUTION on this wide gravel path; it is also used by fast-traveling bicyclists.) Pass under the twin highway bridges of I-271.

2. Just past the bridges, turn left (east) on the Buckeye Trail. (The Towpath Trail continues straight ahead.) Cross the field and watch for a left turn of the BT going uphill, avoiding the marshy track straight ahead and a right turn. The trail climbs upward through a mixed forest.

3. At about 1 mile reach the grassy area next to I-271, cross a drainage culvert and climb a set of log steps. After a short stretch of more woods hiking, reach Boston Mills Rd.

4. Cross Boston Mills Rd. and, after walking 0.1 mile south along the left side of the road, watch for the double blue tree blaze where the Buckeye Trail enters the woods again (on the left). Continue walking along a ravine, staying on the main trail and avoiding the right turnoff.

5. At about 1.5 miles reach Boston Mills Rd. again. Cross the bridge overpass (over I-80, the Ohio Turnpike) and watch for the blue blaze of the Buckeye Trail on the right at the end of the bridge. Here enter a white pine forest. The trees were planted neatly in straight rows by Girl Scouts many years ago. Far over to the right is a land depression that remained after construction of the I-80 highway bridge.

6. Follow the Buckeye Trail as it curves gently through towering oak trees, past ravines and gullies, on this generally flat trail. Cross a small creek and a clearing just before reaching Akron-Peninsula Rd. (3 miles).

7. Turn left (east) on A-P Rd. and walk along it about 0.3 mile until the Buckeye Trail turns off on the right (south) and enters the woods.

8. Reach the wide stream of Boston Run flowing west into the Cuyahoga River. Cross the brook on stones (if the water is low) or on the log lying across the stream (if the water is high). This is a lovely river valley with many springtime wildflowers. Descend some log steps and cross a small side creek, still following the blue blazes.

9. At a trail intersection under the power line, bear left and soon reach Pine Lane Trailhead at SR 303 (4 miles).

Exit from the trailhead to the old, brick-paved road on the right, the former Rte. 303.

10. Follow Buckeye Trail signs westward to the town of Peninsula.

Peninsula was a busy Ohio & Erie Canal town from the 1820s onward—larger than Cleveland—with many homes, mills, hotels, and a boat-building company. When the railroad was built in 1880, Peninsula's importance as a commercial center diminished, as did its population. The town got its name because it once was a peninsula surrounded on three sides by the Cuyahoga River, which originally curled back upon itself. Peninsula is listed as an historic district on the National Register of Historic Places, and is a favorite destination of arts and crafts shoppers.

11. No longer following the Buckeye Trail, turn right (north) through the restaurant parking lot and pass the train depot of the Cuyahoga Valley Scenic Railroad. (The CVSR offers scenic rides all year long through the Cuyahoga Valley National Recreation Area, from Independence to Hale Farm and Village and to Quaker Square in Akron. For ticket information and schedules call 800-468-4070. Information is also available at the CVSR office in Peninsula, 1664 West Main St., Peninsula 44264.)

Ahead on the left, cross the tracks to the Lock 29 Trailhead and the Canal Towpath Trail. The spectacular Cuyahoga River waterfall on the left is a favorite photo spot. Here the old Ohio & Erie Canal switches from the west side of the river to the east side. An exhibit describing the canal and lock system is shown on signs. It is also well worth the climb up the steps to view the interior of Lock 29.

12. Take the gravel Canal Towpath Trail to the right (north). There are fast-moving bicyclists on this trail much of the time; hikers usually keep to the right. The path follows the winding river on the left and the old watered canal on the right. Boston Run stream enters the Cuyahoga River near this point.

13. Pass another old lock on the right (Lock 30). Here also is the foundation of the old Petrie House. (For more information about the Ohio & Erie Canal, and to see a restored working lock, visit the Canal Visitor Center at 7104 Canal Rd. [south of Rockside Rd.] Valley View, OH 44147; 216-524-1497.)

14. Continue past a railing overlooking the scenic Cuyahoga River and through a tunnel under the Cuyahoga Valley Scenic Railroad (6.3 miles). Interpretive signs are posted along the way.

15. Pass another old lock on the right and enter a long boardwalk over pretty marshland and open water. This scenic bird-watching spot, where canal boats used to turn around, is called Stumpy's Basin. I-80 is to the right (northeast).

16. Continue ahead. Pass under the I-80 bridge and rejoin the Buckeye Trail at the turn described in Note #2. Continue under the twin bridges of I-271 and return to the Boston Trailhead and parking area.

31 CASCADE VALLEY METRO PARK

Easy

Directions: From I-271 take Exit 12 (SR 303); follow SR 303 east to Peninsula. Just past the Cuyahoga River bridge in Peninsula, turn right (south) at Akron-Peninsula Rd. Follow it through the Cuyahoga Valley National Recreation Area to its juncture with West Portage Trail. Turn left (east) on West Portage Trail and continue to Northampton Rd. Turn right (south) on Northampton Rd. The roadway changes to Cuyahoga St. The entrance to Cascade Valley Metro Park's Oxbow Area (Hike A) is off Cuyahoga St. on the left, opposite from the Valley View Golf Course. If you wish to take Hike B first, continue south on Cuyahoga St. another 3/4-mile to the park entrance on the left marked for Chuckery Area.
- From the I-77/76 merge in Akron, take SR 59 (Innerbelt), then N. Howard St. north to Cuyahoga St. Continue north on Cuyahoga St.; park entrances are on the right for Chuckery Area and for Oxbow Area.

Akron's Cascade Valley Metro Park is among the newest of a series of parks along the Cuyahoga River developed by the city and Metro Parks Serving Summit County. Its name derives from the numerous cascades that are visible from the trail along the river's edge.

In 1982 the 89-acre Oxbow Area to the west of the river was opened, and in 1986 the 310-acre Chuckery Area opened, featuring remains of a manmade water channel called Chuckery Race, now listed on the National Register of Historic Places. In 1844, city leaders decided to divert the Cuyahoga River through a small channel, or race, to a planned industrial town to be called Summit City. Economics forced them to abandon this project before it could be completed. Although it is now filled in, remnants of the old race can be seen on the Chuckery Trail.

At Gorge Metro Park east of here, the Cuyahoga River makes a sharp turn westward from its long southerly course through Geauga and Portage Counties as it encounters the higher land of Summit County. Here in Cascade Valley Metro Park, the river flows south again, briefly, before turning north to flow through Sand Run Metro Park, Cuyahoga Valley National Recreation Area, and on to Lake Erie.

The Indian Signal Tree is a feature of Cascade Valley Metro Park, but its history is hazy. It is an unusually shaped Bur Oak tree with horizontal limbs on either side of a massive trunk. Legend says that Indians dwelling here may have shaped the tree as a directional signal or perhaps used it for

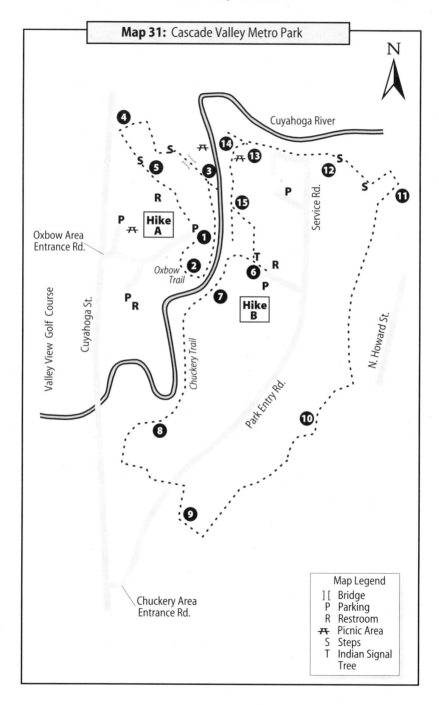

Map 31: Cascade Valley Metro Park

N

Cuyahoga River

Oxbow Area
Entrance Rd.

Hike A

Oxbow Trail

Service Rd.

N. Howard St.

Valley View Golf Course

Cuyahoga St.

Chuckery Trail

Hike B

Park Entry Rd.

Chuckery Area
Entrance Rd.

Map Legend
] [Bridge
P Parking
R Restroom
🛦 Picnic Area
S Steps
T Indian Signal
    Tree

ceremonial purposes. History indicates that the tree was a marker for the beginning of a canoe portage overland from the Cuyahoga River to the Tuscarawas River.

The flood plain of the Cuyahoga River valley supports beautiful wild-flowers in this park, especially the white trillium. Excellent views of this river, with its cascades and rapids, are available from several vantage points in both the Oxbow and Chuckery Areas. The park offers baseball, softball, soccer, tobogganing, and sledding.

The trailheads for the two marked trails—the 1-mile Oxbow Trail (Hike A) and the 2.4-mile Chuckery Trail (Hike B)—are separated by the Cuyahoga River and require a short car trip if you wish to hike both loops.

HIKE A: OXBOW AREA

Distance: 1.2 miles

Hiking time: Less than 1 hour

Description: The first half-mile of the Hike A loop is on a flat path along a beautiful stretch of flood plain alongside the Cuyahoga River. If the river water is high, alternate paths are available. There are lovely views of the small cascades that give the park its name. The second half-mile ascends a steep hill for a long view of the valley before descending to the parking area.

Parking & restrooms: After entering the park, drive past the first parking area on the left (sledding hill) and past the next one (ball fields), to the parking area at the end of the road. Restrooms are at the sledding hill and the ball fields.

1. Enter the Oxbow Trail, marked with a sign containing a pair of paral-lel ripple marks, at the northeast end of the parking area. Immediately turn right (south). The path leads across the flat flood plain of the Cuyahoga River. Many oaks, maples, and cottonwoods flourish in this rich environ-ment. Because the plain is frequently flooded, the soil is thick, moist, and silty. Sycamore, silver maple, and especially cottonwood trees are the dom-inant species here, because they are shallow-rooted and fast-growing.

2. At 0.25 mile reach the south-flowing Cuyahoga River. A short side trail leads to the river for a nice view up and down stream.

The path now goes north and reaches a trail junction. If the high-water bypass is needed turn left. Otherwise, go right for the riverside path. The bypass trail will join the main trail along this very pleasant river walk.

3. After another high-water bypass, continue north past a picnic area. The trail bends west, crosses a small wooden foot bridge, and ascends a steep hill on 103 timber steps.

4. At the top, the path bends west to a bench from which you can enjoy a long view of Cascade Valley below. Continue north through a lovely forest of oaks, maples, and white pines.

5. At 0.7 mile begin to descend to the valley on 47 timber steps, then 20 more, and yet another 21 steps before reaching an open field and the sledding hill on the right. Cross the field to the parking area.

HIKE B: CHUCKERY AREA

Distance: 2.5 miles

Hiking time: 1-1/2 hours

Description: The Chuckery Trail is well marked and wide in most places, and follows a short section of the Cuyahoga River. The first part of the hike is on a flat pathway. Then it ascends a steep hill on the former Chuckery Race and finally descends to the river level on sets of stairs.

Parking & restrooms: From Oxbow Area, drive south on Cuyahoga St. to the Chuckery Area entrance on the left. Follow the park road to the first parking area on the left. Restrooms are located here.

6. Enter the path to the left of the restroom building. It leads to the impressive, fenced-in Indian Signal Tree. A 1986 plaque describes the tree's history.

7. Go west across the field to the Chuckery Trail entrance, marked with an arrowhead symbol on the left. The swift south-flowing Cuyahoga River soon appears on the right. Note the many large eastern cottonwood trees, which are often found beside streams. Their leaves are roughly triangular with toothed margins. American sycamore trees also enjoy living along streams and are characterized by peeling bark that leaves irregular patches of whitish-brown color on their trunks. Their leaf resembles a very large maple leaf.

On the opposite side of the river a stone retaining wall has been built at a strategic spot to retard erosion where the river makes a sharp oxbow (U–shaped) turn.

8. The trail bends south away from the river and passes through an open meadow, a reclaimed landfill from the 1950s and 1960s.

9. At 0.7 mile cross the park road and continue on the Chuckery Trail. Ascend a steep hill through an oak-maple forest. The trail bends left and goes northeast on a wide gravel trail. This is the former Chuckery Race ditch (described in this chapter's introduction) now filled with dirt and gravel.

10. Continue climbing steeply uphill. At about 0.9 mile a bench near the top presents an inviting rest stop. Continue under a power line, hiking in a northeast direction. At 1.2 miles pass an old oval-shaped brick-and-concrete vent on the right that may be a relic of the days when a sewer line used to run along here. The houses on the hill above on the right are on North Howard St.

11. Watch for a sharp left (west) turn in the trail, where it begins to descend the hill and winds through lovely woods. Pass some old stone steps on the left and continue to follow signs with the Chuckery Trail's arrowhead symbols, avoiding any side trails.

Near the approach to the Cuyahoga River descend a set of timber steps, and again, you will see the shimmering river cascades for which the park has been named.

12. (2 miles) Take a set of stone steps downhill (left) toward the river and service road.

CAUTION: Use the hand railing on these slippery, moss-covered steps.

Upon reaching the service vehicle road, stay left and continue alongside the river on the service road (also the trail). A river-bank bench overlooks this scenic view.

13. Where the service road bends to the left toward the soccer fields, stay on the Chuckery Trail as it continues ahead alongside the river going west.

14. Pass through a riverside picnic area (2.1 miles). On the opposite side of the river is the Oxbow Trail, taken earlier on Hike A. Follow the Chuckery Trail as it bends left (south) alongside a tributary stream, leaving the riverside path, which continues straight ahead.

15. At a trail intersection, bear left (southeast). The trail emerges at an open field where you will see the fenced-in Indian Signal Tree. Cross the field to the tree and follow the same path back to the parking area.

This chapter was reviewed by Walter Starcher, Chief Naturalist, Metro Parks Serving Summit County.

32 CASCADE LOCKS METRO PARK

Distance: 1 mile

Easy

Hiking time: 1 hour

Description: This walk is mostly on a marked mulched trail and entails climbing up and down several sets of stairs from which to view the canal and each of the locks. The southerly walk begins at North St. and goes upward 0.4 mile from there to Lock 10 and back. The northern 0.1-mile section from W. North St. to the Little Cuyahoga River is on a level grassy trail.

Directions: From Akron go north on N. Howard St. to W. North St. Turn left (west) on W. North St. and cross the bridge over the canal. Turn right onto the driveway and into the parking lot for Faith Tabernacle Church. From I-77 (in Akron) take Exit 21C, SR 59 east (Innerbelt). Follow the Innerbelt until it narrows down near the Steam Plant on the left. Turn left at the Steam Plant onto N. Howard St. going north. At the first traffic light, turn left (west) on North St. Cross the bridge over the canal to the parking lot next to Faith Tabernacle Church, on the right.

Parking & restrooms: Park in the lot adjacent to the church. There are no restrooms here. Special arrangements have been made with the church and CLPA for parking, but visitors are asked to refrain from parking here on Sunday mornings.

Cascade Locks Metro Park is officially known as the Canal Unit of Cascade Valley Metro Park, both administered by Metro Parks Serving Summit County. Cascade Valley Metro Park is located just north of here on Cuyahoga St. (Ch. 31).

The 309-mile Ohio & Erie Canal once extended from Lake Erie at Cleveland to Portsmouth on the Ohio River and for 80 years was the most important means of transportation in this part of the state; the height of activity was 1827-1850. The entire length of the canal was opened from Cleveland to Portsmouth in 1832 with great fanfare because it transformed this part of Ohio from a rather primitive wilderness state into one of the nation's most prosperous areas. Products from this region could now be shipped north to Cleveland, and from there to East Coast markets by way of Lake Erie, or south to the Ohio River and then as far south as New Orleans.

The 38-mile Akron-to-Cleveland section of the canal was built in

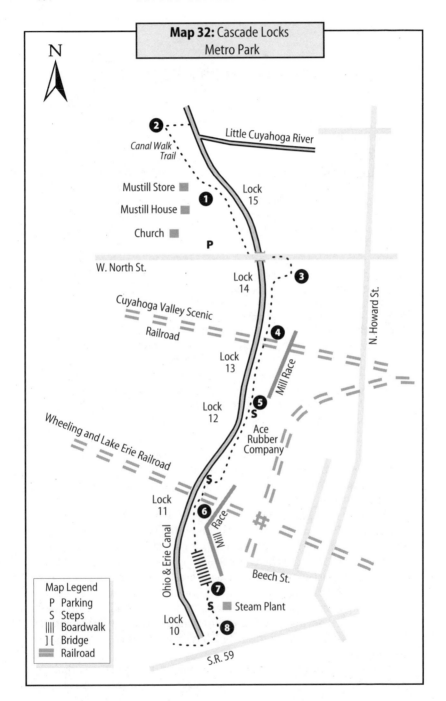

Map 32: Cascade Locks Metro Park

N

Little Cuyahoga River

❷

Canal Walk Trail

Mustill Store ■

Mustill House ■

Church ■

❶

Lock 15

P

W. North St.

Lock 14

❸

Cuyahoga Valley Scenic Railroad

Lock 13

❹

Mill Race

Lock 12

❺
S

Ace Rubber Company

N. Howard St.

Wheeling and Lake Erie Railroad

Lock 11

S

❻

Mill Race

Ohio & Erie Canal

Beech St.

Map Legend
P Parking
S Steps
||| Boardwalk
] [Bridge
▒ Railroad

❼
S

■ Steam Plant

Lock 10

❽

S.R. 59

record time between 1825 and 1827. It required 44 locks (later reduced to 42) to lift or lower canal boats the 395-foot elevation difference between the two cities. Because Akron's Locks 1 through 21 were close together (within a two-mile span) and were the steepest on the canal, they have been called the "giant staircase." Cascade Locks includes Locks 10 through 16 of this historic waterway. Canal water (and excess storm-sewer water) cascades over the sills of Locks 10 through 15, where it is diverted into the Little Cuyahoga River near Mustill Store.

Many of the Ohio & Erie Canal locks were severely damaged in the great flood of 1913. They were subsequently abandoned and some became filled with debris and trash. The canal's demise had already been sealed when railroads became the dominant mode of transportation for both goods and people soon after the Civil War.

In order to preserve an important part of Ohio's history and create new opportunities for recreation, a short segment of the lock staircase was opened to the public in 1994 by the city of Akron. Cascade Locks Park Association (CLPA) spearheaded this effort, and the park is now under the management of Metro Parks Serving Summit County. The Canal Walk Trail extends from North St. south to Akron's Innerbelt. A short segment of the trail goes from W. North St. north to the juncture of the canal with the Little Cuyahoga River. Plans are underway to extend the trail northward, connecting it with the Canal Towpath Trail in the Cuyahoga Valley National Recreation Area.

Other portions of the locks are being opened for public use in nearby locations. A comprehensive canal corridor plan is under development includes a canal footpath that would ultimately extend from Lake Erie to Zoar.

For more information about Cascade Locks call 330-374-5625 or Metro Parks Serving Summit County (330-867-5511).

1. Begin the walk by going north on a driveway to the 1853 locktender's home, Mustill House, and the unpainted building next to it, Mustill Store. These are two of the oldest surviving buildings in Akron and are being restored by Cascade Locks Park Association and the City of Akron as part of the Ohio & Erie Canal Corridor Coalition. (The office for CLPA is in the house.) Lock 15, with 10 feet of lift, is east of the store and is presently the last restored lock before the canal reaches the Little Cuyahoga River.

Lock 15

The locks on the Ohio & Erie Canal were built of locally quarried sandstone blocks. The 90-foot channels were 15 feet wide to accommodate the 70-to-80-foot-long and 14-foot-wide canal boats. Boats traveled only four miles per hour and, even riding low in the water with 50-80 tons of cargo, drew only three feet of the water.

The locks were closed at either end with wooden (oak) gates that formed a "V" pointing upstream to resist the pressure of water.

Lock hydraulics worked by gravity. A "wicket" operated by means of an iron crank handle at the top of the gate permitted water to flow into or out of the lock. As the water entered or left the lock, the boat was then carried either up or down to the next water level.

There were several kinds of canal boats: freight boats (the most valuable), passenger packets, and state boats for the maintenance of the canal.

The boat was pulled by mules on the adjacent canal towpath. Occasionally the canal towpath switched from one side to the other, depending upon the terrain. Here at Lock 15 the towpath is on the same side as the store.

Mustill Store

For 35 years in the mid 1800s Fred Mustill sold food, supplies, and drinks to area residents and canal travelers from this dry goods store and its attached building (no longer existing). Behind the store is an old outhouse and some concrete steps and stanchions that remain from the early days. Still evident at the back of the store is some of the original wood siding, probably dating from the 1840s.

2. Follow a trail north of the store about 0.1 mile down to a wide-open view of the canal, where the flowing water is now level with the land. Here, look over beyond the canal to the confluence of the canal with the Little Cuyahoga River.

After the great flood of 1913, many changes occurred in the water flow of the canal. Lock 16, unwatered and not visible on this trail, was originally the last lock on the "giant staircase." Farther inland and west of here, it is not visited on this hike.

Return on the same path to the Mustill Store and House.

3. Cross North St. and the bridge over the canal, to the trailhead for the south section. Enter the trail at the kiosk sign for Cascade Locks Park. The sandstone wasteway near the bridge was used for runoff of excess water that flowed around Lock 14 at times of peak traffic on the canal.

In 1907, the original sandstone-block walls inside Lock 14 were chiseled and faced with concrete to waterproof them yet still maintain the 15-foot width that enabled the 14-foot wide boats to pass. Near the bottom of the lock the original 1827 stone blocks (not faced with concrete) are still exposed. Large notches at either end of the lock are the cavities into which the water gates were folded to preserve the 15-foot clearance for the boats.

Lock 14 is located in what was once a very busy valley. East of the trail is an open field, a former water basin. Beyond it was the a woolen mill, later the Cascade Grist Mill and, still later, Cascade Mills. It was owned and operated by Ferdinand Schumacher, the innovator and industrialist who ultimately became president of Quaker Oats Co. Schumacher's 1876 mill was powered by an immense, 37-ton, iron overshot wheel with a 10-foot face. It was 36 feet in diameter, with 96 steel buckets receiving canal water through an underground pipe system called Cascade Race. The ruins may be seen near Lock 12. Waste water and water discharged from the wheel flowed out through underground conduits to the Little Cuyahoga River. This huge wheel powered purifiers, iron rolls, cockle machines, ending stones, brush machines, and other appliances used in the manufacture of flour. The mill retained the large water wheel and also added tall chimneys for coal-burning steam engines, when steam power eventually replaced water power.

An interesting history of the 37-ton water wheel has been uncovered by local historians. Apparently the wheel was turned on its side and buried in the basin in the 1920s when it was no longer useful. In the 1950s, when Ohio Edison constructed a steel tower on the site for high tension wires, the wheel was lifted by crane off to a location a short distance east of the pit. In all likelihood it lies buried there still.

4. The concrete conduit near the path carries voltage lines for Ohio Edison.

The railroad trestle farther ahead supports the Cuyahoga Valley Scenic Railroad, an excursion line that carries visitors from Independence near Cleveland to Hale Farm and Village and continues to Akron, going through the heart of Cuyahoga Valley National Recreation Area. (Train information is available by calling 800-468-4070).

The three stone arches on the east once supported a wooden bridge over Lock 13, originally constructed by the Valley Line Railroad in 1879-80. A few of the trestle's original wooden pilings are visible at both.

When the Valley Line RR went bankrupt in 1895, it was reorganized as Cleveland Terminal & Valley Co. The railroad was taken over by Baltimore & Ohio in 1909, which, in a 1910-1916 capital improvement program, replaced the original wooden trestle with a steel railroad trestle to carry freight. In 1963 B & O merged with Chesapeake & Ohio, became CSX. This bridge is about 300 feet long and crosses 40 feet above Lock 13.

Lock 13 also contains exposed original sandstone blocks at its bottom. The concrete walls connecting some of the locks were built in 1937 to prevent erosion of the canal banks.

5. Down a few steps and up another set of steps is Lock 12 on the right and Ace Rubber Co. on the left.

At the top of the steps at Lock 12, look left (east) to see the old Cascade Race. The water for the race originated from a dam on the Little Cuyahoga River in Middlebury (near Goodyear Headquarters). Dr. Eliakim Crosby built the race (sometimes called "Crosby's Ditch"), taking advantage of the downhill terrain to power his Old Stone Mill at Lock 5 (Cascade Plaza Hotel). Along the race were mills, factories, an iron furnace, a distillery, and other businesses that enabled the town of Cascade (North Akron) to thrive.

CAUTION: Watch for vehicles in the open area behind the factory.

Ace Rubber Co., built as American Rubber Co. in 1919, is still in operation and produces rubber floor mats for industry. It is located on the site of the old Aetna Mill (1843), which was built near the even earlier Aetna Iron Furnace.

South of the multistory Ace building is a sump, surrounded by a screened-in shed. The water inside is used for cooling during the manufacturing process and is constantly recirculated.

Originally the millrace water powered two more mills and eventually flowed down to the Little Cuyahoga River.

At the north end of Lock 12 are the remains of a canal basin where boats tied up to take on cargoes. West of Lock 12 is a water wasteway that took excess water around the lock.

6. Continue up the next set of steps and under the next railroad trestle to Lock 11.

The concrete structure that crosses the canal at this point is another conduit for Ohio Edison power lines.

The railroad trestle above Lock 11 is an active freight line of the Wheeling & Lake Erie Railroad. The bridge is about 875 feet long and crosses 70 feet above Lock 11.

The old stone towers on the left and right are pilings that remain from a trestle built by Pittsburgh, Akron & Western RR in 1890-91.

The present bridge, with its steel supports, may have been built after the 1913 flood when stone piers had been undermined.

Continue on the trail. At the far end of Lock 11 the date "1907" is cast into the wall, indicating when the concrete lining was added to the locks to waterproof them. Lock 11 shows an internal sluiceway on the west wall into which water flowed through an open gate to fill the lock; the sluiceway acted as an alternative to the wickets. Note another open boat basin at the end of Lock 11.

7. The ditch for the millrace is now obvious on the left (east). Also to the east are the ruins of what some authorities think was Schumacher's Dam, built to create the necessary "head" (or altitude) for his overshot wheel. Constructed in the early 1870s, this concrete dam may have provided water through a 48-inch pipe to the huge overshot wheel at Schumacher's mill below.

From the left side of the boardwalk, view the concrete dam and box containing the opening for the 48-inch pipe. The bolts that you see inside the hydraulic box supported a screen to keep debris out of the pipe. A pool behind the dam accumulated water for the pipe; excess water flowed over twin spillways on either side of the box.

The wall alongside the boardwalk and the dam itself are made of early Portland cement, a product first manufactured in the U.S. in 1868. Schumacher must have realized that this new construction material was ideal for the dam he wanted to build. One has to admire Schumacher as an entrepreneur and an innovator on the cutting edge of industrial progress.

8. After ascending the next set of steps, you will reach the former Ohio Edison Steam Plant.

CAUTION: Stay well away from the fence surrounding the modern transformers.

This large brick building was originally the Beech St. Steam Plant and for many years produced steam for heating buildings in downtown Akron. An even earlier plant on this site produced Akron's first electricity to operate a street railway. Ohio Edison now uses these transformers for voltage conversion.

A viewing platform on the right offers another view of the canal water racing downward. Although the west wall of Lock 10 has been demolished, the east wall remains totally intact.

The trail ends here at the fence. The Ohio & Erie Canal, however, continues under the Innerbelt and Market St. and may someday become part of a fully-restored canal park system.

Retrace your steps back down the "staircase" of locks to North St. and the parking area.

Jack Gieck, author of *Photo Album of Ohio's Canal Era,* and producer of the video series, *Ohio's Canal Era,* provided substantial assistance in the preparation of this chapter and carefully reviewed it for accuracy of information.

33 FIRESTONE METRO PARK

Distance: 2.8 miles

Easy

Hiking time: 1-1/4 hours

Description: The flat 1.6-mile Willow Trail begins near the shelter, follows the shoreline of Little Turtle Pond, and goes alongside the small Tuscarawas River and Tuscarawas Race. The 1.2-mile Red Wing Trail ascends and descends a small hill to cross the marsh on a boardwalk and follows the river briefly in the opposite direction. Although both trails are short, they offer a surprising amount of variety, both in terrain and natural beauty.

Directions: From I-271 take SR 8 (Exit 18). Follow SR 8 south past I-77/76 to the Waterloo Rd. exit (now on I-77). Take Waterloo Rd. eight blocks west to Glenmount Rd., watching carefully for this left turn. Follow Glenmount south, past I-277, until it ends at Swartz Rd. Turn left (east) on Swartz and right (south) on Harrington Rd. (at Coventry Crossing). Go past the first park entrance on the right (Little Turtle Pond) to the second park entrance (also on the right).
From Akron, take I-277/US 224 to S. Main St. and go south to Swartz Rd. Then take Swartz Rd. east to Harrington Rd. and follow the directions above.

Parking & restrooms: Near the Tuscarawas Picnic Shelter.

Firestone Metro Park, one of Akron's Metro Parks Serving Summit County, was organized in 1941 when Firestone Tire and Rubber Co. donated 189 acres of land across from Firestone Country Club. Now consisting of 255 acres of rolling farmland, the park includes a fishing and ice skating pond, picnic areas, a new reservable picnic pavilion (330-867-5511), a large sledding and kite-flying hill, and three short trails. The narrow Tuscarawas River runs north through the park before eventually turning south to empty into the Muskingum River in Coshocton. Alongside the Willow Trail is Tuscarawas Race, a canal dug originally to feed water to the Ohio & Erie Canal but now providing water for industrial use and fire protection. A large marsh, the centerpiece of Firestone Metro Park, attracts a variety of birds and other wildlife. This wetland was formed by a rise in the water table resulting from a dam constructed in 1956 on Harrington Rd. to form Firestone Reservoir.

1. The Willow Trail, marked with a leaf symbol, begins north of the Tuscarawas Shelter on a wide dirt road going north, a track used also by

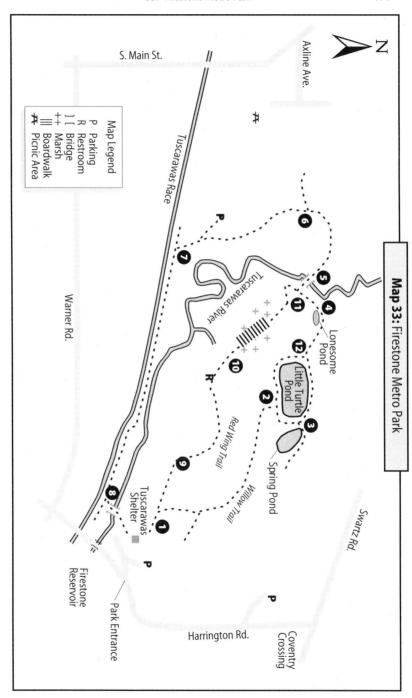

Map 33: Firestone Metro Park

N

S. Main St.

Axline Ave.

Tuscarawas Race

Map Legend
P Parking
R Restroom
] [Bridge
++ Marsh
≡ Boardwalk
⊼ Picnic Area

Warner Rd.

Tuscarawas River

Lonesome Pond

Little Turtle Pond

Spring Pond

Red Wing Trail

Willow Trail

Tuscarawas Shelter

Firestone Reservoir

Park Entrance

Harrington Rd.

Swartz Rd.

Coventry Crossing

park vehicles. Some of the trees carry identification labels. Pass a side trail on the right.

2. Reach Little Turtle Pond at 0.3 miles and bear right to follow the edge of the pond. Special summer fishing programs for children under 15 years are held in this stocked pond (330-867-5511). Lighted ice skating is available in the winter (330-836-0239).

3. The trail continues between Little Turtle Pond and Spring Pond, where many waterfowl usually congregate. Continue along the north side of Little Turtle Pond until the trail bears west into the forested area.

4. Pass Lonesome Pond (filled with marsh cattails) on the left. The narrow Tuscarawas River is now on the right, flowing northward through the park. (This river flows westward after it leaves the park, then south in Barberton, and eventually reaches the Muskingum and Ohio Rivers far south of here.)

5. (0.7 mile) At a trail junction turn right to cross the river on a wooden footbridge and follow the trail as it bends west.

6. At a trail intersection, turn left (south). (The side trail ahead goes out to Axline Ave. and a new picnic pavilion.) Continue south on the Willow Trail alongside the river, which is now on the left. Pass a side trail on the right (leading out to a parking area).

7. Reach Tuscarawas Race at 1 mile and bear left (southeast). The race, built to channel water to the Ohio & Erie Canal northeast of Barberton, now channels it from Firestone Reservoir to lakes west of here and then on to another part of the Tuscarawas River.

The Tuscarawas River is now on the left below. On this wide embankment a railroad once carried coal from a mine southeast of here. Continue along the race to a trail junction.

8. Turn left (north) at this junction to cross the river on an arched wooden bridge and return on the trail to the Tuscarawas Shelter (1.6 miles).

From the shelter building, cross the field in a northwest direction to the edge of the woods and a sign indicating the Red Wing Trail, marked with a wing symbol.

9. Follow the Red Wing Trail westward uphill through a lovely upland forest of oak, maple, and beech trees.

10. The trail goes downhill to an open area with restrooms on the left. Continue to the west then north to enter the marsh on a plastic boardwalk. Here you may see frogs, turtles, raccoons, or muskrats. Cross the marsh to reach the Tuscarawas River again (2.1 miles).

11. Bear right onto the path to follow the river north. Reach the junction with the Willow Trail and the bridge crossed earlier (Note #5). Stay to the right (north) on the Willow/Red Wing Trail and follow it back northeast alongside the river, past the sign for Lonesome Pond, to Little Turtle Pond.

12. Turn right (south) at Little Turtle Pond. Stay to the right at the next trail intersection and follow the trail back to the parking area.

This chapter was reviewed by Walter Starcher, Chief Naturalist, Metro Parks Serving Summit County.

34 FURNACE RUN METRO PARK

Distance: 3.5 miles

Easy

Hiking time: 2 hours

Description: This is an easy, flat walk under magnificent sycamore (button-wood) trees and a cool place on a hot day. Along Furnace Run stream there is abundant evidence of beavers at work. There are several small stream crossings on bridges.

Directions: From I-77 south take Exit 147, Miller Rd. (NOTE—Miler Rd. has no exit from I-77 northbound). Go left (east) on Miller Rd. to SR 21. Turn right (south) on SR 21 and continue past I-80 (Ohio Turnpike) to just past the I-77 overpass bridge. On the right, immediately past the overpass, turn right (north) onto Townsend Rd. Follow Townsend Rd. north to the Furnace Run park entrance on the right. (A sign may identify this park as Brushwood, Akron Metropark.)
From Akron, take I-77/SR 21 north to the Wheatley Rd. exit. Go west on Wheatley to Cleveland-Massillon/Brecksville Rd. and turn right (north) here. Follow this road past SR 303 to Townsend Rd., then follow the directions above.

Parking & restrooms: At the park entrance.

Metro Parks Serving Summit County was organized in 1921 as Akron Metropolitan Park District, the second park district in Ohio. Furnace Run and Sand Run Metro Parks opened a few years later. Today the Metro Parks system includes over 6,600 acres of park land, of which only about one-fifth is developed.

Furnace Run Metro Park, 890 acres, is situated in Cuyahoga Valley National Recreation Area. The park is separated by I-77 into north and southeast sections. The hike described in this chapter is in the north section, in Richfield, west of I-77 and south of I-80.

Furnace Run, for which the park is named, flows southeast from Brushwood Lake for about six miles before it enters the Cuyahoga River near Everett Covered Bridge. The north section of the park contains three short connecting trails that meander through a beech-maple woods and along Furnace Run and Rock Creek, neither of which is a very wide stream here.

The park contains picnic areas and playing fields, Brushwood Lake, and newly-built Brushwood Pavilion adjacent to the lake. Enclosed and heated, this modern building contains a food service area, restrooms, and

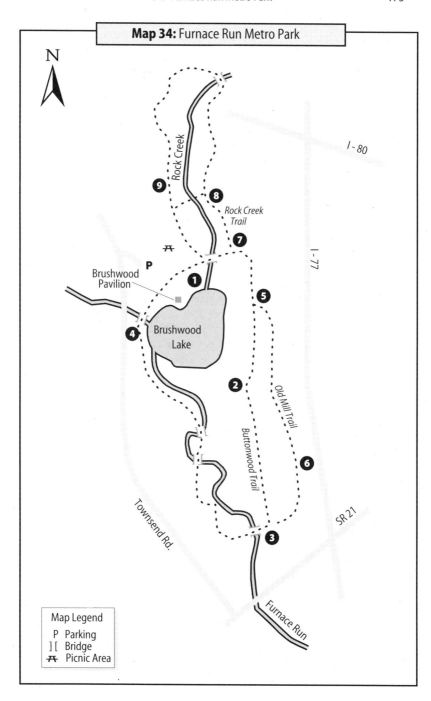

Map 34: Furnace Run Metro Park

N

I-80

Rock Creek

9

8

Rock Creek Trail

7

P

Brushwood Pavilion

1

Brushwood Lake

5

I-77

4

2

Old Mill Trail

Buttonwood Trail

6

SR 21

Townsend Rd.

3

Furnace Run

Map Legend
P Parking
] [Bridge
⚲ Picnic Area

seating for 100 people (330-867-5511 for reservations). Both the pavilion and lake were named for Charles Francis Brush (1849-1929), the inventor of the electric arc lamp. His family donated much of the land for this public recreation area to Akron's Metropolitan Park District in 1929.

1. This hike starts on the walkway east of Brushwood Shelter. At the end of that path, cross a small bridge to the signs for the three north-south trails in the park. Each path is about one mile long. The Buttonwood Trail is marked with a pine tree symbol, the Old Mill Trail with a deer hoof-print, and the Rock Creek Trail with an oak leaf. Turn right (south) on the Buttonwood Trail, which initially runs in tandem with the Old Mill Trail. Stay on the Buttonwood Trail where the Old Mill Trail bears left.

2. Along the Buttonwood Trail are many maples and beeches felled by beavers, who work industriously and persistently to dam up Furnace Run. Their chisel work on trees and shrubs provides ample evidence of their presence. Well known for their engineering feats, these large rodents have cut trees to construct dams that create ponds on Furnace Run. There may or may not be evidence of a beaver lodge, as often these animals dig burrows in the streamside mud as living spaces.

Buttonwood trees (sycamores) that dominate the woods are identified by their pale, peeling bark. These shallow-rooted, fast-growing trees are commonly found along river banks growing in thick, moist, silty soil.

3. Without taking any side trails, reach a bench at the far south end of the Buttonwood Trail (0.5 mile). Turn right and continue following the loop northward, keeping Furnace Run mostly on the right as you cross and recross the brook on bridges.

4. Just past the dam at the south end of Brushwood Lake, the trail crosses a small bridge. Go through the woods to the north edge of the lake, where a variety of ducks and water-birds can often be found enjoying the water.

5. Skirt the edge of the lake and return to the same trail entrance sign described in Note #1. Turn right again, following the Old Mill Trail south in tandem with the Buttonwood Trail initially. But this time turn left at the first intersection as the Old Mill Trail goes up a small hill to a huge glacial boulder. On this giant rock is carved a memorial to Charles Francis Brush.

6. The Old Mill Trail continues east of the boulder and descends to the south. (The cars you hear nearby on the left are on I-77.) After 0.5 mile the trail again reaches the same bench described in Note #3. Turn north (right) on the previously walked Buttonwood Trail.

7. At the trail sign at the north end of the Buttonwood Trail, stay right (north) on the Rock Creek Trail. Follow Rock Creek (on the left), crossing several small brooks.

8. After about half a mile on this trail, reach a cross-over trail, an optional short-cut back to the parking area.

9. Continue to the north end of the loop and circle back south along the west side of the creek. This path goes through a stand of pines and ends at a picnic area. The parking area is over the hill to the west of the picnic tables.

This chapter was reviewed by Walter Starcher, Chief Naturalist, Metro Parks Serving Summit County.

35 MUNROE FALLS METRO PARK

Distance: 3 miles

Hiking time: 1-1/2 hours

Description: The 2.2-mile Indian Spring Trail undulates over moderately hilly terrain through deciduous forest and past two ponds southeast of the swimming lake. The walk is on a wide, well-marked trail and on grass bordering the beach around the swimming lake.

Directions: From I-271 take Exit 18 (SR 8). Follow SR 8 south to the exit marked Graham Rd./Silver Lake/Stow. Follow Graham Rd. east to SR 91. Turn right (south) on SR 91 to Munroe Falls. (On the left, just before the Cuyahoga River bridge, is a parking area for the Metro Parks' Bike & Hike Trail, a good spot for viewing the town's very scenic waterfall.) Continue south on SR 91, crossing the river and railroad tracks, for a 1/2-mile more to South River Rd.; turn left (east). Follow South River Rd. one mile to the park entrance on the right.
From Akron, take SR 8 north to Portage Trail. Turn right (east) on Portage Trail, then take an immediate left onto Munroe Falls Ave. Go east on Munroe Falls Ave. to SR 91. Turn right (south) on SR 91 about 1/4 mile to South River Rd. Turn left on S. River Rd. about one mile to the park entrance on the right.

Parking & restrooms: After entering the park, continue to the right and circle around the swimming lake to the parking lot marked for trails, just before the Shady Beach Shelter. Restrooms are at Shady Beach picnic area.

Munroe Falls Metro Park, a unit of Metro Parks Serving Summit County, is located near the Cuyahoga River in the town of Munroe Falls, close to the scenic waterfall for which the town is named. The central feature of this park is a 13-acre swimming lake, a former private swim club owned by the John Renner family. Metro Parks purchased the property in 1978 and made extensive improvements that included picnic shelters, tennis, volleyball and basketball courts, and playgrounds. A new bathhouse complex was built in 1995. A park admission fee is charged during the swimming season from Memorial Day to Labor Day, and visitors who wish only to hike are still charged this fee. A pleasant loop trail through the woods is enjoyed by hikers and, in winter, by cross-country skiers.

1. Enter the Indian Spring Trail at the south end of the parking lot at the trail marked with a tomahawk symbol.

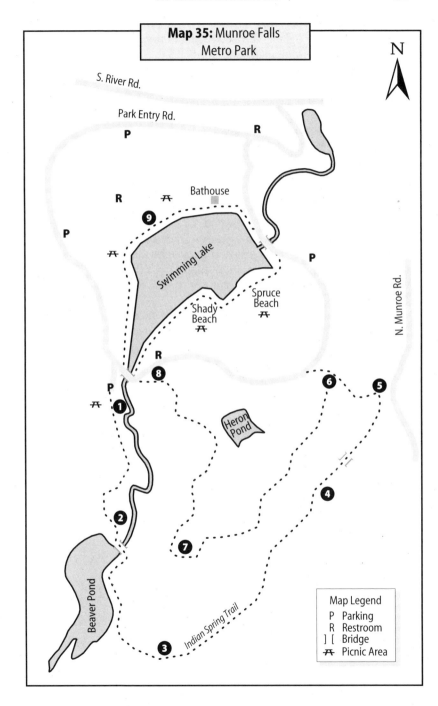

Map 35: Munroe Falls Metro Park

N

S. River Rd.

Park Entry Rd.

P

R

R

Bathouse

⑨

P

Swimming Lake

Spruce Beach

Shady Beach

R

P

⑧

①

Heron Pond

⑥

⑤

②

④

⑦

③ Indian Spring Trail

Beaver Pond

N. Munroe Rd.

Map Legend

P   Parking
R   Restroom
] [Bridge
🎍 Picnic Area

2. At 0.2 mile bear left over the dam at the north end of Beaver Pond. The trail goes to the right (south) and uphill to overlook this pretty little pond, often crowded with many waterfowl.

3. The broad trail bends east through a forest of oak, maple, beech, and cucumber trees.

4. At 1 mile the trail bends slightly toward the north, then east, crosses a small footbridge, and ascends a small rise. Here are bigtooth aspens whose unusual leaves are ovate with rounded marginal teeth.

5. Just before the trail turns west, pass a park bench. The road to the right (east) is North Munroe Rd. At about 1.2 miles the path gently descends through an oak forest.

6. Turn left. (The short-cut trail on the right leads out to the park road that encircles the park and swimming lake.) The trail now bends to the southwest as it snakes through the woods.

7. Soon the path turns toward the northeast past an open field. At about 2 miles reenter the woods going eastward through a former farm field now in succession growth with short stubby maple trees. Pass Heron Pond, on the right, and continue on the trail at the northwest end of the swimming lake dam.

8. After rising gently then descending down stone steps, the Indian Spring Trail crosses a footbridge to the parking area. This hike can be ended here or may be extended by walking 3/4 mile more around the fine swimming lake.

9. Continue in a clockwise direction on the grassy area around the swimming lake and past a new bathhouse. Cross the bridge at the east end of the lake and continue under a stand of spruce trees shading the Spruce Beach Picnic Area. Reach the parking area just beyond the Shady Beach Shelter.

This chapter was reviewed by Walter Starcher, Chief Naturalist, Metro Parks Serving Summit County.

36 SEIBERLING NATUREALM

Distance: 2-3/4 miles

Hiking time: 2-1/2 hours

Description: The trails in Naturealm are generally short and include flat paved paths and dirt trails over somewhat hilly terrain. The Arboretum Trail goes past flowering, weeping, and pyramidal trees and shrubs, and a collection of fruit and nut trees. On Cherry Lane Trail an observation deck overlooks Echo Pond, and a suspension bridge over a ravine joins that trail with Fernwood Trail. The longest trail in Naturealm is the 1.1-mile-long Seneca Trail loop, which begins near Seneca Pond and continues through former farmland, now a deciduous forest. A booklet available at the visitors center interprets the numbered signs on this trail. For visitors walking through the rock and herb garden near the center, there is another interesting brochure available containing herb lore.

Directions: From I-77, exit at Ghent Rd. (Exit 138) to SR 175. Follow Ghent south to Smith Rd. Turn left (east) on Smith Rd., and continue east past Revere and Sand Run roads. The entrance for Seiberling Naturealm is on the right.
From Akron, take I-77 or Market St. northwest to Smith Rd, then Smith Rd. east to Naturealm.

Parking & restrooms: At the visitors center.

F. A. Seiberling, co-founder of Goodyear Tire and Rubber Company, donated 400 acres of his land to establish Sand Run Metro Park, of which Seiberling Naturealm is a part. Opened in 1964, this 100-acre nature preserve offers an arboretum of 16 acres with more than 300 kinds of trees and shrubs. A rock and herb garden contains a collection of 85 glacial rocks and more than 75 species of herbs. There are many flowering trees here that are especially beautiful in the spring, and several attractive trails surrounding Seneca and Echo Ponds.

A unique visitors center, built into a hill, contains a series of striking nature exhibits portraying plants and animals of woodlands and marshlands. A spectacular underwater walk-in display is a child's delight, with oversized snails, crayfish, water bugs, and other pond life depicted. There is also an observation beehive, a bird-watching room (with binoculars provided), and a weather station. Park naturalists offer a variety of programs, classes, and nature walks that originate here. The center, open daily from 10-5, is located on Smith Rd. east of Sand Run Rd. (330-836-2185).

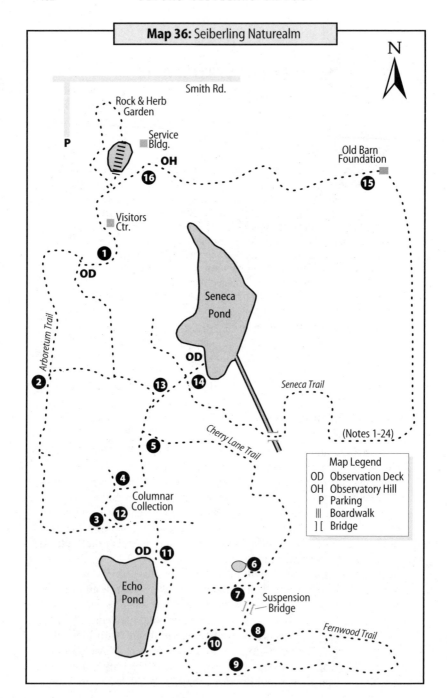

Map 36: Seiberling Naturealm

N

Smith Rd.

Rock & Herb Garden

Service Bldg.

P

OH

Old Barn Foundation

16

15

Visitors Ctr.

1

OD

Seneca Pond

Arboretum Trail

OD

2

13

14

Seneca Trail

Cherry Lane Trail

(Notes 1-24)

5

4

Columnar Collection

Map Legend
OD Observation Deck
OH Observatory Hill
 P Parking
||| Boardwalk
] [Bridge

3

12

OD

11

6

7

Suspension Bridge

Echo Pond

8

Fernwood Trail

10

9

1. From the parking lot take the brick walkway to the visitors center. Begin the walk southwest of the visitors' center on the asphalt Arboretum Trail, identified with a tree symbol; a sign here points toward Echo Pond. Pass an observation deck on the left and continue south past the flowering tree collection.

2. At the next trail intersection, stay to the right and go past several unusual weeping trees. Stay right at the trail junction.

Continue south past the pyramidal collection.

3. Turn left at the next dirt trail. (The trail on the right goes to Echo Pond.) Pass the tall columnar collection.

4. At the next intersection stay to the right where Cherry Lane Trail (identified by a double cherry symbol) merges with the Arboretum Trail. Here there are interesting labeled plant species to study under an attractive shady bower.

5. Turn right (east) going off the asphalt walkway onto a soft pinebark path, now marked as Cherry Lane Trail. A large glacial boulder containing an interpretive label is on the right. Follow this path as it gently winds downhill. This area was once open farmland but has become heavily overgrown with trees.

6. At this point on the trail take a right turn onto a short loop to see a small newly constructed pond, formerly a bog.

7. Turn left (east) at the end of the pond loop, and right (south) at the next intersection. Cross over the suspension bridge to Fernwood Trail (identified with a fern symbol).

8. After crossing the bridge take the left (east) section of Fernwood Trail.

9. On Fernwood Trail watch for a sharp right turn just above a deep ravine. Do not follow this old trail, which winds down into the ravine, but remain on the ridgetop on the Fernwood Trail and follow it around as it bends to the west. Note the unusually large double beech tree on the left.

10. This loop trail bends northeast toward the suspension bridge again. But before reaching the bridge, turn left (west), and follow the trail to an opening in the woods where a small, pretty Echo Pond emerges.

11. At the north end of Echo Pond, pause at the observation deck for a lovely view of the water and a chance to watch for wildlife. Amphibians and ducks frequent this pond; it is stocked with bluegills and large-mouth bass, but fishing is not permitted.

12. From the pond follow the trail northward to the first intersection. Bear left at this intersection, then turn right at the asphalt Cherry Lane/ Arboretum Trail intersection (described in Note #3). Pass the columnar collection again and continue on the paved trail until you reach the same intersection described in Note #5.

13. Continue straight ahead on the asphalt walkway, staying to the right at a junction to pass the fruit and nut trees.

14. Straight ahead is a deck overlooking Seneca Pond, another lovely, restful spot; to the right (east) is the Seneca Trail, identified with an arrow-head symbol. Turn right here to follow the 1.1-mile Seneca Trail generally east. This pleasant forest path loops through beautiful woods and winds gently up and down. A descriptive booklet available at the visitors' center is a helpful guide to numbered indicators you will pass on this section of the trail. A brief notation of these numbered landmarks is offered below:

1. *Seneca Pond.*

2. *Butternut or white walnut tree.*

3. *Forest of beech, maple, tulip, cherry, oak and aspen trees.* The sign is posted before a large shagbark hickory.

4. *American beech tree.*

5. *Tributary stream* of Seneca Pond. The ravine was carved by large amounts of water resulting from the melting of Ohio's last glacier; note the evergreen hemlock trees living in the cool, shaded ravine.

6. *Tuliptree* (yellow poplar), one of the tallest (100 feet) and oldest in Naturealm, with a 10-foot circumference. The tuliptree is the most distinctive and common tree of the forest canopy. It is a marker for this kind of forest on a terrace above a stream. Its towering, pyramidal shape and bright yellow autumn leaves make it stand out among other species.

7. *Tree Finder Wheel* pointing to white-labeled trees with corresponding descriptions. Take time to find each specimen with this ingenious 360-degree wheel: hop-hornbeam, pignut hickory, sassafras, tuliptree, white oak, eastern hemlock, and shagbark hickory.

8. *Native wildflowers* that may be found here in April and May: Jack-in-the-pul-pit, trout lily, large-flowered trillium, Solomon's seal, black cohosh, and hepatica.

9. *American chestnut log*, killed by the blight of the early 1900s.

10. *Glacial Erratics* (rocks) left by the melting glacier, having originally come from eastern Canada.

11. *Bigtooth aspen*, one of the first trees to reforest an abandoned farm field; it has an ovate leaf characterized by coarse, rounded marginal teeth.

12. *Grapevine tangles* (on the hill to the right) often climb to the top of a tree, kill it, then fall to the ground.

13. *Forest glade*, a former farm field that has become overgrown with Virginia creeper, staghorn sumac, poison ivy, flowering dogwood, crab apple, hawthorn trees, and other flora.

14. *An old farm fence-line,* a north-south hump in the trail that was made by farmers plowing the field every year in the same direction; birds sitting on the fence posts may have dropped seeds of wild black cherry trees that now mark the edge of the field; on the right is a bench off a very short side trail overlooking the deep valley of Sand Run Metro Park.

15. *Erosion* of topsoil on a steep hillside that was once cultivated by farmers.

16. *Old barn foundation* lying north-south in the middle of the trail, about 30 by 60 feet, with evidence of several doorways and a trough in the floor for collection of manure; black walnut trees are growing within the foundation; the barn seems to have been poorly located, receiving drainage from the hillside.

15. The barn foundation marks a point about two-thirds of the way around the Seneca Trail loop. The trail now bends toward the north, then crosses a small wooden bridge and continues to wind gently through the woods. The cars you begin to hear beyond the ravine on the right are on Smith Rd.

17. Swamp with a few drain tiles exposed, which were placed by farmers trying to drain the spring-filled soil; skunk cabbage, marsh marigold, ferns, and other moisture-loving plants thrive here; a line of willow trees marks an old lane from the farmhouse on Smith Rd. to the barn.

18. Seneca Springs, one of many springs flowing from the hillside, with tiles marking settling and collecting tanks.

19. Poison Ivy above a deep ravine carved by a stream flowing toward the Cuyahoga River below.

20. Sassafras tree, which often has three leaf shapes on the same specimen: elliptical, two-lobed, and three-lobed.

21. Raccoon wash, a culvert where raccoon pawprints are often found. Their distinctive footprint shows their delicate long toe and a wide reach between prints. They are fond of foraging in wetlands; here they may be searching for worms, crayfish, eggs, nuts, or seeds.

Leave the mulched trail and enter a firmly packed dirt road.

22. Hercules-club tree, with characteristic spiny branches and twigs and twice-compound leaves; also called toothache-tree and devils' walkingstick.

23. Observatory hill, once used by astronomers because of its height, 1,020 feet above sea level.

24. Prairie, with species that once covered vast areas of the Midwest: black-eyed Susan, Indian paintbrush, purple coneflower, goldenrod, and bluestem grass.

16. Just before the service building, turn left (west). A paved walkway straight ahead leads to the visitors' center. On the right, off the paved walkway, is the entrance to the rock and herb garden.

This chapter was reviewed by Walter Starcher, Chief Naturalist, Metro Parks Serving Summit County.

37 GORGE METRO PARK AND RIVERFRONT WALK

Distance: 5.7 miles

Moderate

Hiking time: 3.5 hours

Description: Hike A is on the Gorge Trail (1.8-mile loop); Hike B is on the
Glens Trail (2.2 miles round-trip) and Riverfront Walk (1.2 miles round-trip
from Front St.). Both the Gorge and Glens trails are wide and well marked
and involve some hills and scrambling over rocks. Because of the boulders,
shoes with traction soles are recommended for this hike.

There are many short sets of steps to climb up and down on Riverfront
Walk. It is reached by climbing up the Glens Trail to Front St. From there it
is a short walk to the observation platform for a stunning view of several
waterfalls on the Cuyahoga River in one direction and a deep gorge in the
other. By continuing on Front St. one more block to the Sheraton Suites
Hotel, one can then take the 0.3-mile Riverfront Walk to the city dock and
back.

Directions: From I-271, take SR 8 (Exit 18) south. Exit from SR 8 at Broad Blvd.
in Cuyahoga Falls. Turn right on Broad, and go 2 blocks to Second St. Turn
left (south) on Second St. which, after several blocks, descends a hill to
Front St. and a traffic signal. After another traffic light partway down the
hill, watch carefully for a Gorge Metro Park sign on the right and a sharp
right turn. The park entrance is just before the Cuyahoga River bridge.
From Akron take SR 8 north to the Howe Ave. exit and follow Howe Ave.
southwest to Front St. Turn right (north) on Front St. to the Cuyahoga River
bridge. Park entrance is on the left at the traffic light.

Parking & restrooms: Parking and restrooms are near the entrance.

Located in Cuyahoga Falls, 205-acre Gorge Metro Park contains some
of the most beautiful and spectacular scenery in Summit County. The
Cuyahoga River most likely created this magnificent gorge during the final
retreat of the last glacier covering Ohio about 12,000 years ago. At that
time melting ice water carved the valley, exposing 320-million-year-old
Sharon Conglomerate rock and sandstone. Sharon Conglomerate contains smooth, white quartz pebbles embedded in the sandstone and is
abundant in the sheer ledges along the trails in this park.

It is thought that the former route of the Cuyahoga River coursed near
what is now downtown Akron, but its path was blocked by glacial debris
creating a land summit, thus forcing the stream to move back to this area.
At the bridge on Front St., near the park entrance, the south-flowing river

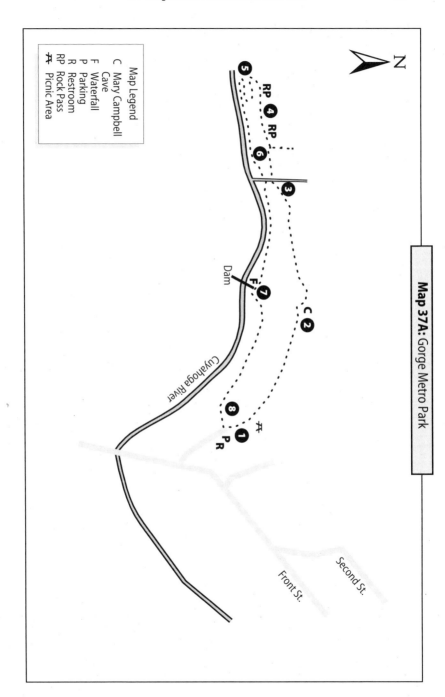

Map Legend
C   Mary Campbell
    Cave
F   Waterfall
P   Parking
R   Restroom
RP Rock Pass
⚲   Picnic Area

N

Cuyahoga River

Dam

Front St.

Second St.

Map 37A: Gorge Metro Park

takes a sharp turn west, then gradually bends north toward Lake Erie. Presently the turbulent river flows over a shale riverbed 850 feet above sea level and 280 feet above the level of Lake Erie.

The land comprising Gorge Metro Park was originally donated to the people of Summit County by the old Northern Ohio Traction and Light Company, predecessor to the present Ohio Edison Company. The Ohio Edison plant across the Cuyahoga River (viewed from the Glens Trail) has been closed since 1992. The dam, built in 1914, creates a beautiful waterfall, Gorge Metro Park's most scenic attraction.

Another notable feature of the park is Mary Campbell Cave, a huge rock overhang that was once home to a group of Delaware Indians who captured a young girl from Pennsylvania in 1759.

Riverfront Walk in Cuyahoga Falls is on a splendid boardwalk along the Cuyahoga River, which cascades over rocks on its way through a magnificent gorge. Here the river drops almost 200 feet on its way to and through Gorge Metro Park. At the end of the walk is the City Dock, from which pontoon boat rides are offered in season (330-971-8225).

NOTE: Along the lower portion of the Gorge Trail an underground sewer pipe carries effluent to a treatment plant farther north of here. Two or three air vents along the lower trail occasionally discharge a whiff of gas that can be unpleasant in hot summer months, thus it is best to hike the lower portion of the Gorge Trail in cool months. As an alternative in the summer, hike the upper Gorge Trail to the last Rock Pass then return along the same pathway to one of the cross-over trails to view Cuyahoga Falls.

HIKE A: GORGE TRAIL

1. The upper segment of the Gorge Trail begins at the sign in the far right-hand corner of the parking lot. After entering the trail, pass an ice-skating field (flooded in winter) on the left, and a picnic area on the right. The trail soon passes a shelter on the left.

The shale rock along this portion of the trail belongs to the Cuyahoga Formation (see Appendix A). It is composed of mud and silt layers laid down at the bottom of an ocean during the Mississippian Age about 350 million years ago. It has subsequently hardened into rock.

Along here and far below are pretty views of the Cuyahoga River flowing westward (and eventually north) to Lake Erie. The river is wide and forms a large lake behind Edison Dam just ahead.

2. There are many connector trails linking the upper Gorge Trail to its lower segment. For views of the waterfall, stay on the wide upper trail, passing a large rock wall. At about 0.2 mile on the right you will reach the Mary Campbell Cave, a massive cliff overhang that once was home to Delaware Indians and Chief Netawatwees. A bronze plaque placed opposite the rock cave in 1934 by the Mary Campbell Society, Children of the American Revolution, tells Mary Campbell's story.

Sharon Conglomerate sandstone is prominent here. This pebbly sandstone was formed during the Pennsylvanian Age about 320 million years ago. The sand was carried here from a quartz-rich area of northern Canada to the shore of an ancient inland sea that once covered land that is now Ohio. The beach sand hardened into sandstone rock embedded with small quartz beach pebbles that have been worn smooth by the action of the inland sea's waves and water at its sandy shore. The sand underfoot on this trail has slowly eroded away from the rock ledge to leave what is actually ancient beach sand. All along the path are many of these quartz pebbles, commonly called "lucky stones," that have fallen from the ledges.

3. Continue on the upper trail, going past small waterfalls that flow over more layers of shale.

Oak, blackgum, tulip, and yellow birch trees are common on both sides of the gorge. The ever-flowing springs and sandy soil provide ideal growing conditions for many varieties of wildflowers and ferns.

At about 0.6 mile you will pass a high waterfall cascading down over huge boulders. Cross carefully.

4. Continue straight ahead, bypassing a trail on the right (which leads up to High Bridge Rd.). Note the private gazebo above the trail that overlooks this scenic area. Next go through the first of two rock passes, which are clefts created by the separation of massive rock formations. Large blocks of the conglomerate break off at the edge of rock ledges, because the underlying rocks of the Cuyahoga Formation are softer and more easily eroded. Settling causes cracks, fissures, and large cave-like crevices to develop subsequently in the Sharon Conglomerate.

At the top of the first pass, do not take the rock steps on the right but continue straight ahead on the main trail to the second rock pass, another spectacular rocky cleft formed of massive sandstone. Note the ledge of Sharon Conglomerate (see Appendix A).

5. As you approach the far west part of the Gorge Trail loop, you will hike up through a narrow rock tunnel, ascending on rock steps to the top of the slope.

NOTE: At this point you have the option of returning on the same trail to the Mary Campbell Cave and taking a side trail downward to view Cuyahoga Falls, or continuing on the Gorge Trail lower loop as described below.

At the next trail intersection, the main trail goes left and at the trail sign it curves around to the east. At the second switchback, the trail curves to the west and makes a gentle descent on log steps. At the bottom of the steps, the main trail goes left (east). There is a fine view of the river below on the right.

6. Continue along the trail to the wooden bridge that crosses a side stream. Below on the right, whitewater rapids appear in the Cuyahoga River, as the water leaves the dam and flows turbulently westward.

Stay on the main trail (though you may want to take one of the several side trails that lead to overlooks for viewing the river and waterfall).

7. At about 1.5 miles on the main trail there is a sign on the left directing you toward the Mary Campbell Cave. Stay to the right heading toward the waterfall.

CAUTION: Stay behind the fence until the trail leads down for a view of the wide waterfall cascading over the concrete dam.

There are large Berea Sandstone boulders upon which you may wish to rest and enjoy the view, the sound, and the cool moist air of this awesome sight. Built in 1914, this dam was only used to generate electricity for a few years before a more efficient coal-fired generator plant was built on the river east of here (it closed in 1992).

8. The trail leads back up to the main trail on log steps and goes east past the shelter and picnic areas to the parking lot. The many connector trails you pass will lead to the upper Gorge Trail.

HIKE B: GLENS TRAIL AND RIVERFRONT WALK

9. Walk south through the parking lot to the exit and cross Front St. at the traffic light to begin the Glens Trail. The entry is located just south of the crosswalk. This trail borders the east bend of the Cuyahoga River and gradually ascends a steep cliff face. All along the left wall of the path are the familiar sandstone boulders, also seen on the Gorge Trail, exposed by the river's relentless cutting action.

10. This scenic trail affords long views high above the Cuyahoga River. Directly across the stream is the huge electric generator plant of the Ohio Edison Company, now closed. The large twin smokestacks remain from the period when electricity was produced by coal-fired steam generators until that process became too costly to continue.

11. At about 0.6 mile on the left is a huge rock overhang and just beyond, a sheer rock wall with a small spring (unsafe for drinking) flowing from its base. The trail bends slightly to the left and soon reaches a set of wooden steps. Continue uphill, taking care to remain behind the protective fence. This quiet, shady trail is a delight in the heat of summer and harbors lovely wildflowers in the spring.

12. At the end of the trail, turn left out to Front St. near the American Legion Hall. Turn right (east) on Front St., walk 0.1 mile to Prospect St., and turn right again.

13. A wooden pedestrian observation platform offers the viewer a spectacular sight of the Cuyahoga River. To the north are the cascading Cuyahoga Falls and rapids, and to the south is a view of a deep, stone-faced canyon with rapids tumbling downstream.

From the platform, go back on Prospect to Front St., turn right, and walk north on Front St. to the Sheraton Suites Hotel.

14. At the far north end of the hotel parking lot, enter Riverfront Walk, a wooden boardwalk with steps. The boardwalk begins at an outdoor cafe (open in the summer). Descend the steps, taking a right turn at the foot to walk under the Broad Blvd. bridge.

15. The boardwalk follows the contours of the river, going up and down several sets of steps along the way, and passes the ruins of an old riverfront building. Here and there are wooden tables and benches inviting a rest to view the ever-changing river and waterfalls. Pedestrians on Front St. may enter or exit the walk at several points. Reach a small riverfront amphitheater at Portage Trail.

Continue past Portage Trail on the sidewalk to view another waterfall. On the left are a broad set of steps and a sign for Riverfront Centre. In the center of the plaza, at the top of the steps, is an impressive stone and marble fountain surrounded by shops along a brick walkway. Back on the Riverfront Walk, continue past River's Edge condos along the sidewalk.

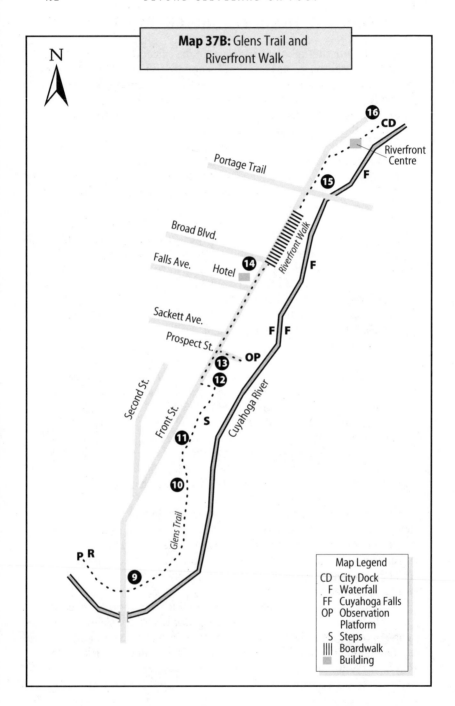

Map 37B: Glens Trail and Riverfront Walk

N

16 CD

Riverfront Centre

Portage Trail

15 F

Broad Blvd.

Riverfront Walk

Falls Ave.   Hotel   14   F

Sackett Ave.

F F

Prospect St.

OP

13

12

Cuyahoga River

Second St.

Front St.

S

11

10

Glens Trail

P R

9

Map Legend

CD City Dock
 F Waterfall
FF Cuyahoga Falls
OP Observation
     Platform
 S Steps
||| Boardwalk
     Building

16. The path ends at the City Recreation and Parks Department's pontoon boat ride. (Fees and operating hours vary seasonally.) Return to the car by retracing your steps along Riverfront Walk to the Sheraton Suites on Front St., then past the Observation Platform at Prospect St. The Glens Trail entrance is near the American Legion Hall and is marked with a small sign.

Follow the path downhill to enjoy new and different views of the Cuyahoga River below. At the traffic light on Front St. cross to the parking area just inside the entrance to Gorge Metro Park.

This chapter was reviewed by Walter Starcher, Chief Naturalist, Metro Parks Serving Summit County.

38 SAND RUN METRO PARK

Distance: 4 miles

Moderate

Hiking time: 2 hours

Description: This hike in Sand Run Metro Park is a very hilly loop hike on the Dogwood and Mingo trails through the west end of the park. The pathway follows the hills up and down and crosses streams on stone blocks or bridges.

Directions: From I-77 exit at Ghent Rd./SR 175 (Exit 138). Follow Ghent Rd. south to Sand Run Pkwy. and turn left (east) opposite Summit Mall. Follow Sand Run Pkwy. eastward, past Revere and Sand Run Rd. roads to the park. Inside the park, drive through the landmark Vehicle Ford of Sand Run stream. (In heavy rain cars cannot drive through the stream and must approach the park from the east rather than the west, taking Smith and Merriman roads to Sand Run Pkwy.) Continue past the Vehicle Ford to Wadsworth Picnic Area, on the right just beyond the Shadowfield Picnic Area.
From Akron take Portage Path north past Stan Hywet Hall to Sand Run Pkwy. and turn west (left) on the parkway to the Wadsworth Area.

Parking & restrooms: At Wadsworth Picnic Area.

Sand Run Metro Park was the first park acquired by Metro Parks Serving Summit County, in 1930, through gifts of land from F.A. Seiberling, the founder of Akron's Goodyear and Seiberling Rubber Companies. Seiberling Naturealm, located within this park on Smith Rd., was named in his honor (Ch. 36).

Sand Run is a hilly, 1,106-acre park that stretches on an east-west axis along Sand Run Pkwy. within Akron city limits. The park's steep ravines enclose several streams that empty into Sand Run, which flows northeast into the nearby Cuyahoga River. Sand Run is so named because of the large amount of sand that was once carried downstream by the river. Wildflowers and ferns thrive in the valleys of this park, as do many birds in its tall trees. Squirrels, woodchucks, raccoons, and other wildlife populate the wooded areas.

This park contains several picnic areas, reservable shelters, playing fields, foot and jogging trails, a sledding hill, a skating area, and an exercise parcours. Many of the shelters and other early park buildings were built by the Civilian Conservation Corps in the 1930s.

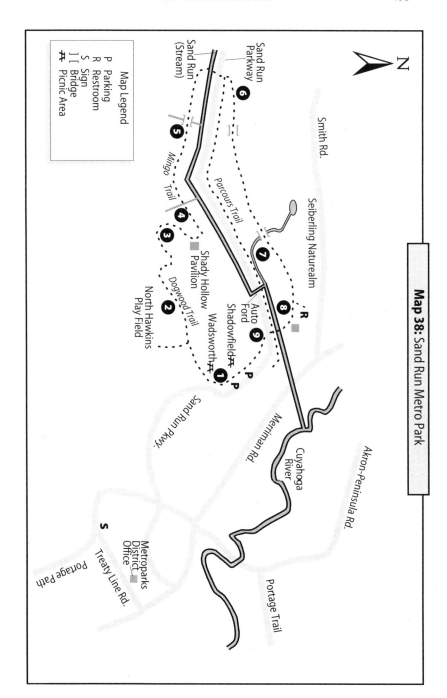

Map 38: Sand Run Metro Park

Map Legend

P   Parking
R   Restroom
S   Sign
⊐⊏ Bridge
⊼   Picnic Area

N

Smith Rd.

Sand Run Parkway

Sand Run (Stream)

Mingo Trail

Parcours Trail

Seiberling Naturealm

Shady Hollow Pavilion

Dogwood Trail

North Hawkins Play Field

Wadsworth

Shadowfield

Auto Ford

Sand Run Pkwy.

Marimum Rd.

Cuyahoga River

Akron-Peninsula Rd.

Portage Trail

Portage Path

Treaty Line Rd.

Metroparks District Office

The Buckeye Trail (BT) goes through Sand Run Metro Park, though here it is not marked with the trail's usual two-inch-by-six-inch blue blazes. It is identified on signposts by the letters BT inside a yellow-bordered arrow.

The BT follows the old Portage Path between the Cuyahoga and Tuscarawas rivers. This important pathway was once the boundary line between the Wyandot and Delaware Indian nations and the United States. Portage Path was the original route used by natives as they carried their canoes over the land between the Tuscarawas and Cuyahoga Rivers. A commemorative sign has been placed at the top of the hill at the junction of Portage Path and Treaty Line Rd. to recognize this historical route. Treaty Line Rd. was named for the 1785 Treaty of Fort McIntosh, which added land west of Portage Path, the former U.S. western boundary, to the United States.

The District Office for the Metro Parks, at 975 Treaty Line Rd., is open on weekdays to provide information, maps, brochures, and shelter reservations (330-867-5511). The district publishes a monthly newsletter called *Green Islands* (free to Summit County residents only, with a small charge to non-residents).

1. Start the hike from the Wadsworth Area. Cross the field to reach the Dogwood Trail (marked with a tree leaf) to the west of and behind the women's restroom. Ascend the hill steeply upward (southwest) on the Dogwood Trail. At the top of the hill stay on the Dogwood Trail, passing any of the turns off this trail.

General Wadsworth, who commanded troops in the War of 1812, used this summit as a lookout point when his forces camped near the Old Portage Picnic Area at the intersection of Portage Path and Sand Run Pkwy.

2. Follow the Dogwood Trail westward through the woods until reaching an open area, the North Hawkins Playfield (0.5 mile). Continue following Dogwood Trail signs past the sledding hill on the left and the soccer field, also on the left, as the pathway curves along the edge of the woods. The trail reenters the woods on the right.

3. The trail next goes steeply downhill to Shady Hollow Pavilion (1.1 miles), open only by reservation. Leave the Dogwood Trail behind at this point and continue around to the back (north side) of the log cabin. Continue going downhill a few steps, then up some stairs to get onto the Mingo Trail, marked with a triangular tree symbol. Follow it to the left (west). (Note that these trail signs have an arrow pointing in the direction opposite from which you are going.)

4. As you follow the ups and downs of this trail going westward, you will see (or hear cars on) Sand Run Pkwy. below on the right. Sand Run stream is just south of the parkway. Cross a small brook flowing north to Sand Run.

5. After ascending and descending more hills, the trail reaches a bridge over another small stream (1.7 miles) and then crosses Sand Run itself, on large stone blocks, and Sand Run Pkwy. (2 miles). Here you have an option of returning to the Wadsworth Area by walking east on the paved parcours jogging trail (marked with a green jogger sign) or continuing east on the Mingo Trail.

6. Continue uphill in an easterly direction, still on the Mingo Trail (arrows still point opposite to the direction of travel). Cross a wooden footbridge and ascend another steep hill. Sand Run Pkwy. is now below on the right.

The terrain undulates through a stretch of forest with tall beech, red and white oak, and maple trees. Then the path descends steeply.

7. At 2.7 miles cross an old stone bridge built in the 1930s that spans a stream outlet from Seneca Pond. (On the hill just above this spot is Seiberling Naturealm, Ch. 36.) Continue steeply uphill until you reach a trail intersection.

8. At this trail junction the path to the left leads to Mingo Pavilion, named for the Mingo Indians who used this hilltop area as a campsite before this land was part of the United States. The path to the right leads down to the paved Parkway Jogging Trail, Sand Run Pkwy., and Sand Run stream.

Take this trail downward to the paved trail. Park Service Area buildings are to the left (east). (Note that Sand Run stream is now on the north side of the road; it crossed over at the Vehicle Ford a short distance west of here.)

9. Cross the bridge over Sand Run and immediately take the dirt trail on the right marked BT. Follow this path out to Sand Run Pkwy. Cross the road to the south side and enter the Dogwood Trail (marked with a leaf symbol) going east. Follow the Dogwood Trail parallel to and above the parkway to Shadowfield parking and picnic area. The wide dirt track leads to Wadsworth parking and picnic area just beyond Shadowfield to complete the loop.

This chapter was reviewed by Walter Starcher, Chief Naturalist, Metro Parks Serving Summit County.

39 SILVER CREEK METRO PARK

Distance: 4-1/2 miles

Moderate

Hiking time: 3 hours

Description: Two loop walks comprise this hike. The first is over flat and mildly rolling farmland and through wooded forests on the 2-mile Chippewa Trail. This trail passes an old barn, circles a small pond, and crosses Silver Creek and its tributaries several times before returning to Silver Creek Lake and the dam.

The second loop (2.4 miles) begins on the Bridle Trail near the new boathouse and follows the shore of Silver Creek Lake to Medina Line Rd. After a short road section, the path continues on a park entry road to the bathhouse, then continues on the road to finish on the Chippewa Trail to Big Oak Picnic Area.

Directions: From I-77 north of Akron, take Exit 136 (SR 21, south). Follow SR 21 south past I-76 and Norton to the exit for SR 585 west. Follow SR 585 west 0.7 mile to Eastern Rd. Turn right (west) on Eastern Rd.; go 1 mile to Medina Line Rd. Turn right (north) on Medina Line Rd. and right again into Silver Creek Park. Turn right at the first driveway marked Big Oak Picnic Area.

An alternate park entrance is off Hametown Rd., which leads across the dam at Silver Creek Lake's south end to a left turn into Big Oak Picnic Area. From Akron, take I-76 west to SR 21 south. Continue to the exit for SR 585 west, then follow the directions above.

Parking & restrooms: At Big Oak Picnic Area (primitive restrooms).

Open since 1966, Silver Creek Metro Park, located in Norton in the southwestern corner of Summit County (adjacent to Wayne and Medina Counties), covers 616 acres. Its major feature is 50-acre Silver Creek Lake, created by the damming of Silver Creek. Gathering many small tributaries along its way, this stream flows south through the former Harter family dairy farm. The water flows year round and comes partly from an underground coal mine on Wall Rd., northwest of Silver Creek Lake. Abandoned coal mines from the 1930s underlie most of this park. One of the largest northern red oaks in Summit County can be seen on the Chippewa Trail at the start of the hike.

A recently constructed 19th-century-style bathhouse includes restrooms, changing areas, first aid and lifeguard stations, and a concession stand. The new public swimming beach (for which a fee is charged)

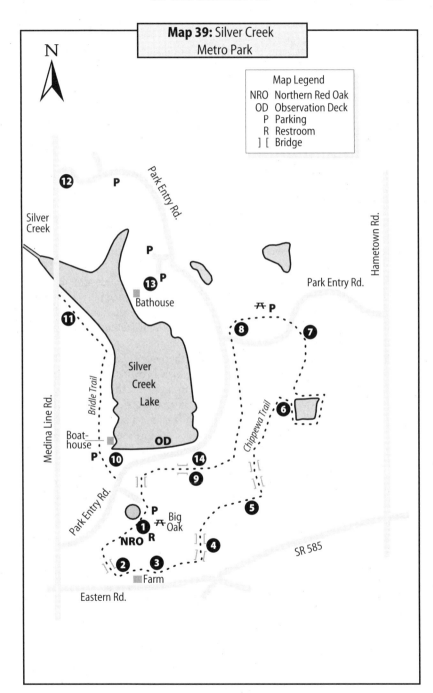

Map 39: Silver Creek
Metro Park

N

Map Legend
NRO Northern Red Oak
OD Observation Deck
P Parking
R Restroom
] [Bridge

Silver
Creek

Park Entry Rd.

Hametown Rd.

Park Entry Rd.

Bathouse

Medina Line Rd.

Bridle Trail

Silver
Creek
Lake

Boat-
house

OD

Chippewa Trail

Park Entry Rd.

Big
Oak

NRO

R

Farm

SR 585

Eastern Rd.

is open from Memorial Day to Labor Day. Hikers and others not using the swimming facilities are not charged the fee. Children's play areas, picnic areas, a bridle path, fishing, boating, swimming, and cross-country skiing are all available at Silver Creek Metro Park.

1. Enter the Chippewa Trail (marked with a tomahawk symbol) at the west side of the parking lot. To the right (north) of the mulched trail there is a small pond. Behind the fence on the left is a huge northern red oak. With a 20-foot circumference around its double trunk, its spreading limbs are supported by several steel cables. This grand old oak, estimated to be 150-200 years old, is considered one of the largest in Summit County. Its leaves, with between 7 and 11 pointed, toothed lobes, turn bright red in the autumn. This oak drops thousands of acorns in the fall, some of which sprout and propagate many smaller red oaks nearby. Continue ahead.

2. Cross a small wooden foot bridge and pass old farm buildings that once belonged to the Harter family dairy farm—two silos, a granary, and a shed. Part of the barn dates from the Civil War.

3. Enter a stand of young Norway (red) pines. These trees were planted as seedlings by Girl Scouts of the Western Reserve Council between 1964 and 1983 in a series of Arbor Day events. Local scouts planted about 40,000 seedlings at various places in the park to initiate the beginning of future forests here.

4. The trail bends around to the east and then north. Cross Silver Creek on a wooden foot bridge. Note the rusty, reddish-brown color of the water in the stream. When it flows out of the coal mine shafts, the water is rich in iron but sterile. Moving south, it picks up oxygen, nutrients, and bacteria that produce an iron-oxide precipitate in the form of a powder that covers the stream bottom. These reddish deposits do not seem to deter fish, amphibians, and other wildlife from living in the creek.

Cross another wooden foot bridge (0.5 mile).

5. The mowed path continues across an open meadow toward the east. In the field you may encounter pheasants, meadowlarks, bob-o-links, bluebirds, or butterflies.

Enter a young beech-oak-maple forest. Note the occasional shagbark hickory tree, with its distinctive bark composed of thin, narrow scales that curve outward. The leaves are 8 to 14 inches long with five leaflets. Often you will find hickory nuts scattered on the ground below this tree. In the spring, there are many varieties of wildflowers in this forest.

Cross two more small foot bridges over tributaries of Silver Creek.

6. Reach a trail junction and turn right (southeast) to a small woodland pond. Follow the pond-edge path by hugging the shore in a counterclockwise direction. The path is somewhat obscure along the south edge, but circles past young white pine and spruce trees to return to the Chippewa Trail.

7. Continue on the Chippewa Trail in a northeast direction and cross a meadow to the park entry drive from Hametown Rd. (1.2 miles). Cross the drive and continue past a parking and picnic area on the right. The trail bends to the west and brings Silver Creek Lake and the dam into view.

8. Next the path turns left (south) and recrosses the park entry road (1.5 miles). Continue toward the dam and lake, enjoying a long view of the lake to the north. Here with binoculars you may spot shore birds and ducks, such as egrets, herons, gulls, terns, Canada geese, grebes, or mergansers.

Reenter the woods and continue going west.

9. The trail leads down below the dam and then crosses a bridge over the lake's outlet stream. Cross the last small foot bridge over another of the rust-colored creeks to reach the Big Oak Picnic Area (2 miles).

10. Optional: the hike may be ended here.

To continue, go north from the parking area and cross the park entry road to a parking area and boathouse. At the east end of this parking lot, enter the Bridle Trail going north along the west shore of the lake.

CAUTION: If you encounter horses on the trail, step off the path and remain still until these skittish animals have passed.

The Bridle Trail initially goes east toward the lake, then bends north to follow the water's edge. In the summer, boating and fishing are popular sports here. Usually there are also many waterfowl enjoying the water, especially ducks and Canada geese.

11. At 2.7 miles reach Medina Line Rd. Cross it to walk north, facing oncoming traffic, to the park entry road on the right.

12. Turn right (east) onto the park entry road and follow it past a service road on the left and a parking area on the right.

13. Continue on the road to the bathhouse entry drive on the right. It is worthwhile to visit the bathhouse. A 1994 award from the Akron Chapter of the American Institute of Architects noted the building's pleasant placement away from the parking lots, its use of an existing tree line, and the fine view the structure affords from the waterfront.

After leaving the bathhouse, continue south toward the dam past the park entry road on the left (3.7 miles).

14. About midway along the road and atop the dam, enjoy a long view of the lake and another view from an observation deck (no fishing permitted).

Walk down the slope of the dam to the Chippewa Trail. Turn right (west) and go across the bridge over the lake's outlet stream to return on the trail to the Big Oak Picnic Area.

This chapter was reviewed by Walter Starcher, Chief Naturalist, Metro Parks Serving Summit County.

40 GOODYEAR HEIGHTS METRO PARK

Distance: 3.1 miles

Moderate

Hiking time: 1-3/4 hours

Description: The trails in Goodyear Heights Metro Park follow rolling hills through beautiful forests of pine, beech, maple, and tuliptrees. Alder Pond, an oasis in this urban park, offers wintertime ice skating.

Directions: From I-76 (in Akron, after it splits from 1-77 on the east side of town), take Exit 26 to SR 91 (north). Follow SR 91 north for 1/2 mile to Newton St. Turn left on Newton and into the park entrance on the right. From Akron take I-76 east and follow the directions above.

Parking & restrooms: After entering the park, continue past the first parking area on the right to the second one straight ahead. Restrooms are here.

Located in Summit County south of Tallmadge, this 410-acre park opened in 1930 after Goodyear Tire & Rubber Co. and local farmer Gilbert Waltz each donated land for public recreation. Crews working in the Civilian Conservation Corps planted thousands of Scotch and white pines and tuliptrees, built a shelter at Alder Pond, and deepened the pond at its southern end. In the 1950s, Goodyear donated money for extensive park development that included a 37-acre playing field, a sledding hill, a much larger picnic shelter building, and other amenities.

Goodyear Heights Metro Park is frequently used by runners and local high school cross-country teams because of its 5-kilometer (3.2 mile) Parcours Trail. Other trails also wind up and down throughout the park, allowing fine hiking opportunities.

1. Start the hike at the northwest end of the parking area, going past the picnic tables on the right to an unmarked path. (Do not take the trails going east and north). Follow the path northwest to Carver St. and continue west on Carver St. past Elko St. to another Metro Parks parking lot.

2. At the far end of this parking area enter the Pond Trail at the trailhead sign. At the first fork in the trail go straight ahead. At the second fork, bear left on the Pond Trail. Continue past the restrooms to Alder Pond.

3. Alder Pond, a popular place for winter ice skating, is a lovely, tranquil spot with pleasant viewing of waterbirds and ducks (0.4 mile).

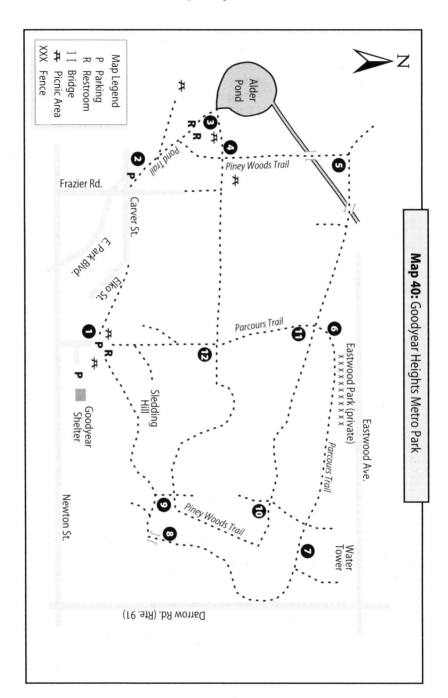

Map 40: Goodyear Heights Metro Park

Map Legend
P   Parking
R   Restroom
][Bridge
⚎   Picnic Area
XXX Fence

Alder Pond

Pond Trail

Piney Woods Trail

Frazier Rd.

Carver St.

E. Park Blvd.

Elko St.

Parcours Trail

Eastwood Park (private)
x x x x x x x x x x x x x

Eastwood Ave.

Parcours Trail

Sledding Hill

Goodyear Shelter

Newton St.

Piney Woods Trail

Water Tower

Darrow Rd. (Rte. 91)

N

Turn right (east) on the path nearest the pond and follow it through the picnic area.

4. At the next trail intersection, turn left (north) onto the Piney Woods Trail, a wide track marked with a pine tree symbol (also the Alder Trail).

Cross a small stream on a dirt and stone bridge.

5. Reach a trail intersection at 0.8 mile and turn right (east), staying on the Piney Woods Trail (the Alder Trail goes to the left). Cross the stream on another bridge and pass a side trail on the right. Continue uphill alongside a fence enclosing Eastwood Park, a privately owned pool and picnic park.

6. Reach a four-way trail intersection and turn left (east) on the Parcours Trail, marked with an arrow symbol. Pass exercise stations 7,8,9,10,and 11. The ball fields and water tower on the left are on Eastwood Ave.

7. Between exercise stations 11 and 12, a trail on the left loops around the water tower. (This optional 0.5-mile loop returns to the main trail just past station 13.)

Continue southeast past exercise stations 12-18 through a forest.

8. The path gradually bends southwest and crosses a wooden foot bridge at 1.8 miles. Continue past a path on the left.

Option: end the hike here by following this path out to the parking area.

Continue the walk uphill through a white pine forest.

These tall trees are some of the small seedlings planted by the Civilian Conservation Corps during the 1930s soon after the park opened. After more than 60 years they have grown to this magnificent size. You can identify the eastern white pine by its bundle of five needles as opposed to the Scot's (Scotch) pine, which has bundles of two needles. Red or Norway pines also have needles in bundles of two, but their needles are longer and break very easily.

Pass exercise station 19.

9. Reach a trail junction (2 miles) and turn right (north) onto an unmarked trail. Follow this path about 150 feet through more beautiful white pine forest, then turn right (east) onto a segment of the Piney Woods Trail. Continue on this loop as it bends north then west.

10. At a four-way intersection continue straight ahead, still on the Piney Woods Trail. Follow the path through a beautiful forest of tall maple and beech trees to the four-way junction reached in Note #6. Eastwood Park is again ahead on the right (2.4 miles).

11. Turn left (southwest) at this next four-way trail junction to reenter the Parcours Trail, marked with an arrow. Continue past exercise stations 7, 6, 5, and 4.

12. Reach another four-way trail junction and continue straight ahead (south) on the parcours trail. Just past exercise station 3 bear left uphill.

(The trail on the right goes to the park service area.) Continue on the main trail as it winds uphill and downhill past stations 2 and 1. Pass a trail on the left (it goes to the sledding hill) and return to the parking area.

This chapter was prepared with the assistance of Charles Briggs, hiker and longtime member of Akron Metropolitan Parks Hiking Club, and was reviewed by Walter Starcher, Chief Naturalist, Metro Parks Serving Summit County.

41 HAMPTON HILLS METRO PARK

Distance: 3.6 miles

Strenuous

Hiking time: 2-1/2 hours

Description: The trails are broad and well marked for the most part. There is a steep hill to climb at the beginning of the hike and an even steeper hill to descend at the end. At Top o' the World the farmhouse is closed, but the grounds are open for strolling to view the old barn and outbuildings. The leaf colors on this land are gorgeous in the fall.

Directions: From I-271 exit at SR 303 (Exit 12). Follow SR 303 east to Peninsula. Turn right (south) on Akron-Peninsula Rd. Drive to the south end of the CVNRA to the park entrance road on the left (east), just before Bath Rd.
From Akron take Akron-Peninsula Rd. north to the park entrance on the right, just beyond Bath Rd. and the CVNRA sign.

Parking & restrooms: Parking is just inside the entrance; primitive restrooms are in the woods along the trail to the left (west) of the trail.

Hampton Hills Metro Park lies inside Cuyahoga Valley National Recreation Area (CVNRA) but is managed by Metro Parks Serving Summit County and supported by Summit County tax levies. It was enlarged in 1967 when Rhea and Reginald Adam donated 162 acres of land, including their summer home (an 1820-1850 farmhouse called Top o' the World), to Akron's Metropolitan Park District. Three years earlier, the city of Akron had leased 116 acres of this land to begin developing the park.

The deep ravines of Hampton Hills Metro Park were formed by Adam Run and its tributaries as they cut through these rugged hills long ago. The debris along the stream embankments is composed of ancient lake sediment and glacial till left from the last glacial retreat about 12,000 years ago. Hiking is challenging in this park because of its steep hills. By combining two trails, Adam Run Trail and Spring Hollow Trail, you will hike a distance of about 3-1/2 miles.

Nearby, on the south side of Bath Rd. west of Akron-Peninsula Rd., is a great blue heronry with huge nests that these magnificent birds have built at the top of large sycamore trees. A very large number of herons may be seen standing guard over their nests during April and May.

1. Begin the hike at the trailhead straight ahead (east) of the parking lot. Picnic tables are in the woods to the right (south) of the parking area.

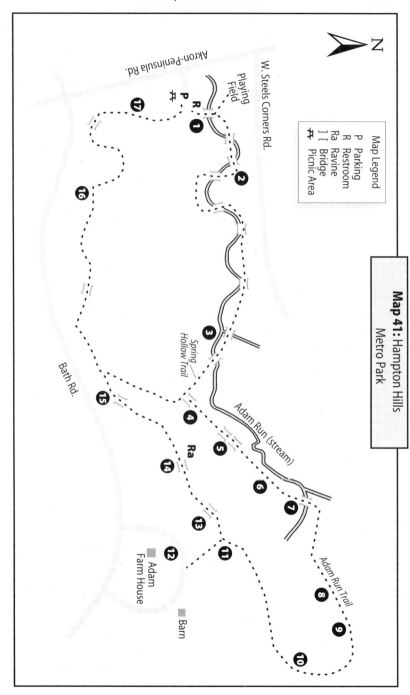

Map 41: Hampton Hills Metro Park

Map Legend
P   Parking
R   Restroom
Ra   Ravine
][Bridge
⚏   Picnic Area

Adam Run Trail, marked with two parallel water or wave symbols, begins (and ends) at the trail sign. It is contiguous with the Spring Hollow Trail, marked with an oak leaf symbol, in the lower (west) part of the park.

Turn left on the trail (north) past the restrooms. Cross Adam Run on an old iron-railed bridge that once was the route of East River Rd. Years ago, this old road was relocated to the present site of Akron-Peninsula Rd. To the left is a trail leading to a soccer and softball field. Follow the Adam Run Trail to the right as it leads onto a broad path through cool woods.

2. You will cross and recross the stream on six wooden footbridges as Adam Run meanders through the forest. Note the extensive erosion of the embankments caused by the brook's constant cutting action through the soft sandy soil. In the spring a wide variety of beautiful wildflowers grow in this favorable environment. All along the banks of Adam Run are green scouring rushes, an unusual hollow-stemmed plant that often grows alongside streams and helps reduce erosion. This ancient plant was used by early settlers to scour pans because its stems contain silica. Many walnut and sycamore trees also thrive in this moist, cool environment.

3. Go up a set of short log steps and soon cross a log bridge over a tributary. Cross another bridge over Adam Run, which will now be to the left (north) of the trail.

4. At about 0.7 mile meet the intersection of Spring Hollow Trail. Stay to the left to remain on the Adam Run Trail.

5. You will cross two more footbridges over tributaries of the main stream and reach a long set of railroad-tie steps that go up a hill.

6. At the top of the hill is a welcome rustic bench that invites a pause to enjoy the tall oak, maple, beech, and shagbark hickory trees. The trail follows the edge of a ravine, which is below on the right, and reaches another set of railroad-tie steps.

7. Descend the hill to cross a small stream before ascending the other side.

8. Arrive at a beautiful, tall forest of white pines, planted as seedlings in 1968 by local Girl Scouts. After a gentle rise on more steps, notice that the trees and shrubs at this higher elevation are in general much smaller than the towering trees below.

9. The well-marked trail crosses a sunny scrub meadow with tall wildflowers. In the fall the field is beautifully covered with yellow goldenrod, pink Joe Pye weed, and white Queen Anne's lace.

10. Shady bowers join each open field to the next one, presenting a variety of long views. The trail bends southwest. At about 1.6 miles you will come to a trailside bench from which to appreciate the birds, butterflies, flowers, fields, and wide open sky.

11. Reach another bench at the intersection of the Adam Run Trail and a side trail to the Adam farmhouse, Top o' the World. Turn left to follow the side trail to the old house.

12. Although the home is boarded up, visitors may walk around the old farmstead and property, which was used by the Adam family until 1967. In late August, gorgeous yellow sunflowers blanket the field to the west of the house. (The circular driveway leads down to Bath Rd.)

Return to the side trail and the intersection described in Note #11. Turn left (west) back onto the Adam Run Trail.

13. The path makes a gradual descent to a bridge (2.3 miles). You will hear (and see) traffic on Bath Rd. now, which roughly parallels the trail on the left. The trail gently descends through cool woods to an open meadow.

14. Cross a small bridge and note another deep ravine on the right. Trees here are larger, because of the decreased elevation and increased soil moisture.

15. At about 2.9 miles cross a longer bridge and meet the intersection of the Spring Hollow Trail. Stay to the left and continue on the main trail without taking any cross trails.

16. Go down several sets of railroad-tie steps, then make a brief ascent before taking another set of several steps downhill.

17. Follow the trail to the sign where the hike started and turn left to the parking lot (3.6 miles).

This chapter was reviewed by Walter Starcher, Chief Naturalist, Metro Parks Serving Summit County.

42 O'NEIL WOODS METRO PARK AND SCHUMACHER WOODS

Strenuous

Distance: 6 miles (The Deer Run Trail is a 1.8-mile loop and the Buckeye Trail in Schumacher Woods is 4.2 miles round trip.)

Hiking time: 3.5 hours (1 hour for the Deer Run Trail alone and 2.5 hours for the Buckeye Trail) in Schumacher Woods.

Description: The Deer Run Trail is marked with a hoofprint symbol. It is worthwhile to take time in this small park to observe the plants and trees, and the variety of birds. White-tailed deer may be seen in the hilltop meadows or down by the creek. (The deer population of Ohio has increased immensely since their reintroduction to the state in the 1930s, to the point where their current number actually exceeds that of pioneer days. Their increased foraging of forest vegetation poses a potential problem, because they have virtually no predators now and have unusually easy access to food.)
NOTE: The blue-blazed Buckeye Trail branches off the Deer Run Trail at the east end of the parking lot. Because there are many other pathways in this section of the woods, hiking through Schumacher Woods on the Buckeye Trail to Ira Rd. requires close attention to the blue blazes.

Directions: From I-271 take Exit 12 for SR 303. Follow SR 303 east to Peninsula. Just before crossing the bridge over the Cuyahoga River, turn right (south) at the traffic light onto Riverview Rd. Take Riverview Rd. south, past Everett Rd. and Indigo Lake, to Ira Rd. Turn right (west) on Ira Rd. (Ira Rd. continues ahead to Hale Farm and Village.) Turn left (south-west) off Ira Rd. onto Martin Rd., and left again into O'Neil Woods at the park sign.
From Akron take Akron-Peninsula Rd. north to Bath Rd. and Bath Rd. west over the Cuyahoga River. At the intersection with Yellow Creek Rd. bear right, still on Bath Rd. At Shade Rd., turn right and follow it to Martin Rd. Turn right at Martin Rd. and right again to enter the park at the park sign.

Parking & restrooms: Parking is at the end of the entrance road, and primitive restrooms are on the hill adjacent to the picnic tables just south of the parking lot.

O'Neil Woods Metro Park is maintained by Metro Parks Serving Summit County. Located in Bath Township at the southern end of Cuyahoga Valley National Recreation Area (CVNRA) and west of Hampton Hills Metro Park, this small, hilly, 274-acre park opened for public use in 1969.

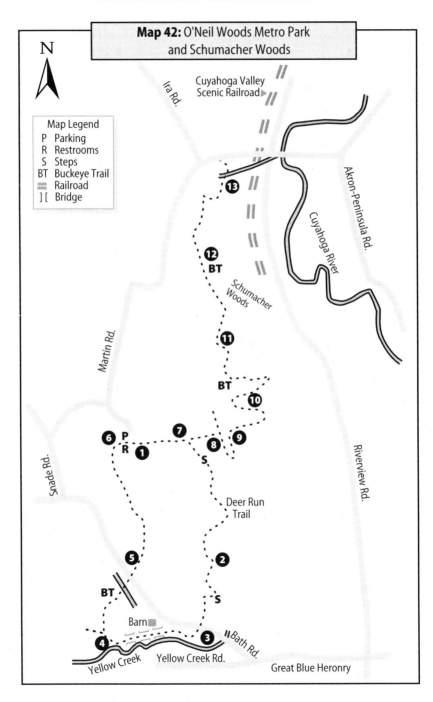

Map 42: O'Neil Woods Metro Park
and Schumacher Woods

N

Cuyahoga Valley
Scenic Railroad▶

Ira Rd.

Akron-Peninsula Rd.

Map Legend
P   Parking
R   Restrooms
S   Steps
BT Buckeye Trail
     Railroad
] [Bridge

Cuyahoga River

⓭

⓬
BT

Schumacher
Woods

⓫

BT
⓾

Martin Rd.

❻ P   ❼   ❾
      R   ❽
      ❶   S

Riverview Rd.

Snade Rd.

Deer Run
Trail

❺   ❷

BT   S

Barn

❹   ❸   Bath Rd.

Yellow Creek   Yellow Creek Rd.   Great Blue Heronry

The family of William and Grace O'Neil first leased and then, in 1972, gave the land outright to Metro Parks. Mr. O'Neil, the founder of General Tire and Rubber Company, and his family had used the land for farming, horseback riding, and family gatherings since the 1930s. Their huge white barn is visible from the trail at Bath Rd.

Deer Run is O'Neil Woods' only trail, a 1.8-mile loop. When taken in a clockwise direction, it descends a steep ridge, follows the course of Yellow Creek a short distance, and then climbs back up out of the valley on the Buckeye Trail.

The blue-blazed Buckeye Trail (BT) then continues from the east end of the parking lot and gradually descends through Schumacher Woods to Ira Rd. The BT is identified by two-inch-by-six-inch rectangular blue tree blazes. In the portion north of the Deer Run Trail, the BT is very well marked but takes many twists and turns as it crosses other trails and old farm roads through the forest. This land originally belonged to Ferdinand Schumacher, the innovator and industrialist who ultimately became president of Quaker Oats Co. in Akron.

There are many varieties of trees, birds, and wildflowers in both the upper hilltop and the stream valley floor; occasionally deer may be spotted here.

Of interest on the drive to the park is a great blue heronry. These huge birds have built their nests in tall sycamore trees on the south side of Bath Rd., west of Akron-Peninsula Rd., near the Cuyahoga River. In April and May these enormous birds can be seen standing guard over their mammoth nests.

Nearby is CVNRA's Hunt Farm Visitor Information Center on Bolantz Rd. just east of Riverview Rd. Information is available about CVNRA's hiking trails, bicycling paths, Cuyahoga Valley Scenic Railroad, and other activities.

1. The trailhead for Deer Run Trail is at the east end of the parking area. This wide, well-marked trail soon enters the woods. Stay to the right, past an intersection for the Buckeye Trail on the left, and ascend an oak ridgetop. (This intersection is where the Buckeye Trail descends to Ira Rd. through Schumacher Woods on the second portion of this hike.) After about 0.4 mile the trail begins to descend the narrow ridge on railroad-tie steps.

2. The 180-foot drop continues steeply downhill on more steps and narrow switchback paths to yet another set of steps at the bottom of the ridge.

3. Cross Bath Rd. at 0.7 mile and note the large white O'Neil barn on the south side of the road. Arrive at broad Yellow Creek flowing eastward toward the Cuyahoga River. The tall trees that thrive in this moist environment are cottonwoods, walnuts, sycamores, and willows. Many wild-flowers, ferns, and bittersweet vines also make their residence here, as do deer and other wildlife. Marked erosion has occurred on the stream banks due to the creek having overflowed many times on top of the loose, sandy soil.

4. Follow the trail westward, keeping Yellow Creek on the left (south). Cross three wooden bridges over side streams as the trail gradually bends away from the creek at a point near the end of a field. At a trail intersection, stay to the right on the main trail (1.2 miles).

5. Cross a tributary stream on rock slabs and reach Bath Rd. again. Cross the road and begin ascending the hill on the Buckeye Trail. Part way uphill is a bench at which to pause and enjoy the tall oak-maple-beech forest. Continue ascending the steep hill and come to another welcoming bench before reaching the summit and parking lot.

6. Just before the trail exit are old apple trees, reminiscent of the former use of this farmland. The blue blazes of the Buckeye Trail (BT) continue across the parking lot to its east end. (Optional: the hike may be ended here.)

7. Reenter the Deer Run Trail, but this time (after 0.1 mile), take the left fork in the trail onto the well-marked, blue-blazed BT.

8. Enter the woods and reach a trail junction (0.2 mile). Follow the BT as it turns right (south), then continues east briefly.

9. At 0.4 mile the BT turns left (north) and quickly makes another turn right (east).

CAUTION: Because of many turns in the trail, and because the BT criss-crosses other paths and old woods roads, watch carefully for and follow the blue blazes painted on trees.

10. At about 1 mile the trail turns west, then north.

11. At 1.4 miles, the path reaches an old woods road and enters a beautiful pine forest.

12. At 2 miles the BT descends the ridge.

13. Cross a creek on stones to reach the exit at Martin and Ira roads.

Turn around and return by retracing your steps through Schumacher Woods, following the BT in reverse. Cross the creek, ascend the hill, and continue following the blue blazes to the junction with the Deer Run Trail. Bear right to the O'Neil Woods parking lot.

This chapter was reviewed by Walter Starcher, Chief Naturalist, Metro Parks Serving Summit County.

The method of nature: who could analyze it? That rushing stream will not stop to be observed. We can never surprise nature in a corner.
—Ralph Waldo Emerson, *The Method of Nature*

MEDINA COUNTY

The most distinctive feature of rural Medina County is the town of Medina's central square, surrounded by restored Victorian-era galleries, studios, shops, and antiques stores. This small-town village square, listed on the National Register of Historic Places, was first constructed in the early 1800s. In 1870, however, a fire destroyed all but one of the town's buildings. By 1880 they were all rebuilt, and the subsequent restoration re-creates its late-19th-century appearance.

The town was to have been named Mecca for the Islamic prophet Mohammed's birthplace, but when it was discovered that another town in Ohio bore that name, it was changed to Medina, the prophet's burial place.

One of Medina's 12 town parks is 316-acre Reagan Park, located northeast of the city off Weymouth Rd. (SR 3). Among its recreational facilities are nature, fitness, and cross-country ski trails.

Once a year, in the autumn, Medina County offers a fall foliage tour through rural parts of the county. The trip includes stops at farms, orchards, and other interesting places. For more information about Medina, contact Medina Area Chamber of Commerce, 145 N. Court St., Medina, OH 44256 (330-723-8773) or the Visitors Bureau, 124 W. Lafayette Rd., Medina, OH 44256 (330-723-5502).

Medina County is home to one of the Cleveland Metroparks recreation areas, Hinckley Reservation. A 90-acre lake in its midst, ancient Whipp's and Worden's Ledges providing an interesting perspective, and an annual celebration of the return of the buzzards (actually turkey vultures), contribute to Hinckley Reservation's popularity.

Medina County Park District includes eight developed parks: Green Leaf, Hubbard Valley, Buckeye Woods, Letha House, Plum Creek, River Styx, and Alderfer-Oenslager; two parks with limited access: Allardale and Hidden Hollow; and two fragile nature areas that are open to visitors only with written permission: Chippewa Lake Nature Areas and Princess Ledges. Information is available from Medina County Park District, 6364 Deerview Lane, Medina, OH 44256; 330-722-9364 or 330-225-7100 ext. 9364.

43 HINCKLEY RESERVATION: WORDEN'S LEDGES

Distance: 1 mile round trip

Easy

Hiking time: 1 hour

Description: The trail is not marked, but it can be followed with this description and map or by referring to the map posted on a garage adjacent to the house. The ledges are located directly under the hill below the homestead, the carvings are not difficult to find. Worden Heritage Homestead is managed by the Hinckley Historical Society and is usually open on Sunday afternoons in the summer (216-278-2154).

Directions: From I-271 take Exit 3 to SR 94 (North Royalton) at Remsen Corners. Take a right (north) on SR 94 (Ridge Rd.). Turn right (east) on Ledge Rd. Pass Kellogg Rd. and Ledge Lake Pool to the Worden Heritage Homestead, about 1 mile ahead on the left.
From Akron, take I-77 north to SR 18 west. At SR 94 go north to Remsen Corners, then follow the directions above.

Parking & restrooms: Very little parking is available at Worden Heritage Homestead, but a few cars can be parked along the side of the driveway. A restroom is available inside the museum, when open.

In 1851 Hiram Worden bought land in Medina County from the estate of Samuel Hinckley that would later become Hinckley Reservation, one of 14 Cleveland Metroparks reservations (and the only one located outside Cuyahoga County). The Worden Heritage Homestead at 895 Ledge Rd. was built by Hiram Worden in 1862, the year his daughter Nettie was born, and was occupied by his farming family and their descendants until the 1980s. Nettie, who lived in the house all her life until her death in 1945, married her third husband, Noble Stuart (20 years her junior), in 1944. Noble and his son, George Stuart, continued to stay in the house until George's death in 1984, when Cleveland Metroparks acquired the home and Hinckley Historical Society became its manager.

Noble Stuart, a bricklayer, homebuilder, wanderer, and, most significantly, folk artist, began carving wood and wet concrete after his marriage to Nettie. He discovered huge sandstone ledges a half-mile beyond the Worden home and proceeded to carve figures and faces and other objects in the ledges over a period of several years. The carvings, which are gradually deteriorating, represent aspects of Stuart's life that were important to

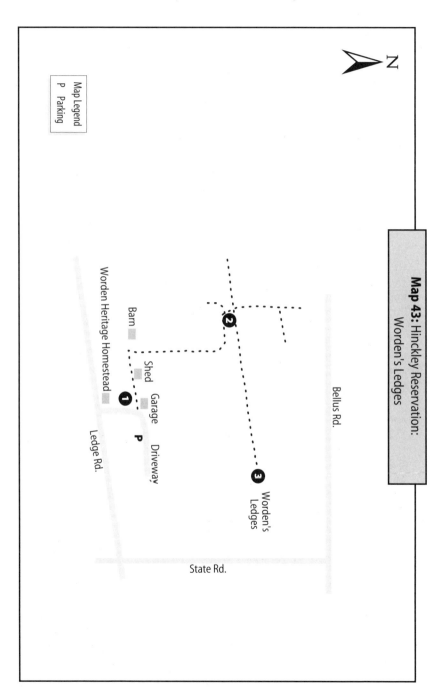

Map 43: Hinckley Reservation: Worden's Ledges

Map Legend

P Parking

N

Worden Heritage Homestead

Barn

Shed

Garage

Driveway

P

Ledge Rd.

State Rd.

Bellus Rd.

Worden's Ledges

1

2

3

him: a cross over an open Bible; baseball player Ty Cobb, whom he took hunting and fishing in Detroit; a schooner, representing his father's death in a shipwreck on Lake Superior; a bust of Hiram Worden on a corner of a rock with his named inscribed; "Nettie," carved in script; George Washington and Marquis de Lafayette, reflecting Stuart's historical interests; and an eight-foot-long sphinx lying atop a large boulder. In addition, Stuart's concrete carving of Christ on the Cross is located on the ground north of a small shed on the property.

Although Stuart was a skillful craftsman, authorities do not consider him a significant artist. He died in 1976 at the age of 94. When asked in 1948 why he did the carvings, he said he simply wanted to keep practicing stone carving and leave something that would last.

West of Worden Heritage Homestead on Ledge Rd. is popular Ledge Lake Pool and Recreation Area (216-234-3026). A small admission charge allows visitors to use the 80-foot by 100-foot pool, changing facilities, and picnic area. Seniors over 65 and children 5 and under are admitted free. It is open 10 a.m. to 8:30 p.m. Memorial Day to Labor Day.

Hinckley Reservation contains hiking trails, picnic areas, and an additional swimming area on Hinckley Lake that can be reached from Bellus Rd.. Trail information is available from Cleveland Metroparks.

1. From the homestead, reach the trail to the ledges by going west parallel to Ledge Rd. (on your left) and past the sheds (on your right). Turn right (north) just before the barn and follow an old farm lane past an abandoned gas well on the left. Soon the path curves around to the left and gently descends a small hill. The trail may be muddy, as it is also used by horses.

2. Near the foot of the slope ignore the minor trail going off to the left and turn right (east) immediately. Follow the trail until you see large Sharon Conglomerate sandstone ledges on the path directly ahead (see Appendix A).

3. At the farthest set of rock outcroppings, you will see on the left a large sphinx carved on top of a rock. This imposing creature seems to guard the entrance to the ledges area. Next is a large rock with "H. M. Worden 1851" carved on its face. On the northwest corner of this rock Stuart carved a bust of his father-in-law, to which he later added a cement beard when he noticed a photo of him sporting this adornment. "Nettie" is deeply incised in the next rock. A schooner can be seen high up on a ledge to the right. Farther along, also on a ledge to the right, is a cross with a Bible intricately carved into the stone. Ty Cobb's face and name are on a north-facing outcropping nearly obscured by moss.

Worden's Ledges were formed by the same ancient processes that shaped Whipp's Ledges (Ch. 46), located in another part of Hinckley Reservation.

Other ledge formations can be found in Nelson-Kennedy Ledges State Park (Ch. 14), Chapin Forest Reservation (Ch. 7), and Virginia Kendall Park in the Cuyahoga Valley National Recreation Area (Chapters 27 and 28).

About 360 million years ago, land that is now Ohio was under a vast inland sea. Over millions of years the sand at the ocean bottom solidified into rock, and as the waters receded and the land uplifted, the rocks became exposed. This rock is called Sharon Conglomerate sandstone because it is composed of sand and quartz. Embedded in it are white quartz "lucky stones" that were washed downstream from a quartz-rich area of Canada. Stream action and ocean waves wore the beach pebbles very smooth during the time they were in and at the edge of the sea. Pebbles mixed with sand and both eventually hardened to form the rock ledges we now see. Glaciers that covered Ohio at various times from 1.6 million years ago to about 12,000 years ago have shaped these sandstone ledges. The rock has not been completely eroded because of its hardness. Erosion and change continue very slowly still.

Return to Worden Heritage Homestead by retracing your steps in the reverse direction.

44 HUBBARD VALLEY PARK

Distance: 1.3 miles

Easy

Hiking time: 1/2 hour

Description: This easy trail encircles Hubbard Valley Lake on a generally flat path. The first half of the hike allows enjoyable views of the water and its wildlife, and the last part, a pleasant walk through the woods.

Directions: From I-71 take Exit 218 (Medina/SR 18). Drive west on SR 18 to Medina, then south on SR 3 about 6 miles to Blake Rd. (SR 118). Turn left (east) on Blake Rd., go 0.7 mile to Hubbard Valley Rd. Turn right (south) on Hubbard Valley Rd., go 0.6 mile to the park entrance on the right. (Hubbard Valley Rd. is closed south of the park due to bridge repairs on I-71).

Parking & restrooms: Park in the parking area just inside the entrance; restrooms are located here.

Hubbard Valley Park is one of Medina County Park District's several scenic parks and is dominated by an 18-acre fishing lake. This small, scenic park, located in the southern part of the county near Chippewa Lake, offers picnic shelters, a boat launching area, an observation overlook, and a hiking trail that surrounds Hubbard Valley Lake. Fishing for several different species of fish is permitted from the shore or in a rowboat. Information about Hubbard Valley Park can be obtained from Medina Park District 330-722-9364.

1. Enter the paved All-Purpose Trail at the southwest end of the parking area, walking clockwise around the large lake. Lakeside Picnic Shelter is on the left.

Ahead is a sweeping view of the water. Often various kinds of waterfowl congregate here in large numbers, especially during migration seasons.

2. Continue on the paved trail past the boat launch facility, then up the slope on the left to a wide, mowed path. From the hill above the lake are nice views of the water and its activity. The trail is bordered in the fall by purple asters and yellow goldenrods. Butterflies often flit around these abundant wildflowers.

3. The path narrows down to a grassy trail near the south end of the lake. Pass by the many fishermen's paths that go down to the water's edge.

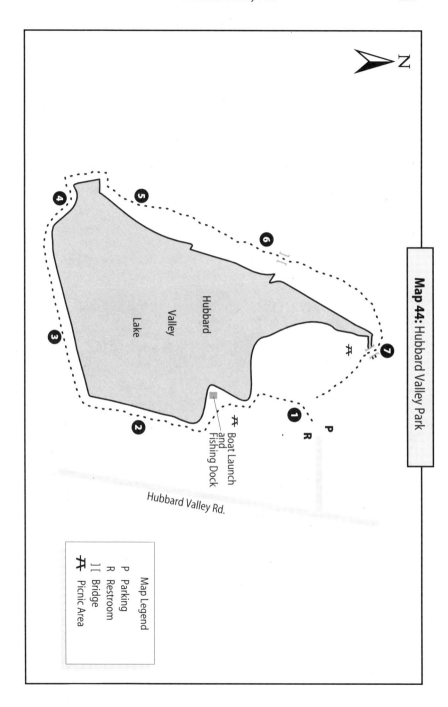

N

Map 44: Hubbard Valley Park

Hubbard Valley Lake

⚓ Boat Launch and Fishing Dock

Hubbard Valley Rd.

P

R

1
2
3
4
5
6
7

Map Legend
P Parking
R Restroom
⅃⅃ Bridge
⚓ Picnic Area

4. Reach a large concrete overflow box at the west side of the lake. The trail turns north through the woods at the edge of the water, then bends left (west).

5. After heading north through a meadow, the trail reenters the woods on a wide dirt track. Hubbard Valley Lake is to the right (southeast). The pleasant path winds through a maple, beech, and tuliptree forest. On the left, an old farm fence lines the pathway.

6. At 0.8 mile pass a park bench on the right overlooking the lake. Cross a wooden bridge as the trail veers farther away from the water.

7. The path bends south at 1.2 miles, then bears left to cross a wooden bridge.

Exit from the trail at a picnic shelter and cross the lawn to the parking area to complete the loop.

Marilyn Dolence

45 PLUM CREEK PARK

Distance: 1.4 miles

Easy

Hiking time: 3/4 hour

Description: This easy hike follows fairly flat terrain on a wide, unmarked trail. Although Plum Creek itself is east of the park (and east of Plum Creek Pkwy.), several other smaller creeks in the park are crossed on wooden bridges. The hike ends on Hidden Creek Interpretive Trail near the Interpretive Center (now closed).

Directions: From I-71 take Exit 222 (Medina/SR 3). After exiting I-71, turn to follow SR 3 south, but take an immediate right turn onto Hamilton Rd. (just to the west of the interstate exit ramp). Follow Hamilton Rd. west 0.8 mile to Plum Creek Pkwy. Turn right (north) on Plum Creek Pkwy. for about 1 mile to the park entrance road on the left. Turn left here onto the dirt road and go to the last parking lot located near a small fishing pond.

Parking & restrooms: A primitive restroom is at the parking area.

Plum Creek Park is located on Plum Creek Pkwy. off Hamilton Rd. in the northern part of Medina County. This pleasant park, once a town landfill, is a good example of land reclamation. Available here are fishing and observation ponds, a nature trail, a tall grass prairie planting, picnic tables, and shelters. Recent acquisition of 74 additional acres of land west of the developed area brings this park's total land area to 191 acres.

Information about Plum Creek Park is available from Medina County Park District, 330-722-9364.

1. Enter the Nature Trail at the sign at the west end of the open grassy area. Walk straight ahead, following the blue arrow sign. This is a new-growth forest consisting predominantly of young maple trees. Wildflowers also abound in this environment.

At 0.2 mile the trail bends to the north, goes down steps and crosses a brook on a wooden bridge. After another 0.1 mile, you will pass a deep ravine on the left, then descend a small set of steps.

2. Cross a boardwalk and bear left (north) to cross another wooden bridge. A bench at the top of a gentle rise invites a pause to contemplate this peaceful woods.

The trail now heads westward above the ravine on the left, then northwest.

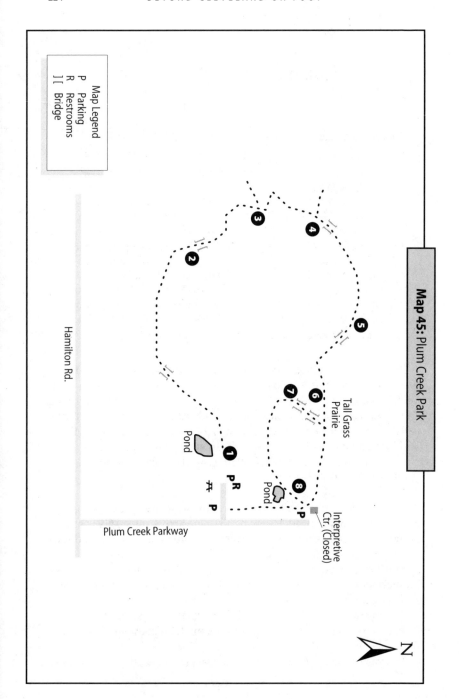

Map 45: Plum Creek Park

Map Legend

P   Parking
R   Restrooms
][Bridge

Hamilton Rd.

Plum Creek Parkway

Pond

Pond

Tall Grass
Prairie

Interpretive
Ctr. (Closed)

N

3. At a trail junction (0.45 mile), stay to the right on the main trail. The path bends north, then west.

4. At another trail junction, where there is a trail identified with a red arrow, stay to the right on the blue arrow trail. Descend some steps, cross a small bridge, and ascend the next set of steps.

5. The trail heads east, then southeast. At 0.6 mile, descend yet another set of steps to cross another bridge. The path now heads south. In the spring there are many beautiful wildflowers along here.

6. (0.7 mile) Reach the Tall Grass Prairie, a small, circular planting of flowers native to the plains states. Turn right (southwest) on the main trail. (Ahead is a mowed, grassy path that leads to the closed Interpretive Center.)

7. Continue westward on the main Nature Trail. Cross a small bridge and hike through a tall beech tree forest. Other tall trees here include the cucumber magnolia and tuliptree. Cross another bridge over a stream.

8. At 1 mile the trail heads east and crosses an open meadow. Head to the left (east) at this meadow and pass a pond on the right. Dogwood trees bloom along here in the springtime.

Bear right to pass the Interpretive Center (on the left) and a small shelter. Continue on the path a few steps (east) to a parking lot.

Turn right (south) on the trail, which parallels the gravel road (Plum Creek Pkwy.). Follow this path back to the main parking area.

46 HINCKLEY RESERVATION: WHIPP'S LEDGES

Distance: 5 miles

Strenuous

Hiking time: 2-1/2 hours

Description: This hike, partly on the blue-blazed Buckeye Trail along Hinckley Lake, goes to Whipp's Ledges and returns on the All-Purpose Trail along the east side of the lake to complete a loop. There is one steep hill to climb.

Directions: From I-271 take Exit 3 at Ridge Rd. (SR 94, Remsen Corners). Go north on Ridge Rd. to Hinckley Hills Rd. (SR 606). Turn right (east) on Hinckley Hills Rd. to Bellus Rd., then turn right (east) on Bellus Rd. Turn right (south) on West Dr., entering the Reservation. Follow West Dr. 3/4 mile to a sign indicating Johnson's Picnic Area.

Parking & restrooms: At Johnson's Picnic Area go to the second (farthest) parking area, where the road dead-ends.

Hinckley Reservation, a Cleveland Metropark, surrounds 90-acre Hinckley Lake, into which the east branch of the Rocky River flows. The river was dammed in 1926 to form this beautiful lake. Hinckley, located in Medina County, is the only reservation of Cleveland Metroparks outside Cuyahoga County. In it are Whipp's Ledges and Worden's Ledges. (A walk to Worden's Ledges is described in Ch. 43.)

The Worden Heritage Homestead, managed by the Hinckley Historical Society, is on the north side of Ledge Rd. between State and Kellogg roads. Here you will find interesting information about the history of Hinckley Reservation.

Hinckley is well known for its celebration (on the Sunday following March 15) of the annual migratory return of the buzzards (actually turkey vultures) from the southern U.S. The buzzards find the open fields, rocky ledges and cliffs, and abundant food ideal for egg-laying and nesting. In the spring and summer they can be seen soaring on the rising, warm-air thermals created by the open fields.

1. Start the hike at Johnson's Picnic Area by finding the blue-blazed Buckeye Trail (BT) heading north on the uphill gravel path just beyond the last parking area. The blue blazes are on the tall trees. The creek will be below on the left. Hinckley Lake comes into view along this route.

2. Turn left on State Rd. at about 0.7 mile and continue on the road

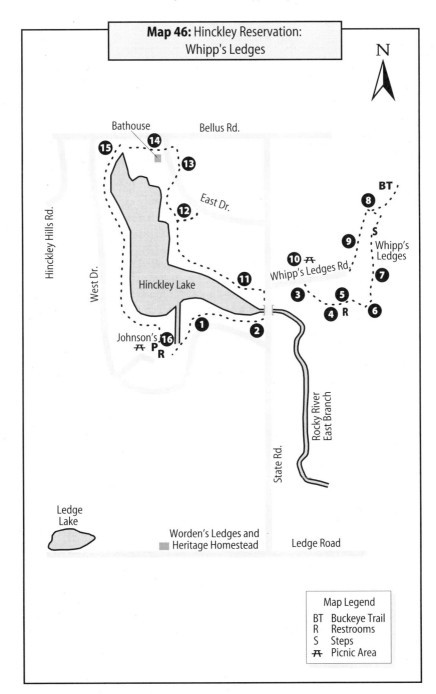

Map 46: Hinckley Reservation:
Whipp's Ledges

N

Bathouse

Bellus Rd.

⓯

⓮

⓭

East Dr.

⓬

BT

❽

S

Whipp's
Ledges

Hinckley Hills Rd.

West Dr.

❾

⓫

❿ 🌲

Whipp's Ledges Rd.

❼

Hinckley Lake

❸

❺

❻

❹ R

❶

❷

Johnson's 🌲 P R

⓰

Rocky River
East Branch

State Rd.

Ledge
Lake

Worden's Ledges and
Heritage Homestead

Ledge Road

Map Legend

BT   Buckeye Trail
R   Restrooms
S   Steps
🌲   Picnic Area

across a sturdy pedestrian/bicycle bridge over the Rocky River East Branch.

3. Cross State Rd. and turn right onto Whipp's Ledges Rd., which leads to a picnic area. Immediately to the right the BT turns east from the road alongside a small creek, a tributary of the Rocky River East Branch.

4. The BT continues through a wet area, past the Rocky River East Branch on the right, then goes into the woods and uphill.

5. At 1.2 miles reach a stone restroom at Whipp's Ledges picnic and parking area. The BT turns right, then continues straight ahead uphill.

6. Still following BT blue blazes, start a very steep uphill climb to the foot of the moss-covered ledges. The BT turns left directly under these striking sandstone cliffs, which are estimated to be 320 million years old. They are composed of outcrops of Sharon Conglomerate, the pebbly sandstone formed during the Pennsylvanian Age. These magnificent rock formations rise about 350 feet above the level of Hinckley Lake. The small, shiny, rounded quartz pebbles that you see embedded in the sandstone are often called "lucky stones." These pebbles originated in a quartz-rich section of Canada and were carried here by streams of water, then rolled along the shores of a great inland sea that covered land that is now Ohio. The sandstone hardened and formed these Sharon Conglomerate ledges that are quite resistant to erosion (see Appendix A).

7. Hike past small caves and huge boulders, still following BT blazes. At 1.5 miles climb a flight of stone steps between two ledges. Because the rocks underlying these ledges (Cuyahoga Formation) are much softer than the sandstone, massive blocks of Sharon Conglomerate sandstone often break off at the edge of the cliffs. Settling then causes cracks, fissures, and large cave-like crevices to develop, as seen here.

8. Hike along the top of the ledges to a trail intersection. Turn left (leaving the BT at this point) and carefully descend a rocky path on the left between a large split boulder, formed by the process described above.

9. Reach the trail under the ledges again and bear right onto a path that descends to Whipp's Ledges Picnic Area (2 miles).

10. At the picnic area walk down Whipp's Ledges Rd. to State Rd. Cross the road and, before the bridge, turn right onto the All-Purpose Trail going north alongside Hinckley Lake.

11. There are fine views of the lake along this well-maintained walkway.

12. At 3.5 miles, continue straight ahead past an intersection with another trail joining from the right. Follow the path as it curves upward to East Dr.

13. Cross East Dr., continuing on the paved All-Purpose Trail, following it left (north) as it leads along the road past Hinckley Lake Bathhouse to Bellus Rd. (3.75 miles).

14. Recross East Dr. to continue on the All-Purpose Trail past the swimming area, bathhouse, and spillway on the left.

15. After a short distance, leave the All-Purpose Trail to turn left (south) at the top of the spillway and follow a dirt trail downhill adjacent to the lake.

16. Continue along this lakeside trail to the boat launch area and return to Johnson's Picnic Area.

My "best" room, however, my withdrawing room, always ready for company, on whose carpet the sun rarely fell, was the pine wood behind my house. Thither in summer days, when distinguished guests came, I took them, and a priceless domestic swept the floor and dusted the furniture and kept things in order.

—Henry David Thoreau, *Walden*

LORAIN COUNTY

Mostly rural, Lorain County extends along Lake Erie from the city of Avon in the east to downtown Vermilion and the Vermilion River in the west, and continues south to Oberlin and Wellington. The county's east-west ridges, formed by ancient Lake Erie beaches, produced natural road-ways for immigrants from the Connecticut Western Reserve and facilitated subsequent development of the county.

Antique dealers abound in Lorain County; in Avon alone there are more than 100. Jamie's Flea Market in South Amherst is one of the largest in Ohio. Oberlin (Ch. 47) is a charming town with an interesting history.

Lorain County Metro Parks offers over 4,500 acres of green space, with a central headquarters at Carlisle Reservation. Its nine parks include Caley National Wildlife Woods and the reservations of Vermilion River, French Creek, Black River, Indian Hollow, Carlisle, Charlemont, and Kipton. Schoepfle Garden, one of Lorain County's Metro Parks, is actually in Erie County (Ch. 56). An annual Pioneer Days Festival is held at Vermilion River Reservation, and yearly Halloween Walks are held at Carlisle Visitor Center. Information about programs and activities is available by calling 216-458-5121 or 800-526-7275.

Findley State Park is in Wellington (216-647-4490) and some of the city parks in this county include Lakeview Park in Lorain and Cascade Park in Elyria.

More information about Lorain County is available from Lorain County Visitors Bureau, 611 Broadway, Box 567, Lorain, OH 44052; 216-245-5282 or 800-334-1673.

47 OBERLIN

Distance: 3.5 miles

Easy

Walking time: 2 hours

Description: This walk is entirely on sidewalks through the campus and town, and leads past college buildings, historical landmarks, and heritage homes. The walk covers several square blocks of downtown Oberlin.

Directions: From I-480 west take the exit (on the left) for SR 10 (Oberlin). Follow SR 10 southwest to SR 511 west, leading directly into Oberlin. At SR 58 (Main St.) in Oberlin, turn left (south) and drive one block to College St. Turn left (east) one block on E. College St., left again (north) on Willard St., then right (east) into one of several free parking lots.

From Akron take SR 18 west to Wellington and turn north onto SR 58 to Oberlin. Turn right (east) on E. College St., left on Willard St., and right into one of the free parking lots.

From Lorain go south on SR 58 (Leavitt Rd.) to Oberlin. Turn left on E. College St., left on Willard, and right into one of the free parking lots.

Parking & restrooms: Park at the free parking lot off Willard St.; restrooms are in any public restaurant or building.

Oberlin is a small, lovely, cosmopolitan town southwest of Cleveland, dominated by internationally known Oberlin College and Oberlin Conservatory of Music. Its population of 8,600 (including 2,700 students) cherishes the town's heritage and history and its many prized 19th-century homes and college buildings. A visitor to Oberlin immediately notices the brick-accented sidewalks, pots of plants hanging from lamp posts, and the beautifully landscaped central green, which offer the impression of a quaint Victorian village. Yet Oberlin is a progressive community with a small but first-rate art museum, a modern hospital only a block from the center of town, an excellent water treatment system, and a new continuing-care retirement community—Kendal at Oberlin—near downtown. An annual celebration of Oberlin's history, called Oberlin Heritage Days Festival, is held on Tappan Square each July. For information call 800-OBERLIN.

Oberlin's history illustrates how the town and college have worked in partnership as a progressive community. When the town was founded in 1833, Oberlin opposed slavery as a violation of Christian principles. The village thus became a haven for abolitionists and runaway slaves. From

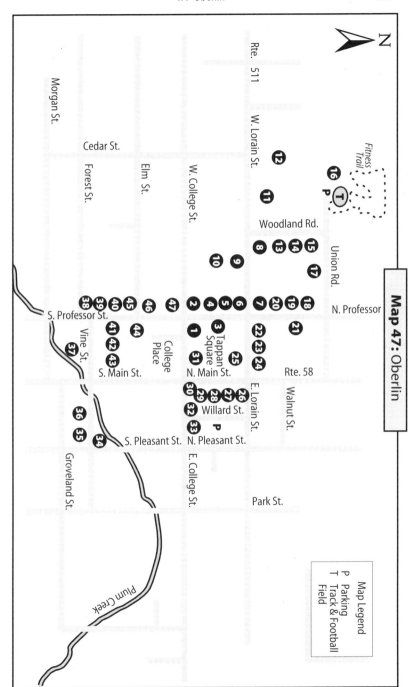

Map 47: Oberlin

N

Map Legend
P Parking
T Track & Football
   Field

about 1833 to the end of the Civil War, Oberlin was one of the major stations (No. 99) on the Underground Railroad network that sheltered fugitives from the south. From here it was easy to transfer runaways to Lake Erie ports and waiting boats that took them to Canada and freedom. Many former slaves stayed in Oberlin, going into farming, business, or other types of employment, and raised their families here, leaving descendants who still live in Oberlin.

When the college opened, also in 1833, it admitted women, thus becoming the first coeducational college or university in the country. By 1835 it admitted African-American students, becoming one of the first colleges in America to do so. Oberlin was also active in crusades for temperance and women's suffrage. The Anti-Saloon League was founded here in 1893.

The 440-acre Oberlin campus has been called one of America's 35 best campuses, in Thomas A. Gaines's *The Campus as a Work of Art.* Oberlin graduates have earned more doctorates than the graduates of any other private liberal arts school in the nation. The college ranks high in scientific education. Three alumni have won Nobel Prizes: Robert Millikan, in 1923 (physics); Roger Sperry, in 1981 (medicine/physiology); and Stanley Cohen, in 1986 (medicine/physiology).

Oberlin calls itself the "City of Music," because concerts are offered by conservatory students and faculty almost every night of the week—and most are free. The outstanding quality of musical performance derives from the conservatory's high national ranking in the education of musicians at the undergraduate level. About 500 students are enrolled in the conservatory, including students who are pursuing double degrees from both the conservatory and the college.

1. From the parking lot, go south on Willard St. to College St. Walk west on College St. past Tappan Square to the corner of W. College and N. Professor streets. Thirteen-acre Tappan Square, with its many tall, mature trees—about 300 trees of 58 different species—was named in honor of Arthur Tappan, a wealthy New York businessman whose generous gifts ensured Oberlin's survival in 1835. His philanthropy was contingent on the college admitting African-American students. Tappan Square is owned by the college but used by both Oberlin College and townspeople. Festivals, concerts, and annual May commencement exercises are held here.

The big round boulder near the southwest corner of Tappan Square, on the lawn near W. College St., was put there by the Oberlin College Class of 1898, who pried it out of Plum Creek. It is painted each year by the graduating class (and the rest of the year by others expressing various messages, a tradition started during the Vietnam War era).

2. The white building on the northwest corner with the lacy facade is the King Building, the college's main classroom building. This beautiful 1964 building was designed by Minoru Yamasaki, who also designed the Conservatory of Music on the opposite corner. Warner Center next to King serves as a theater and dance center.

3. On the west side of Tappan Square is the 1903 Memorial Arch recognizing Oberlin missionaries who were killed in the Boxer Rebellion of China in 1900. A new plaque has been in honor of Chinese civilians who lost their lives.

4. On the left is historic Peters Hall (1885), constructed, like Baldwin and Talcott Halls, of rough-textured Ohio sandstone. This complex structure was the college's main classroom building from the 1880s to the 1960s.

5. Cox Administration Building (1915) was designed by the well-known architect of the U.S. Supreme Court Building, Cass Gilbert, in an ornate Northern Italian Renaissance style. Gilbert designed several more of the college's buildings.

6. At the corner of Professor and W. Lorain streets is beautiful Finney Chapel, a 1908 design also by Cass Gilbert. Its 1,376-seat sanctuary is the site of many artist recitals, orchestral concerts, assemblies, and religious gatherings. The chapel was named in honor of Rev. Charles Grandison Finney, a prominent evangelist, antislavery advocate, and second president of Oberlin College.

7. Turn left (west) on W. Lorain St. On the northwest corner of Professor and W. Lorain is Severance Hall, housing the college's psychology department. Named for trustee Louis Henry Severance, it was built in 1900 and designed by Chicago architect Howard Van Doren Shaw.

8. To the west of Severance, on the corner of W. Lorain and Woodland Ave. is the Kettering Science Building (1961), housing the Chemistry and Biology departments, and the Roger Sperry Neuroscience Wing. This recent addition was named after the 1981 Nobel-Prize-winning scientist (a 1935 Oberlin graduate) who won the award in medicine/physiology. The building was designed by Reed Axelrod in 1990 to blend in with the older Kettering building and the brick dormitories at this end of the campus.

9. Wilder Hall (1911), on W. Lorain opposite Kettering, is the student union, a former men's dormitory. Most of Oberlin's student organizations have offices located here. In the basement are campus night spots—the Rathskeller and Disco. The main lounge and former residential library is now used as a performance space and multipurpose meeting room—"Wilder Main."

10. Behind and to the west of Wilder is Mudd Learning Center (1974), the college's central library, with over one million volumes.

Of the library's most important collections, several are outstanding. The Violin Society of America/Goodkind Collection on the History and Construction of the Violin has been called the world's most important collection of information about the making, playing, and teaching of stringed instruments. The Antislavery Collection is one of this country's most historically significant assortment of pamphlets and books on slavery. The Collection on the History of the Book holds examples of bookmaking, binding, typography, and illustration from 1450 to the present. The Architecture Collection is almost a duplicate of Thomas Jefferson's architecture library.

11. Continue west on W. Lorain. On the right is Hales Gymnasium (1939), housing Crane Pool (no longer in use), a six-lane bowling alley, and a favorite student hang-out, Cat in the Cream Coffeehouse.

Oberlin's impressive Athletic Complex extends north from here to the Jesse Philips Physical Education Center (1971) and beyond.

12. To the west of Hales is the medical campus serving the entire community. Here is 100-bed Allen Memorial Hospital (1925) and the Oberlin Clinic.

Return to Woodland St. and walk north. Several of the small homes on the left are rented by students and faculty.

13. Part way up the block on the right is Barrows Hall (1956), a large dormitory reserved entirely for first-year students.

14. Next to it is Noah Hall, a neo-Georgian, coed dormitory built in 1932. Its high ceilings, chandeliers, wood paneling, and lounges with fireplaces create the feeling of an old English country home.

15. Zechiel House (1968) at the end of the block is a small men's residence occupied by many of the college's male athletes. It is just across from the Jesse Philips Physical Education Center.

16. On the left and extending for some distance are the buildings comprising the Athletic Complex. Inside huge Philips Gymnasium are an Olympic-sized pool, basketball, squash, racquetball, and tennis courts, and other facilities. Also located in the complex are field houses, an ice rink, the Savage football stadium, athletic fields, tennis courts, and a Fit Trail. Students, faculty, staff, and townspeople all use these facilities.

The 1.25-mile Fit Trail is a pleasant gravel path available to anyone for either running or walking. The trail was given to the college jointly by Southwood Corporation and the late Jim Fixx, a 1957 Oberlin College graduate who was a well-known marathon runner and author. The Fit Trail begins at the southeast end of the football stadium, near Woodland and Union roads. (If you wish to walk on this trail only, parking is available in the lot at the southwest end of the football stadium.)

17. Turn right (east) on Union Rd. Langston Hall (1963), named for John Mercer Langston, Oberlin's most famous 19th-century black graduate, is on the right.

18. Turn right (south) on N. Professor St. On the right is Walter Bailey House (1968), also known as "French House," for French-speaking students. Two graduate assistants from France and a French faculty member also live here. All take their meals in a French-speaking, private dining room in Stevenson Hall.

19. East Hall (1964), next on the right, is unique in that the third floor is designated as a "quiet hall."

20. Next to East Hall is Barnard Hall (1968), a small residence for upperclass students.

South of Barnard is Wright Laboratory of Physics (1942), named for Wilbur and Orville Wright. Their sister, Katherine Wright Haskell (an Oberlin College graduate), donated funds for the construction of the building in her brothers' names.

21. Across from Barnard is the recent (1991) Stevenson Hall, the college's main dining hall. One of the newest structures on campus, it was designed by architect Charles Gwathmey.

22. On the corner of N. Professor and W. Lorain streets is the Carnegie Building, built in 1908 as the library and now housing the admissions office. You may stop here to pick up information about the college.

23. Turn left (east) on W. Lorain. Bosworth Hall (1931), containing Fairchild Chapel, is another of Cass Gilbert's Mediterranean-style architectural designs. Behind Bosworth is Asia House-Quadrangle, also designed by Gilbert in 1931. The 60 coed students who live in Asia House share a common interest in Asian culture. Look for the relief sculptures which adorn the columns on a walkway located on the southwest corner of the quadrangle. The complex formerly served as Oberlin's Graduate School of Theology.

24. First Church, at the corner of N. Main St. and W. Lorain St., was built of red brick in 1844 in Greek Revival style. It has been well preserved both inside and out. It served as an early meeting place for all town gatherings and was the center of community life in Oberlin for many years. First Church was once the largest structure west of the Allegheny Mountains. It is the only substantial building remaining from the original Oberlin colony.

Turn right (south) on Main St.

25. Tappan Square's unusual Clark Bandstand (1987), designed by Oberlin College graduate Julian Smith, was constructed to be handicapped accessible and resembles a large Asian festival wagon. The bandstand is named for its benefactor, A.C. "Kenny" Clark, a businessman and member of the Oberlin College Class of 1948.

26. On the southeast corner of E. Lorain and N. Main streets is Allen Memorial Art Museum, designed by Cass Gilbert in 1917, with a modern extension, designed by Robert Venturi, added in 1976. This fine museum contains one of the finest collections of art on a college or university campus in this country. The 14,000-object collection ranges from ancient Egypt to contemporary America. Its particular strength is in 17th-century Dutch and Flemish paintings, 19th- and 20th-century European art, contemporary American art, and Japanese woodblock prints. On the grounds around the building are a number of museum sculptures. The museum is open Tuesday-Saturday 10 a.m.-5.p.m., and Sunday 1-5 p.m. (closed Mondays and major holidays). Admission is free (216-775-8665).

27. Adjacent to the museum is the Women's Gateway monument. It commemorates the admission of women to Oberlin College in 1833, making Oberlin the country's first coeducational college.

28. Under a gorgeous weeping beech tree is the Bacon Arch.

29. Hall Auditorium, named for Charles Martin Hall, an Oberlin College graduate, aluminum manufacturer, and philanthropist, is the home of Oberlin Opera Theater and other theatrical and dance performances. Architect Wallace Harrison's design for the curved-concrete structure was the focus of much controversy when the auditorium opened in 1953. Harrison also designed the U.N. Building in New York a few years earlier.

30. The Oberlin Inn, on the corner of College and Main streets, was built in 1954; a large addition was constructed in 1969. It is the fourth hotel to be located at this spot. The first was a log cabin built for pioneer travelers in 1833.

31. Directly across Main St., on Tappan Square's southeast corner and surrounded by flags, is the site of an historic elm tree, removed several years ago. It is the spot where John J. Shipherd and Philo P. Stewart knelt in prayer, having located what they thought was the perfect place for a new village and college. They named their proposed village and school "Oberlin" after a European pastor, John Frederick Oberlin. The first settler, Peter P. Pease, built a log cabin near this site in April, 1833. Here also is a memorial for Charles Martin Hall, whose method of aluminum extraction enabled him to establish the Aluminum Company of America.

32. Turn left (east) on E. College St. past the Oberlin Area Chamber of Commerce on the left (216-774-6262).

33. Continue to the restored 1853 Charles Martin Hall House at 64 E. College, now a college faculty residence and formerly the boyhood home of the college's most generous benefactor. Hall, working in a woodshed behind his house in 1886 (a year after his graduation from Oberlin College), discovered the electrolytic process for extracting aluminum from bauxite ore, essential in making aluminum a common material with many uses.

34. Turn right (south) on S. Pleasant St. past Plum Creek to Martin Luther King, Jr. Memorial Park at the corner of Vine and Pleasant streets. This three-part tribute to African-Americans was created by the town's Parks and Recreation Department and other persons, and dedicated in

1987. The tall, incised-brick portrait of Martin Luther King, Jr. was designed by Paul B. Arnold, an Emeritus Art Professor. King visited Oberlin many times and was awarded an honorary doctorate of Humane Letters Degree in 1965.

Continue west on the walkway. The second memorial is a photographic monument remembering the Oberlin-Wellington Rescuers. In 1858, fugitive slave John Price, who came from Kentucky to Oberlin, was seized by slave-catchers and driven to the town of Wellington. A group of abolitionists then marched on Wellington, rescued and protected him by returning him to Oberlin, then helped him gain his freedom in Canada. This event was significant in inflaming antislavery sentiments nationwide leading up to the Civil War. The third monument commemorates three Oberlin men (John A. Copeland, Shields Green, and Lewis Sheridan Leary) who were killed in John Brown's 1859 raid on Harpers Ferry, another important event leading up to the war. This 1860 cenotaph was originally in Westwood Cemetery and was moved here in 1971.

35. The white frame house set back from the road is the 1847 Wack-Dietz House at 43 E. Vine St. It is the former home of Chauncey Wack, a tavern keeper and prominent Democrat who was a witness in the trial of the Oberlin-Wellington Rescuers.

36. The small two-story brick house at 33 E. Vine St. is the former home of Wilson Bruce Evans. It was built in 1856 for Evans, a free black carpenter and cabinet maker from North Carolina. Evans, his brother, Henry Evans, and Lewis Sheridan Leary, their brother-in-law, were arrested in the Oberlin-Wellington Slave Rescue. Evans is said to have opened his home to fugitive slaves and made it a stop on the Underground Railroad. The house is owned by an Evans descendant and is not open to the public.

37. On the southwest corner of Vine and S. Main streets is Wright Park (dedicated in 1932), honoring Clarence J. Wright, a grocer whose first store once stood on this corner.

Across Plum Creek is the Soldier's Monument honoring 96 Civil War casualties of both town and college, and those killed in the Spanish-American War of 1898, World War I, World War II, the Korean War, and the war in Vietnam.

Continue walking west on Vine St. to Professor St. Here are several college residences for students with special interests.

38. Ahead is Max Kade House (the German House), home for German-speaking students.

39. Harvey House (1968), adjacent to Kade, is for Spanish-speaking students, and is also known as the Spanish House.

Price is located to the rear of Harvey and was founded by a group of Asian-American, Latino, and Native-American students for those interested in these cultures.

40. At 68 S. Professor is the 1894 Lewis House, the Religious Life Center. Located here is the Office of Chaplains, which oversees the student-volunteer Community Outreach Program that serves 50 agencies throughout Lorain County annually.

41. On the east side of the street at 73 S. Professor are three old buildings maintained by Oberlin Historical and Improvement Organization. Jewett House (1883) was once the home of Frank Fanning Jewett, an Oberlin College chemistry professor who taught chemistry to Charles Martin Hall. Both the house and barn are on the National Register of Historic Places. The house is open to the public for tours by calling 216-774-1700.

42. Down the walkway, also off the Conservatory parking lot, is the 1837 Little Red Schoolhouse, the first school for Oberlin children. It was originally built near First Church and later used as a residence on S. Main St. The schoolhouse was restored in 1958 and moved here in 1968. Third-graders use the building each June when they study Oberlin's history.

43. Another historic building south of the Conservatory parking lot is the James Monroe House, a brick Italianate building constructed in 1866 and moved here in 1960. This home belonged first to General Giles Shurtleff, Oberlin's leading Civil War hero. James Monroe, an abolitionist and classics professor at the college, lived in it after 1870 with his wife, Julia Finney Monroe, the daughter of Rev. Charles Finney, Oberlin's great religious leader.

44. Next on Professor is the prestigious Oberlin Conservatory of Music, this country's first conservatory when it opened in 1865. To most people just hearing the word "Oberlin" conjures up thoughts of music. Rev. Charles Grandison Finney, an amateur cellist, was instrumental in starting the conservatory and Charles Martin Hall, a piano student, provided funding and established America's first music professorship at the college. Other firsts in the country for the conservatory were: the first full-time chair in music history and appreciation (1892); the first four-year degree program in public school music (1921); the introduction of the Suzuki method of string pedagogy (1958); establishment of a pioneer program in electronic music (1969); and creation of the first arts exchange program between the former U.S.S.R. and the U.S. with the American Soviet Youth Orchestra, consisting of 100 students from both countries.

The conservatory building, designed in 1964 by Minoru Yamasaki, the architect of New York's World Trade Center, is one of the most unusual on campus. The structure contains three distinct sections, each with a different function: Bibbins Hall, used primarily for teaching, contains classrooms, studios, a chamber music hall, offices, and space for other educational uses; the Central Unit contains two performance halls, Warner Concert Hall and Kulas Recital Hall, and an extensive music library, rehearsal rooms, and a lounge; the third section in the complex is Robertson Hall, containing individual practice rooms, each with its own grand piano and window overlooking the campus.

45. Fairchild House (1950) at Elm St. and S. Professor is another residence hall.

46. At 30 S. Professor, opposite the Conservatory of Music, is historic Baldwin Cottage, home of the Women's Collective, a community of women who share an interest in feminist issues. This lovely old building was originally built as a dormitory in 1885.

47. At West College St. and Professor is Talcott Hall (1887), another architecturally distinguished residence hall. Its stone construction is Romanesque in style.

The Underground Railroad Monument in front of Talcott was designed and installed by students to commemorate the historical events that took place here during the mid-19th century. Oberlin was one of the first small towns in America to promise freedom to all who came within its borders.

Turn right at W. College to College Place and the car parking lot.

Geoffrey Blodgett, Danforth Professor of History at Oberlin College, Oberlin resident, and 1953 Oberlin College graduate generously reviewed this chapter for historical accuracy.

Ran Taylor, Oberlin resident, and Flora Burkholder also contributed to this chapter.

Lorain County Visitors Bureau

48 BLACK RIVER RESERVATION: BRIDGEWAY TRAIL

Distance: 3 miles from north to south or 6 miles round trip [Easy]

Walking time: 2 hours one-way or 3 hours round-trip

Description: The flat, 12-foot-wide Bridgeway Trail, the major trail in the park, has information panels along its length describing the history and natural features of the Black River Valley. Mile markers along the path make it a favorite for hikers and joggers. Two loop trails offer interesting side visits—one to a big cottonwood, one of the largest trees in Lorain County, and another to a tall waterfall below E. 36th St. in Lorain.

Directions: From I-90 take Exit 148 in Sheffield (SR 254). Follow SR 254 (Detroit Rd.) west about 1 mile to East River/Gulf Rd. (The Sheffield Fire Department is on the southeast corner.) Turn right (north) E. River Rd.; follow it north to E. 31st St. Turn left (west) onto E. 31st St. Cross the bridge over the Black River to the park entrance marked Day's Dam on the left. From Lorain take SR 57 (E. 28th St.) east to Elyria-Lorain Rd. (still SR 57). Turn left (east) onto E. 31st St. to the park entrance for Day's Dam on the right.

Parking & restrooms: Located at both Day's Dam and Bur Oak picnic and parking areas.

The Bridgeway Trail, dedicated in 1994, is part of Black River Reservation, one of Lorain County's nine developed public recreation areas. Lying in an urban corridor along the Black River Valley between Elyria and Lorain, its 833 acres consist mainly of scenic bottom lands, forests, meadows, and wetlands. The park's most outstanding feature is an impressive Cleveland Shale cliff exposed by the relentless cutting of the Black River. This black shale contains dark organic matter that has given the river its name.

A three-mile, asphalt-paved trail with interpretive signs extends from Lorain to Elyria and provides access to hikers, bicyclists, and people in wheelchairs and strollers. A free electric tram, operating on weekends from May through October, takes visitors who otherwise would be unable to negotiate the trail into the valley from Day's Dam picnic area at 31st St. to Bur Oak picnic area. Another feature of the park is a 1,000-foot bridge spanning the Black River that crosses it twice and provides rewarding views of both the river and a treetop forest.

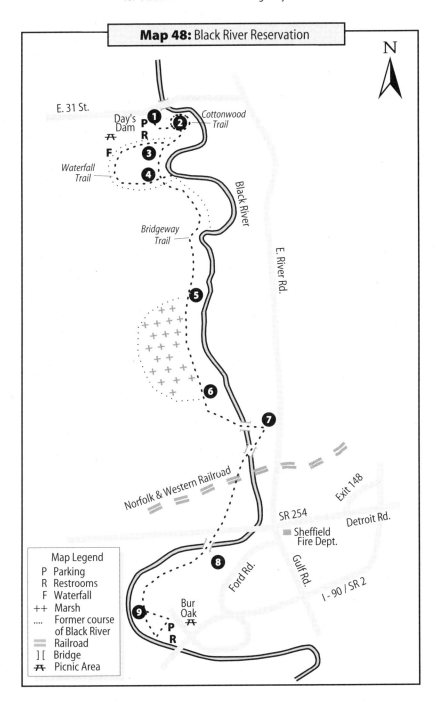

Map 48: Black River Reservation

N

E. 31 St.

Day's
Dam

P
R

Cottonwood
Trail

F

Waterfall
Trail

Bridgeway
Trail

Black River

E. River Rd.

Norfolk & Western Railroad

SR 254

Sheffield
Fire Dept.

Exit 148

Detroit Rd.

Ford Rd.

Gulf Rd.

I - 90 / SR 2

Bur
Oak

Map Legend
P Parking
R Restrooms
F Waterfall
++ Marsh
.... Former course
     of Black River
     Railroad
] [Bridge
⊼ Picnic Area

NOTE: Because this hike is on a north-south linear trail with a substantial round-trip distance of 6 miles, you may optionally park a second car at Bur Oak picnic area at the south end of the reservation to end this hike after 3 miles. To reach the reservation's south end from SR 254 west, follow the directions above to the Sheffield Fire Department intersection at SR. 254 (Detroit Rd.) and East River/Gulf Rd. Turn south onto Gulf Rd. Almost immediately (about 500 feet) turn right onto Ford Rd. and follow Ford Rd. downhill about a half-mile to the Bur Oak park entrance on the right.

1. Begin the walk at Day's Dam at the overlook to the Black River. Go south on the asphalt-paved walkway lined on either side with black Cleveland Shale (see Appendix A). This layer of shale was formed about 360 million years ago when the land that is now Ohio was covered by a warm, deep, stagnant inland sea. Thick extensive deposits of mud accumulated on the sea floor and eventually solidified; the sea drained away and left dry land, and the hardened mud became shale. Carbonized plant fragments and numerous fish fossils have been found in Cleveland Shale. Note how this soft rock breaks up into thin, sharp-edged, slaty fragments. Although it appears gray on the surface, the typical black color of this shale is revealed when it is broken in half. Here and there are brownish-red pieces that have been changed by weathering; occasionally marcasite or pyrite ("fool's gold") can be found in this shale.

2. At 0.3 mile on the left, a 0.1-mile woodchip-lined path, the Cottonwood Trail, leads to one of the largest trees in the area. At a fork in this trail, bear left to cross a small bridge to the huge cottonwood, surrounded by a viewing deck. The age of this tree is unknown, but it has been growing to a spectacular size for many years in this moist, rich bottom land. Return on the Cottonwood Trail to the paved Bridgeway Trail.

3. Cross a small meandering stream, a remnant of the river's former course, flowing eastward to join the Black River. The broad, open meadow on the right was the old river's flood plain, and the Cleveland Shale cliff, also on the right, was cut by the river's old channel.

4. Go off the main trail to follow another woodchip trail on the right (southwest), the Waterfall Trail. This path leads to a 25-foot-high waterfall over a Cleveland Shale cliff just below E. 36th St. Near the falls, bear left off the path to go near the foot of this little-known scenic spot. This half-mile trail continues along the old river channel to return to the Bridgeway Trail. On the right (west) in the center of this loop is a natural prairie, dominated in the summer by big bluestem, a native prairie grass.

Continue south on the Bridgeway Trail.

5. Just past the 0.5-mile marker, cross another arm of the old river channel.

6. Near the 1.5-mile marker on the right (west) is a large wetland. This marsh, offering a fine habitat for wildlife, represents another remnant of the river's former course. The Cleveland Shale cliff on the edge of the marsh was also cut by the river's previous course.

7. Cross two spectacular steel bridges over the Black River. These marvelous bridges were strategically placed to bypass the Cleveland Shale cliff on the right (west) and to provide beautiful views of the river below. Because the bridges are so high, you look down at the tops of some of the trees growing below.

Cleveland Shale, a Devonian-Age rock, contains few fossils but is famous, however, for its giant armored fish fossil, *Dunkleosteus*, found in Cuyahoga County. (This huge fossil is on exhibit at the Cleveland Museum of Natural History.)

Follow the trail under the Norfolk & Western Railroad trestle and the SR 254 bridge.

8. Cross a third steel pedestrian bridge at the 2-mile marker and enjoy more views of the river, which flows north to Lake Erie.

9. At the 2.5-mile marker, a paved side trail loops over to the river for a closer look at the stream and then leads back to the Bur Oak picnic and parking area.

At this point, end the hike if a second car is parked here or return on the Bridgeway Trail to the start of the walk at Day's Dam.

This hike was prepared with the generous assistance of Flora Burkholder and reviewed by Lorain County Metro Parks.

49 VERMILION RIVER RESERVATION

Distance: 2.5 miles

Hiking time: 2 hours

Description: Flat trails provide views of high shale cliffs, pass a few of the old mill sites along the river, and take quiet paths through woods and meadow. Over the years, the Vermilion River has changed course many times because of its vulnerability to storm floods. Several traces of its old channel can be seen along the Bacon Woods and Bluebird trails. The southeast section of the park provides magnificent views of the high Cleveland Shale cliff, views of wildlife at a waterfowl pond, and traces of the old mill town. The northwest section provides views of the river and its old course and trails, both wooded and open.

Directions: From I-90/SR 2, follow SR 2 west to the Vermilion/Sunnyside roads exit. (Be sure to stay on SR 2 where I-90 separates from SR 2, about 1.4 miles west of SR 57.) Follow signs for Vermilion Rd. by turning left (south) to cross over the highway and right (west) on Jerusalem Rd. to Vermilion Rd. Turn left (south) on Vermilion Rd. for about 1-1/2 miles to N. Ridge Rd. and turn right. After driving downhill, pass the Bacon Woods entrance on the right and cross the bridge over the Vermilion River. Take an immediate left turn into the parking area for the Benjamin Bacon Museum.
From Lorain take US 6 west to Baumhart Rd. and go south on Baumhart to N. Ridge Rd. Turn right (west) onto N. Ridge Rd. and follow it until the road seems to dead-end. Turn right (north) for 0.3 mile, passing Vermilion Rd. and enter the reservation straight ahead and downhill. Cross the bridge over the river and turn left into the Benjamin Bacon Museum parking area.
From I-90 (Ohio Turnpike) exit at 7A, Baumhart Rd. Go north on Baumhart Rd. 1.8 miles and turn left (west) onto N. Ridge Rd. After another 1.8 miles (where the road seems to dead-end), turn right (north) for 0.3 mile, passing Vermilion Rd. on the right and entering the reservation by continuing straight ahead and downhill. Cross the bridge over the river and turn left into the Benjamin Bacon Museum parking area.

Parking & restrooms: Park adjacent to the Benjamin Bacon Museum. Indoor restrooms are located at the new carriage barn behind the museum.

One of the most frequently visited parks in Lorain County is 950-acre Vermilion River Reservation. It is located alongside the Vermilion River,

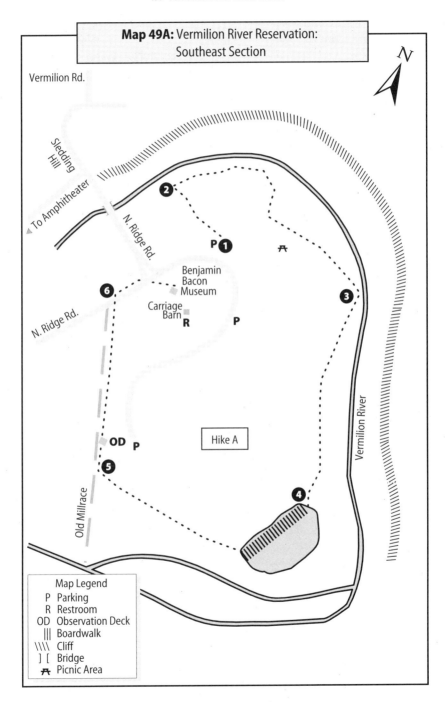

Map 49A: Vermilion River Reservation:
Southeast Section

Vermilion Rd.

Sledding Hill

To Amphitheater

N. Ridge Rd.

N. Ridge Rd.

Benjamin
Bacon
Museum

Carriage
Barn
R

P

P

Vermilion River

Hike A

OD P

Old Millrace

Map Legend
P   Parking
R   Restroom
OD Observation Deck
||| Boardwalk
\\\\ Cliff
] [Bridge
⌐ Picnic Area

south of SR 2 in Brownhelm Township, and about three miles south of the city of Vermilion. The park's outstanding feature is its spectacular 100-foot shale cliff composed of rock estimated to be 360 million years old. It has taken thousands of years of erosion to carve out the valley and expose these ancient cliffs. Also contributing to the park's popularity is its interesting past, when it was known as Mill Hollow. In its heyday in the 1860s, the hollow supported a busy mill town with many homes and commercial buildings.

In July 1817, Benjamin Bacon and other early settlers from New England established homes and built a sawmill, gristmill, and millrace at the neck of a wide bend in the Vermilion River. A church, school, and post office were soon added, and then a tannery, ashery, and blacksmith's shop. They called their settlement Brownhelm Mills; it later became known as Mill Hollow.

Benjamin Bacon's Greek Revival home (1845) and 110 acres of land were given to Lorain County Metro Parks in 1958 by the last Bacon descendant, Grace A. B. Demuth. Now fully restored with period furnishings, the Benjamin Bacon Museum is open to the public during the summer months (800-LCM-PARK). It is listed on the National Register of Historic Places.

Annual events that occur in this reservation are Pioneer Days Festival, on the second weekend in September, and Keel Haulers Canoe Race, on the last Sunday in March. This race starts eight miles upriver in Birmingham and ends in the southeast section of the park.

HIKE A: SOUTHEAST SECTION

1. Start at the carriage barn for information about activities and programs in this and other Lorain County Metro Parks. This new barn was recently constructed with a pegged timber frame.

If the Benjamin Bacon Museum is open, it is worthwhile to take a tour (for information call 800-LCM-PARK). Modeled on New England architecture of the time, the central portion of this 2-1/2 story house was built in 1845; a wing and summer kitchen were added later. The mill room off the main entry served as Mr. Bacon's office, where he bought timber, wheat, corn, and oats, and sold flour, horse feed, and lumber. This room also was a social center and courtroom—Bacon was a Justice of the Peace for Brownhelm Mills. Other downstairs rooms are a parlor, bedroom, dining room and kitchen; upstairs there are four bedrooms. The summer kitchen wing to the north served as woodshed, milkhouse, and wash house.

2. From the west end of the parking area walk north toward the river's edge and the Cleveland Shale cliff. The path is on the grassy embankment and in and out of the trees along the river's edge. Because of beach erosion, it is not usually possible to walk along the beach, especially if the water is high.

The almost-vertical Cleveland Shale cliff has been carved by the Vermilion River over many millennia. It took 100 million years for the sediments that comprise these rocks to accumulate at the bottom of an ancient ocean floor during the Devonian Age (see Appendix A).

The lower two-thirds of this 100-foot-high cliff is composed of thin layers of dark, slaty Cleveland Shale. The upper third of this cliff is Bedford Formation. In sequence, from bottom to top, it consists of a thin layer of grayish shale, then a protruding layer of sandstone, then a thick layer of soft, grayish-red shale. The sandstone is composed of fine sand and silt particles strongly cemented together to form very hard rock. The reddish-hued shale tints the cliff reddish-orange when it washes down in a rainstorm. (This shale is thought to have caused early inhabitants to name the river Vermilion, French for reddish-orange.) Glacial deposits and soil form the cliff's top layer.

Sometimes found along the edge of the river are small "turtle rocks." These are concretions of a particular form, called septaria by geologists, that have fallen out of the Cleveland Shale layers; they resemble rusty-brown turtle shells with prominent veins. (The "turtle" appearance is a result of water having been expelled from a colloidal mass, leaving a shrinking center and cracking of the surface.)

Occasionally found here are iron concretions of various shapes and siltstones or "flow-stones" that originally formed contorted masses in the sediments of the ancient sea. These stones solidified into unusual shapes and later fell from the Bedford Formation layer in the top portion of the cliff.

"Fool's gold," composed of the minerals pyrite and marcasite, may also be found as small nodules protruding from fallen slabs of Cleveland Shale. Often found near the base of Cleveland Shale are whitish limestone rocks that appear to be fossils (some resemble a large tooth) but are actually part of a thin layer of crystallized limestone that produces this unusual pattern.

3. Continue along the mowed grass. Note the various colors in the cliff: white, black, gray, red, and yellowish-brown. Some of these tints are a result of the reddish shale running down, some from soil washing down, and others from iron and sulphur compounds exposed to air and erosion. Plants have started growing in the slope created by an accumulation of rocks and debris having fallen down. Springs emerge from the shale at various points, allowing moss and algae to grow. In winter, especially January, these springs freeze into spectacular icicle formations, and ice falls along the cliff faces.

4. Walk toward the pond, then take the boardwalk/observation deck across it. Any of several varieties of waterfowl may be enjoying the pond. Follow the boardwalk across the pond to the river's edge.

Near the water's edge is shale that is bluish, very soft, and easily broken. This 360-million-year-old Chagrin Shale lies beneath the Cleveland Shale and is the oldest exposed rock in northeast Ohio (see Appendix A).

Turn right, heading toward the picnic shelter to find the path going north. This path leads to a wooden walkway/observation deck overlooking the old millrace.

5. The millrace was originally a ditch built in 1825 to cut across the horseshoe bend of the Vermilion River. The race diverted water north to supply power to a sawmill and gristmill on N. Ridge Rd. South of here, at the river's edge where the stream flows eastward, a mill dam was constructed to raise the level of the river, thus enabling water to enter the millrace.

At the wooden walkway is a concrete dam that blocks the millrace; it was built to keep N. Ridge Rd. from washing away when the river flooded. The road, put through after the mill ceased operation in 1900, replaced a bridge over the millrace.

Continue on the path alongside the millrace north to N. Ridge Rd. On the left, just before crossing the road, is the site of the original Brownhelm Mills blacksmith shop. The site of the original sawmill was opposite, on the west side of N. Ridge Rd.

CAUTION: Cross N. Ridge Rd. carefully, as there is fast-moving traffic here.

6. A few yards down the west side of the road and into the woods is the site of the original gristmill built by Benjamin Bacon for grinding wheat, oats, and corn into flour and meal. The mill was in operation from 1820 to 1876, when it burned down. A year later it was replaced by a three-story building with the latest milling equipment that used steam power to accommodate times when the water was low or the river was iced over. Only an old foundation remains.

Return to the parking area past the Benjamin Bacon Museum.

A short walk (or drive) takes you to trails at the northwest end of the reservation. Exit from the museum area and cross the bridge over the Vermilion River again. Take the first park entry road on the left and continue to the last parking area, near the trail information display area.

In the winter months, bald eagles may be seen in this part of Vermilion River Reservation, as they often nest near here.

HIKE B: NORTHWEST SECTION

7. Park near the trail information display area. After visiting the displays, begin the walk on the Bacon Woods Trail.

NOTE: There are *two* entrances to the Bacon Woods Trail. Take the trail to the northeast, the trail entrance that is closest to the cliff on the right. (The other is the path that you will be returning on.)

8. Continue on the Bacon Woods Trail, a wide gravel path. Considerable damage was done to the trees along this trail by a 1992 tornado that opened up the woods to more light and sun, thus changing the vegetation. The wet ground is caused by frequent flooding along the river plain and poor drainage of the soil. This moist environment supports beech and maple trees, some of which have been uprooted or had their tops twisted and snapped off in the tornado. Here also are recent vegetation changes in the growth of plants and smaller trees. Other trees that grow here are the sycamore, with its mottled white, green, and brown bark, black walnut, Ohio buckeye, box elder, tulip, and American elm. Spring wildflowers are especially abundant along this trail.

9. Stay to the right (east) on the Bacon Woods Trail where a trail goes off to the left. Cross a wooden boardwalk. These new walkways have been placed over swampy land that is prone to flooding; at an earlier period, the river flowed over this land.

10. Spicebush may be found along here. It is recognized by its yellow flowers in the spring, red berries in the fall, and spicy fragrance of leaves and twigs when crushed.

Sensitive fern also thrives in this moist environment. This fern has nearly opposite pinnae and grows with a separate fertile stalk alongside its fronds.

Black and honey locust trees grow abundantly here and can be differentiated by the size of their seed pods: black locust pods are small (2-4 inches long), while honey locust pods are much longer (8-16 inches). Both trees have short spines on the trunk and limbs. Black locust is an introduced species brought here by early settlers because its hard wood was useful in making fence posts and poles. Now it is an important tree for erosion control.

Poison ivy is plentiful in this woodland and has twined itself up some of the locust trees with a thick, twisting stem. Other large vines that grow well here are grape vines, which sometimes form giant swings, and Virginia creeper vines, distinguished from poison ivy by having five leaflets rather than three.

11. After crossing the short second boardwalk you will find the Bluebird Trail on the right. Follow the path a few steps to the open meadow, then take the branch to the left to walk the loop path in a clockwise direction. This open area used to be a farm field where, until the 1970s, corn and soybeans grew.

Birding is excellent in this meadow and river flood plain. Black locust trees have gained a strong foothold here, and wild roses, cow parsnips, blackberry bushes, and a variety of summer wildflowers enjoy the open sunshine and rich soil. Ground nut, also called wild bean, is especially abundant along this trail. The pungent fragrance of its flower clusters is quite noticeable in August.

Side trails on the left lead over to the old river channel. A new river

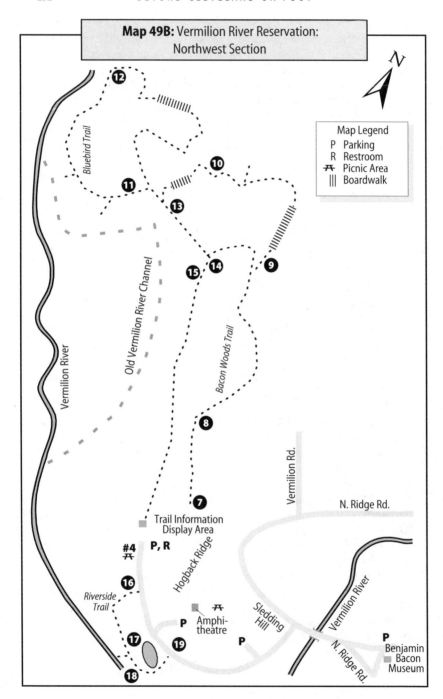

Map 49B: Vermilion River Reservation:
Northwest Section

Bluebird Trail

Map Legend
P   Parking
R   Restroom
⊼   Picnic Area
||| Boardwalk

Old Vermilion River Channel

Vermilion River

Bacon Woods Trail

Trail Information
Display Area

#4

P, R

Hogback Ridge

Vermilion Rd.

N. Ridge Rd.

Riverside
Trail

Amphi-
theatre

Sledding
Hill

Vermilion River

P

N. Ridge Rd.

P
Benjamin
Bacon
Museum

channel was created to the west during a huge flood in 1969. The old channel still carries water when the river is high but is often dry with only a scattering of water holes. Just ahead is a pleasant view of the Vermilion River on the left.

12. The wide mowed path of the Bluebird Trail is especially enjoyable for cross-country skiing in the winter as it is flat and only about 3/4 mile long. A new boardwalk crosses a muddy area where it is thought the river channel may have lain at one time.

13. Meet the end of the loop and leave the Bluebird Trail by turning left on the short connector, then bear right (south) to enter the woods on another section of the Bacon Woods Trail.

On both sides of the trail is beautiful Ostrich Fern, here thriving in wet soil and reaching 5-7 feet in height. Note the smaller fertile frond, which is stiff and woody, growing alongside the much taller sterile fronds. The fertile fronds remain all winter after the leafy fronds have been killed; they release their spores the following spring, a feature unique to this particular fern. (Most other ferns release their spores the same season that they are produced.)

14. Turn left (east) on a connector trail for 100 feet to briefly see an old hollow sycamore tree that is still alive, though its center is gone. Names and dates have been carved on the tree's south side but are nearly obliterated by the tree's growth rings around the scar.

15. Retrace your steps to the Bacon Woods Trail and turn left (south) to walk parallel to the old Vermilion River channel (on the right). Continue south on the path, passing trees twisted and cracked off by the 1992 tornado, to return to the trail information display area.

Continue south on the road past picnic shelter No. 4.

16. Turn right onto the wide, grassy trail located south of picnic shelter No. 4 and north of the pond. Follow this trail westward a short distance to the Riverside Trail, identified by old blue blazes. Turn left (south) onto this section of the now mostly eroded Riverside Trail. In the spring the wildflowers are beautiful along this riverside path.

17. Of interest on this trail are ice scars on the upstream (southeastern) faces of some of the larger trees, such as sycamore and cottonwood. The river flows from south to north, and in late winter or early spring blocks of ice flow down the flooded river and are forcefully jammed against trees, causing damage to the bark. A fungus then enters the wound, causes the tree to rot, and eventually it dies. Many trees along the river have been lost.

18. Near the end of the trail, follow a side path to the right (south) to the stone beach of the river, and a good view of the Cleveland Shale cliff. Seepage of water from the layers of shale form spectacular ice falls and giant icicles in January. Return to the trail. Bear right and uphill to the grassy area just south of the small pond, where the trail ends.

19. After reaching the pond, turn left (north) and head back to the parking area near the trail information display area or return to the Benjamin Bacon Museum.

Flora Burkholder, hiker and geologist, supplied substantial information for this chapter, hiked the trail with and without the author, and carefully reviewed material for accuracy. This chapter was also reviewed by Lorain County Metro Parks.

50 CARLISLE RESERVATION

Distance: 5.3 miles

Easy

Hiking time: 2-3/4 hours

Description: The trails in the reservation are flat or gently rolling. The most interesting landscape feature of Carlisle Reservation is the West Branch of the Black River and several creeks that feed it.
This hike consists of three loop hikes—a short loop north of the Visitor Center and two longer loops near the equestrian center to its west of the Visitor Center.

Directions: From I-480 west take the exit marked SR 10/Oberlin. Follow US 20/SR 10 west to the exit for SR 301 (LaGrange Rd.). Drive south on SR 301 about 0.5 mile to Nickel Plate-Diagonal Rd. (SR 27). Turn right on Nickel Plate-Diagonal Rd. (opposite the Fire Station) and follow it about 1.5 miles to the Carlisle Visitor Center entrance on the right. (You will pass the Duck Pond Picnic Area entrance on the right *before* reaching the main entrance.)
From Sheffield, Elyria, and Lorain's east side, take Rte. 301 south. Just past US 20/SR 10, turn right onto Nickel Plate-Diagonal Rd., then follow the directions above. From the center of Lorain take SR 57 south, bypassing Elyria, then turn right (south) on US 20/SR 10 and follow the directions above. From Lorain's west side, take SR 58 south to Russia Rd. and turn left. Continue east on Russia Rd. until it ends. Turn left then right onto LaGrange Rd. (SR 301). Go 2 miles south to Nickel Plate-Diagonal Rd. and follow the directions above.
From Akron take I-76/US 224 west to Lodi, then SR 83 north to SR 303 at Belden. Turn left (west) on SR 303 past LaGrange to Nickel Plate Rd. Turn right (north) on this road. As it bends northeast, it becomes Nickel Plate-Diagonal Rd. The park entrance will be on the left.

Parking & restrooms: At the Carlisle Visitor Center.

Lorain County's Carlisle Reservation is located south of Elyria and east of Oberlin. The West Branch of the Black River courses west to east through Carlisle's 1,720 acres of wooded forests, meadows, and lowlands. Approximately eight miles of hiking and bridle trails are maintained in the park. Cross-country skiing is popular on Carlisle's trails, as well as in nearby Forest Hills Golf Center.

The park contains a beautiful new visitor and administrative center with a large wildlife observation area, nature exhibits, a children's nature

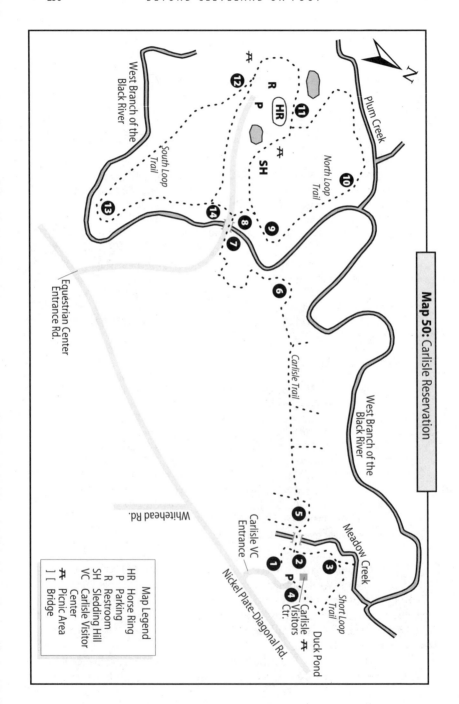

Map 50: Carlisle Reservation

Map Legend

HR	Horse Ring
P	Parking
R	Restroom
SH	Sledding Hill
VC	Carlisle Visitor Center
🌲	Picnic Area
] [	Bridge

room, seasonal displays, and a nature store. Here park naturalists provide maps, programs, guided hikes, and information about all of Lorain County's parks. The center is open daily from 8 a.m.-4:30 p.m. at 12882 Diagonal Rd., LaGrange, OH 44050; 216-458-5121 or 800-LCM-PARK.

An equestrian center is located west of the West Branch of the Black River and is open to people owning their own horses. On weekends during September and October, Lorain County Metro Parks offers free 30-minute, horse-drawn hayrides along these trails. Although designed primarily for horseback riders, the equestrian trails (a 1.5-mile north loop and a 1.1-mile south loop) are eminently suitable for hiking. Hikers are cautioned to step off the trail when encountering a horse and rider, and to remain still and quiet until they have passed, so as not to frighten these skittish animals.

NOTE: Because of ongoing trail construction in Carlisle Reservation, please inquire at the visitor center about trail conditions.

The West Branch of the Black River and Meadow Creek contain dark-colored water caused by mud and silt dissolved in it from constantly eroding stream banks. The West Branch cuts across a pre-glacial river valley that once was 192 feet deep and almost a mile wide in places. When glaciers pushed across this area, they brought mud, silt, and sand, all of which filled in the old valley as the glaciers melted. The present West Branch of the Black River follows the same course it started with the melting of the glaciers; it has now cut a valley about 35 to 55 feet deep in Carlisle Reservation. The river continues to gouge out the leftover glacial debris above bedrock and leaves a very unstable, muddy valley that is prone to flooding after heavy rains.

The first inhabitants of this area were archaic Indians who lived here about 4,000 years ago, as revealed by spear points and flint scrapers that have been found in cultivated fields. Most of the Indian settlements occurred on higher ground away from the river's flood plain, as did those of later inhabitants. Farmers chose this area for settlement because of the fertile soil for crop growing. They cleared the tall timber (black walnut, cherry, and chestnut trees), built lumber mills and homes, and used the fields for pastures. Occasionally the stumps of these tall trees can be seen off the trail. Today the land is being left undisturbed, to allow it to return to its original forested condition. The woods provide a fine habitat for white-tailed deer and other wildlife species.

1. Begin the hike at the south end of the parking lot. Enter the 0.4-mile Short Loop Trail, a handicapped-accessible gravel trail. Follow the path as it curves northwest. The small, meandering stream on the left is Meadow Creek, a tributary of the West Branch of the Black River; it is flowing north toward the river.

2. Stay on the Short Loop Trail, passing the trail junction and bridge on the left.

3. Continue northwest. At a trail intersection, stay to the right as the path curves around to the east. (The trail on the left leads down to the river. You may wish to take it for a closer view of the stream.)

Circle around the loop to now head southeast. This path is also called the "Halloween Trail," because it is traditionally used for a Halloween evening hike, when the path is lined with goblins, ghosts, and pumpkins.

Pass a set of steps on the left. The trail now gradually ascends a slope.

4. Continue on the main trail, which leads back to the visitor center.

Cross the parking area south of the visitor center to enter the same trail (Note #1), and continue to the trail junction described in Note #2. Now turn left here, crossing the bridge over Meadow Creek.

5. A newly-created wetland is just over the bridge. You are now on the Carlisle Trail, which you will follow westward. Avoid several side trails to the right and left.

6. At the power line, the Carlisle Trail curves left (south). (Another trail goes off to the left.) Soon you will follow alongside an old barbed-wire farm fence that marks the edge of the woods above the steep bank of the West Branch of the Black River.

7. Continue south and southwest on the trail. A pond and large maintenance building appear ahead on the left. Soon the path leads down to the entrance road to the equestrian center.

8. Turn right on the road and cross the bridge over the river. Take an immediate right turn on a path to get to the North Loop Horse Trail.

9. Once on this wide gravel trail, follow the loop counterclockwise. This section of the North Loop Horse Trail offers some very scenic views of the West Branch of the Black River.

CAUTION: If you meet a horse and rider on this trail, step off to the side and remain still until they have passed.

10. The trail enters the forest above the river. Note the unusual sycamore tree on the right with its bifurcated trunk, exposed by constant erosion of the soil along the riverbank. The path now circles around to the west to the confluence of Plum Creek with the West Branch.

11. Continue alongside Plum Creek—this is the same creek that flows through the town of Oberlin (Ch. 47). Reach a trail junction between the Horse Ring and a large fishing pond and turn right (west). Continue on the trail past new restrooms and a picnic and parking area.

12. At the sign just off the road, turn right (southeast) onto the South Loop Horse Trail (marked with red and blue). Continue across a meadow and alongside the West Branch.

13. The path enters the forest above another bend in the West Branch and then circles north.

14. At the approach to the entrance road, go off the main trail to reach the road.

Once on the road, turn right and cross the bridge. Reenter the Carlisle Trail going eastward. Follow the same path previously hiked (in reverse), avoiding any of the side trails off the main Carlisle Trail until you again reach the visitor center.

This chapter was prepared with the assistance of Flora Burkholder, who walked and re-walked the trails, clarified descriptions and maps, and reviewed the final narrative. Personnel of Lorain County Metro Parks also reviewed this chapter.

51 FINDLEY STATE PARK

Distance: 5 miles

Moderate

Hiking time: 2-1/2 hours

Description: This hike follows trails that are generally flat, but includes two very short, steep hills near the beginning and another short hill later on. A wide variety of trees and pretty views of Findley Lake make this a very enjoyable hike in almost any season.

The walk follows a loop around the lake on various trails, beginning and ending on a short section of the Buckeye Trail. It crosses the north end of the lake on an earthen dam and affords a view of a large spillway.

(An optional 1.5-mile, self-guided nature trail created by the Black River Audubon Society begins in the woods just east of the camp check-in station. Its 10 stops follow part of the old Wyandot Trail, the Meadow Trail Loop, and the Buckeye/Hickory Grove Trail.)

Directions: From I-480 west exit onto SR 10 (Oberlin). Take US 20/SR 10 to SR 58. Turn left (south) on SR 58 (Oberlin Rd.). From this intersection it is about 9 miles to the park entrance on the left, 2 miles past Wellington.

On I-76/US 224, go west to Lodi, then take SR 83 north to Chatham. Turn left (west) on SR 162 to Huntington. Turn right (north) on SR 58 to Findley State Park on the right.

On SR 58, the park entrance is 2 miles south of Wellington.

Parking & restrooms: After entering the park, turn right onto Rd. No. 3 and follow it around to the park office. Park in the parking area south of the office building. Restrooms are here.

Findley State Park, located near Wellington, is an 838-acre tract of forested land surrounding 93-acre Findley Lake. It offers hiking, camping, boating, hunting, fishing, swimming, and picnicking. Park regulations pertaining to these activities can be obtained from the Park Office at 25381 SR 58 South, Wellington, OH 44090-9208; 216-647-4490.

The park, named for Judge Guy Findley, a local conservationist, offers nearly 10 miles of hiking trails, including a portion of the blue-blazed Buckeye Trail. Judge Findley purchased this land in 1936 and donated it to Ohio as a perpetual state forest for timber production and experimental foresting. The Division of Forestry then supervised the planting of nearly half a million trees by the Civilian Conservation Corps. By 1950 the park was transferred to Ohio's Division of Parks and Recreation, a dam was

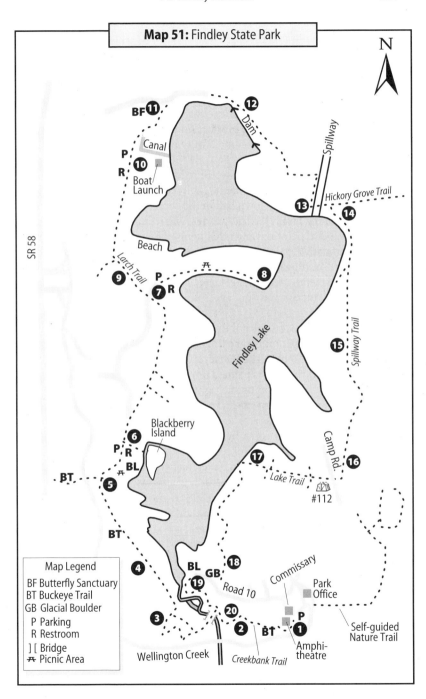

Map 51: Findley State Park

N

BF ⑪

⑫

Dam

Spillway

Canal

P
⑩
R

Boat
Launch

Beach

Hickory Grove Trail

⑬

⑭

SR 58

Larch Trail

⑨

P
⑦ R

🏕

⑧

Findley Lake

⑮

Spillway Trail

Blackberry
Island

⑥
P R
BL

BT

⑤

⑰

Camp Rd.

⑯

Lake Trail

🏕
#112

BT

④

BL
⑲

GB

⑱

Road 10

Commissary

Park
Office

Map Legend
BF Butterfly Sanctuary
BT Buckeye Trail
GB Glacial Boulder
 P Parking
 R Restroom
] [Bridge
🏕 Picnic Area

③

⑳

② BT ①

Self-guided
Nature Trail

P

Amphi-
theatre

Wellington Creek

Creekbank Trail

built, 93-acre Findley Lake created, and further developments made that led to the present public recreation area. The park's beautiful forest, consisting mainly of white and red oak, red maple, white ash, black cherry, red and white pine, and American beech trees, is a regrowth secondary forest on abandoned dairy farmland.

Although this section of Lorain County was settled slowly, by the early 1800s New Englanders had begun to develop the present town of Wellington. Dairy farming and cheese production were the dominant industries of the area and eventually Lorain County became known as the cheese capital of America.

The present town of Wellington still reflects a New England influence. Many of its buildings are listed on the National Register of Historic Places, including the ornate 1885 town hall in the center of town. At the Herrick Memorial Library, on E. Herrick Ave. near Main St., is a large collection of Archibald Willard paintings and other items of historical interest. Willard, a Wellington native, painted the classic Revolutionary War image called *The Spirit of '76*. Information about the painter is also preserved in the Spirit of '76 Museum on N. Main St., just north of Herrick Ave. (open free of charge on Saturdays and Sundays from 2:30-5 p.m.).

1. Enter the Buckeye Trail at the edge of the woods west of the parking lot and south of the Commissary Building. The trail entrance is near the Naturalist Activity Center. The Buckeye Trail is blazed with two-inch-by-six-inch light blue rectangles painted on trees. Follow the blue blazes west past the camp amphitheater on the right.

2. At 0.3 mile the trail meets an old woods road. Turn left (west) here onto this wide path. Cross a bridge over Wellington Creek, which flows into Findley Lake at this point. In 1954, the creek was dammed up north of here to create this beautiful, one-mile-long lake. Metal bird boxes standing in the water are nesting sites for wood ducks. Cross another small wooden bridge over a side creek. Maple, ash, and pawpaw trees thrive in this habitat.

3. At 0.5 mile the trail bends to the right (north) to go up a steep hill and, further on, a ravine.

Option: an alternate trail on the left, marked with white tree blazes, goes around these two steep sections.

Tall red pine trees were planted here in the 1950s to reforest the former farmland.

At 0.6 mile in the ravine on the left (north slope) is trash dumped here years ago by farmers, who customarily disposed of their rubbish this way, leaving myriad debris. At the top of the hill the Buckeye Trail is rejoined by the white trail on the left.

4. Views of Findley Lake begin to appear on the right. Continue north on the Buckeye Trail through a pine forest. After descending to the low-lands, note evidence of beaver activity along here. Their ever-growing incisor teeth maintain a sharp edge that ensures their ability to down small trees for eating and for construction of dams and large domed lodges. Aspen, willow, and birch trees are their favorite foods.

5. At 0.9 mile reach Picnic Pines picnic area. (Here the BT veers off to the left and continues its journey westward.) Continue straight ahead (north), heading to the right of the wooden restroom building, then cross a footbridge to a large parking lot for the boat launching area.

6. Walk through the parking and picnic area toward its north end. Near the restroom, unmarked side trails lead to the right (east) down the slope for a view of Blackberry Island. This is the only island in Findley Lake. Shells of large lake snails are often seen along the edge of the lake.

North of the restroom, take the unmarked trail straight ahead, and bear right at the north end of the parking lot. At the next two forks in the path, bear left. These two side trails lead down to the lake.

7. At 1.3 miles turn right on a road leading to Peninsula picnic area. Here there are picnic tables, a picnic shelter, and a new restroom building. A lovely circular grove of white pines is straight ahead.

8. Continue out onto the peninsula for beautiful views of the water in all directions. Again, along the edge of the lake there may be large fresh water snails. Attractive bigtooth aspen and pine trees have been planted here.

9. Return to the parking area and turn right to enter the Larch Trail at the southwest end of the parking lot. This trail goes northwest and is marked by a sign pointing to the beach.

10. At the 2-mile point on this hike you will pass the swimming beach and concession area. To the left of the restroom building note the beautiful larch trees, which drop their needles in the winter.

Pass the boat dock and a small canal used for launching boats (electric motors only) and canoes.

11. Enter a gravel path which leads northeast into the woods to a park road.

Just to the west of the road/trail juncture is a sanctuary for the Duke's Skipper butterfly. A relatively large colony of this rare butterfly was first discovered in 1963. The small, brown, inconspicuous butterfly feeds on wetland sedge, a plant found only in this environment that resembles tall blades of grass. It is of interest to butterfly enthusiasts not only because it is uncommon but because the distribution of its small colonies is a mystery. It is theorized that the species made its way north after the last glacial age, inhabiting sedge meadows that are the result of glacial carving. (Collecting this extremely rare species is prohibited.)

Turn right (east) on the service road to the top of the 1954 earthen dam.

12. Cross the top of the dam, stopping to take a look at the peninsula just visited lying in the middle of the lake. The concrete house near the dam is a floodgate; it is periodically opened to allow the lake to drain down to a lower level. This operation permits removal of silt in the lake and allows park staff to make repairs to the beach or other shoreline facilities. The deepest part of the lake, at 25 feet, is here at the north end.

13. At the end of the dam, bear left (east) to walk over and view the spillway. In the spring, this grassy meadow becomes a stream-bed for floodwaters that flow into Wellington Creek to the north, which then flows into the West Branch of the Black River.

Walk south along the top of the spillway toward the lake, then turn left (east) and cross the bottom of the dry spillway.

14. (3.0 miles) Pass the marked Hickory Grove Trail on the left and turn right (south) onto the Spillway Trail (unmarked), following the east edge of the lake.

At a fork in the trail, stay to the left as the trail curves around the edge of the lake. There are fine views of the water here.

15. Follow the wide path past an area cleared for utility poles.

16. The trail exits at a blacktop camp road (3.5 miles). Cross the road to a post marking campsite No. 112. Enter the woods to the right (west) to follow the Lake Trail. Continue straight ahead on this trail past side trails to the camping area to the south and the lake to the north.

17. Go up a short hill ahead, passing a trail to the left, and continue westward on the wide Lake Trail until reaching a lookout point overlooking the lake. Here are more fine scenic views of Findley Lake.

The trail now narrows and turns left (southwest) through a lovely forest area and continues along the shoreline.

18. Reach Rd. No. 10, a park road leading to the boat launch area. Turn right (west) and follow this road past a large glacial boulder (on the right) left here after the last glacier retreated from Ohio about 12,000 years ago. The reed grass growing near the lake often reaches 10 feet in height.

19. Turn left (south) off Rd. No. 10 at the sign for the Creekbank Trail and enter this path following the edge of Wellington Creek.

(OPTIONAL: In the spring or after a hard rainfall this trail may be too wet and muddy to walk on. If so, take Rd. No. 10 past the glacial boulder and past roads No. 13 and No. 12 to a sign for the commissary. Turn right to return to the parking area where the hike started.)

The Creekbank Trail bends away from the creek to follow another loop of the stream and then returns alongside the main creek.

20. At 4.4 miles reach the Buckeye Trail (BT) again. Turn left (southeast), bypassing the bridge over Wellington Creek that was crossed earlier (Note #2).

Follow the blue-blazed BT eastward in the reverse direction from that hiked earlier. Watch for a sharp right turn where the BT goes off the wider old woods road. Continue southeast until the trail exits at the parking area.

This hike was prepared with the generous assistance of Flora Burkholder, who carefully reviewed the material, helped map the trails, and hiked with the author.

52 FRENCH CREEK RESERVATION

Distance: 2.1 miles

Moderate

Hiking time: 1-1/4 hours

Description: This hike follows paved or gravel trails over moderately undulating terrain past French Creek, Fish Creek, and Sugar Creek. The trails go through woods, along old farm lanes, and past outcrops of ancient Cleveland Shale. The farm lanes were first used by the original owner Jabez Burrell in 1815, and later by his descendants, who farmed the land until the 1940s. Of additional interest in the reservation are traces of an old railroad that once ran through the property.

Directions: From I-90 take Exit 151 to SR 611 (Lorain-Avon Rd.). Go west on SR 611 (Colorado Ave.) for 2-1/2 miles (passing SR 301) to the French Creek Nature Center entrance. The building is somewhat obscured behind the large grassy hill on the left.
From Lorain take SR 611 east past Lake Breeze Rd. to French Creek Nature Center on the right.

Parking & restrooms: At the nature center.

Beautiful French Creek Reservation, one of the Lorain County Metro Parks developed public recreation areas, is located on SR 611 in Sheffield, just east of Lorain. Its 428 forested acres include a nature center, two picnic shelters and a playground, and almost five miles of hiking and cross-country skiing trails. The Fish and Sugar creeks run through the park to join larger French Creek, which flows westward to eventually join the Black River on its way to Lake Erie. These park streams furnish a rich environment for wildlife and vegetation and provide the area with scenic wetlands, ravines, and exposed rock formations.

French Creek Nature Center, built in 1990, continues the ongoing development of this park, which was acquired in 1964. This fine center offers nature exhibits, a gift shop, library, program hall, classrooms, and a wildlife observation area. A periodical called *The Arrowhead* describes the many nature activities, programs, and guided hikes offered by the center. The building is open daily from 8 a.m. until 4:30 p.m.

Information pertaining to any of Lorain County's parks may be obtained from Lorain County Metro Parks, 12882 Diagonal Rd., LaGrange, OH 44050, 216-458-5121 or 800-LCM-PARK.

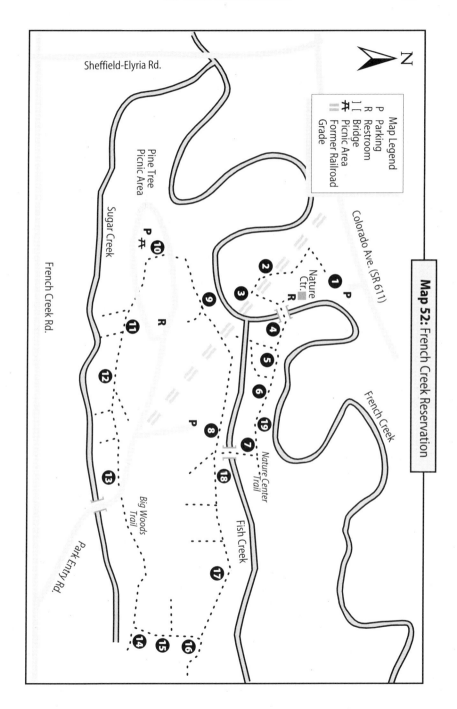

Map 52: French Creek Reservation

1. The hike begins at the west edge of the entry road parking lot on the Nature Center Trail, an asphalt-paved path. This trail follows part of an abandoned railroad grade that once ran from northwest to southeast through the reservation.

Bear left at a Y fork.

2. On the left is a line of old osage orange trees marking the location of a former farm fence row. This hedge tree was frequently used to mark boundaries; its leaves are ovate with smooth margins that turn bright yellow in the fall. The inedible round fruit, three to five inches in diameter, oozes a milky juice when squeezed.

3. A fenced overlook of French Creek valley marks the location of an old railroad bridge that once crossed the creek and valley, part of the abandoned railroad that extended across the property.

4. The path goes toward the nature center and a set of steps down to the valley. Cross a bridge over French Creek and note the layers of dark Cleveland Shale exposed by the stream. This 360-million-year-old shale layer is very dark because it contains carbonized plant and other organic material (see Appendix A).

5. The trail ascends and reaches a fork. Turn right (south) on the unmarked, mulched trail to the right (the green-marked Nature Center Trail bears left).

Where this mulched trail begins to turn left, look below to note where Fish Creek enters larger French Creek. (Avoid taking the trail on the right that goes down to Fish Creek.)

At the next junction, turn sharply left to stay on the mulched trail. Continue on the wide mulched trail as it loops back along the ridge to the Nature Center Trail.

6. Turn right (east) to rejoin the Nature Center Trail. Pass another trail intersection and continue on the green Nature Center Trail to the right (south) toward Fish Creek.

7. Cross the bridge over Fish Creek and the observation platform and boardwalk; continue uphill on the steps.

8. At the top of the hill, turn right (southwest) at a trail intersection. (Avoid taking the boardwalk ahead.) This now is the gravel-paved, yellow-blazed Big Woods Trail.

The path bends to the south and crosses the former railroad grade.

9. Pass a trail on the left. Continue ahead to the Pine Tree Picnic Area. The lovely pine trees at this picnic spot were planted about 1950 in former Burrell farm fields.

10. Near the picnic shelter is a Norway maple, called the Freedom Tree, that was planted in 1973 by local Girl Scouts. Beside it are two granite markers honoring servicemen who died in the Vietnam War.

11. Cross the parking area going southeast on the gravel path to stay on the Big Woods Trail.

12. Continue east on the main trail bypassing any of the trails on the right that lead down to Sugar Creek.

This wide trail is partly on the old Burrell farm road that connected their home west of this spot (on Sheffield-Elyria Rd.) with farm fields to the east. It was used by the family through the 1940s.

Captain Jabez Burrell of Sheffield, Massachusetts, purchased this land in 1815 from the Connecticut Land Company when it was still part of the Connecticut Western Reserve. After clearing the land, the Burrells settled here and kept the farm in the family until World War II. The 1825 Burrell family home, listed on the National Register of Historic Places, is still occupied and is not open to the public.

13. Reach a park road, the south entry to the park from French Creek Rd. This road was built on the old abandoned railroad grade, whose bridge abutments were seen earlier (Note #3).

Cross the road and continue eastward on the gravel path, still on the Big Woods Trail.

14. At the fence turn left (north) to continue on the gravel trail.

15. Continue northward through a young forest as the path soon curves toward the west. You will pass several trail junctures marking older woods trails that are now blocked with fencing.

16. Turn left (west) on the Big Woods Trail, now just above Fish Creek.

17. Pass trail intersections on the right and continue ahead on the main trail.

18. Where a parking area and shelter are nearby on the left, turn right (north) onto the Nature Center Trail again. Descend the steps, cross the boardwalk and Fish Creek bridge.

Bear left (west) at the intersection toward the Nature Center.

19. Continue on the Nature Center Trail as it descends the hill then rises to an observation deck for a view of French Creek and any wildlife that may be evident here.

Continue across the French Creek bridge and up the steps to return to the French Creek Nature Center.

This chapter was prepared with the generous assistance of Flora Burkholder, who carefully reviewed the material for accuracy and hiked the trails both with and without the author. This chapter was also reviewed by Lorain County Metro Parks.

53 ELYRIA'S CASCADE / ELYWOOD PARK

Distance: 4 miles for all three hikes (A, B, and C)   Moderate
Hiking time: 3-1/2 hours for all 3 hikes
Description: The trails in Cascade Park vary from flat to very steep.

Hike A requires a hike up a steep, rocky embankment (1.3 miles) and goes to West Falls and to several historic and natural features of the park, with names such as Ancient Falls, Bear's Den, Natural Bridge, Camel's Hump, Old Auto Trail, West Falls, Old Quarry, Shelter Cave, and Oyster Rock.

Hike B, across the Black River via the Automobile Ford, is a 1.3-mile woods trail in Elywood Park.

Hike C, on the Two Falls Trail, requires a short car ride to another park entrance road, off Lake Ave. This 1.2-mile round-trip walk goes to East Falls, Power Plant Ruins, Big Cave, and a view of West Falls from the opposite side.

Directions: From I-90/SR 2 west, take Exit 57 for Lorain-Elyria. Go south on SR 57 for 2 miles (passing I-80), then turn left (east) onto SR 57/113 (Northeast By-Pass). Continue east 0.4 mile to the tall, blue Elyria water tower, then turn right (south) onto Furnace St. Follow Furnace St. 0.6 mile, then turn left (east) into Hillsdale Court and descend on the park entry road to Cascade Park.

From I-77 take I-80 (Ohio Turnpike tollroad) west to Exit 8 (Elyria). Go south on SR 57 and turn left (east) onto SR 57/113 (Northeast Bypass), then follow the directions above.

From SR 204 (Elyria/Lake Ave.) go south to SR 113. Turn left (east) on SR 113/57 (Northeast Bypass) and follow the directions above.

Parking & restrooms: Park at the foot of the entrance hill in the first parking area on the left, just past the stop sign. Restrooms are near the trailhead to the south.

Both Cascade Park and adjacent Elywood Park are located in downtown Elyria at the confluence of the East and West Branches of the Black River. Cascade Park, which celebrated its centennial in 1994, is maintained by the Elyria Parks and Recreation Department (216-365-7101). It is also supported by a volunteer organization, Friends of Cascade Park. Smaller Elywood Park is also supported by these groups.

Cascade Park's 155 acres include short hiking trails in a deep gorge with two 40-foot waterfalls, a huge cave with stalactites, and many other features of historic and natural interest, most of which have been given

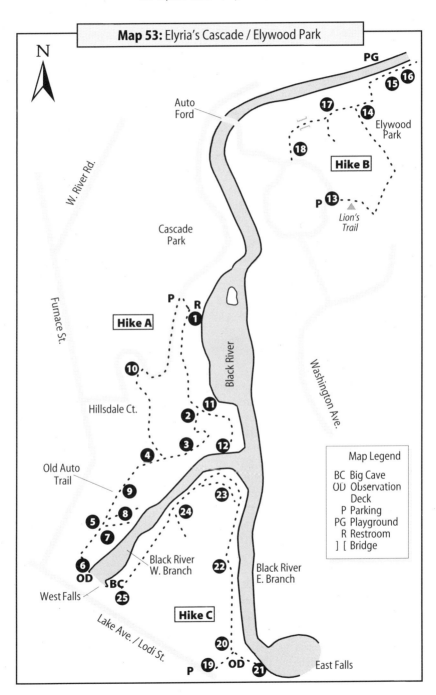

Map 53: Elyria's Cascade / Elywood Park

N

Auto Ford

W. River Rd.

PG

16
15

17
14

Elywood Park

18

Hike B

P 13
Lion's Trail

Cascade Park

Furnace St.

P   R
Hike A   1

10

Black River

Hillsdale Ct.

11

2

3

12

4

Old Auto Trail

9

8

23

5

24

7

6
OD
BC
West Falls   25

Black River W. Branch

Washington Ave.

22

Black River E. Branch

Map Legend

BC Big Cave
OD Observation Deck
P Parking
PG Playground
R Restroom
] [Bridge

Lake Ave. / Lodi St.

Hike C

20

P 19 OD 21   East Falls

descriptive names. A one-car-wide automobile ford of the Black River takes visitors to Elywood Park on the river's opposite side, where there are more short trails. Both parks offer picnic areas, playgrounds, and fishing in the Black River, but no swimming. A $6-million master plan for these two parks calls for a total renovation into a family recreation center by the turn of the century. A new nature center, new concession building, improved hiking trails, facilities for rollerskating, bicycling, canoeing, and other sports are planned.

Because the steep park entrance roads are closed in winter, and because the rocks and cliffs in the park can be slippery when wet or snow-covered, it is best to visit Cascade Park on a dry day in the spring, summer, or fall. The Auto Ford to Elywood Park is open only when the river water is low, usually in the summer and fall, and ordinarily does not allow a crossing on foot. Since this is a city park, it is best to visit between 10 a.m. and 2 p.m. to avoid traffic congestion on nearby roads. April and May are usually good times to observe the waterfalls, as they have their greatest flow in those months.

HIKE A: WEST FALLS

1. Walk south toward the restroom building and enter the trail. After about 100 feet, there is a sign pointing toward Ancient Falls. In the Black River on the left, note the large Berea Sandstone blocks that have fallen from the ledges above and the softer and older Bedford Formation (shale) that has eroded and undercut the sandstone (see Appendix A).

This sandstone was formed about 360 million years ago during the Devonian Age. Massive, thick delta deposits of sand were formed by freshwater streams carrying the sand to an ancient ocean covering the land that is now Ohio. This extensive layer of sand later hardened into rock and became erosion-resistant sandstone. It is called Berea Sandstone because so much of it was quarried in Berea, Ohio, known as the grindstone capital of the world. This very hard rock has been quarried in many places within 25 miles of Elyria, the best known of which is a 225-foot-thick layer quarried west of here in Amherst, Ohio.

Beneath Berea Sandstone lies older Bedford Formation (shale), formed from silt and mud deposited in the shallow ocean, also about 360 million years ago. Continue past an intersection on the left that goes down to the river.

2. The wide gravel trail leads to a Berea Sandstone arch, called Natural Bridge, probably formed about 18,000 years ago at the time of the final retreat of Ohio's last glacier. This is the location of the feature called Ancient Falls, which is now dry rock. The river once dropped over this precipice thousands of years ago.

The imminent confluence or meeting point of the East and West branches of the Black River is just behind this 45-foot sandstone ridge. The present waterfalls (East Falls and West Falls) of each branch have retreated over thousands of years, and both are now much farther upriver than they once were.

The flat rock at the base of the cliff is the former foundation of another park feature called Bear's Den. Here a fenced-in bear cage and shed housed a black bear from 1920 to the early 1970s. Over the years four different bears were kept here, an attraction that became popular with summertime tourists. Sophie, the last bear, died of old age in 1985. Ash-laden soil from the days when the park was occupied by Native Americans has been found underneath Bear's Den.

3. The trail turns to the right under the cliff and follows the path steeply uphill over the rocky ledge. About halfway up, turn left toward the cliff and take the cut sandstone steps to the top. You are now standing on narrow Natural Bridge. The West Branch of the Black River is below on the right. The top of the hill has been named Camel's Hump because its color, shape, and texture resemble that animal. This prominence is also called Lookout Point because from here one has a long view of the city of Elyria to the south and a panoramic view of the park in all directions when the leaves are down.

The pitted pattern on the surface of the large sandstone block on top of Camel's Hump has been formed by honeycomb weathering. This process involves rainwater dissolving the weaker "cementing" minerals (on the exposed area of the sandstone block) quicker than the more durable silica sand grains, thus developing a texture resembling a honeycomb. Honeycomb weathering is sometimes seen on conglomerate rocks as well as on sandstone.

The rounded boulders partially embedded in the soil are not native to this area. They were transported here thousands of years ago from the Precambrian Shield area of northern Canada by glacial action, then dropped in place when the glacier melted. The pressure of that mile-thick sheet of ice gouged and smoothed the pieces of rock carried along with it. Most of these boulders are granite, but gneiss and quartzite can also be found. Scratches called striae are sometimes visible on the glacially scoured "erratics."

CAUTION: Use considerable care on this partially fenced-in area, because it contains very loose, gravelly glacial soil. A continual process of erosion makes it extremely hazardous to venture close to the edge. (The Cascade-Elywood Park Master Plan calls for revegetation of Camel's Hump so as to slow the erosion rate of the loosely consolidated till composing this hill.)

When the leaves are off the trees, you can see the river confluence down below, where the East and West branches come together to form the Black

River. Also visible are the remains of two concrete structures that formerly crossed the West Branch—a footbridge near the confluence and the ford of the Old Auto Trail. This former vehicular road was used by cars driving around the park until a 1969 flood destroyed it.

Return to the flat, fenced-in area of the Natural Bridge where there are four trails. The trail to the far right is the one just ascended; the one next to it (to the south) goes uphill to the Old Auto Trail; the trail straight ahead goes 150 feet to a precipice overlooking the Old Quarry; the one on the far left descends steeply over a treacherous cliff.

4. Take the second trail to the Old Auto Trail. Turn left (southwest) when out on the old road and follow it down.

5. Partway down the hill stay to the right (southwest) to go off the road and follow a trail about 200 feet towards an Observation Deck overlooking West Falls (0.5 mile).

Underfoot and on the hillside to the right are pieces of old slag and glassy, rocky debris remaining from an 1832 iron foundry that existed on the top of the hill. Some of the shiny slag has a bluish cast to it from the high temperatures used to extract iron from the rock. The Old Auto Trail originally was used to bring ore and fuel to the foundry furnace, hence the name of Furnace St., which is just above this hill.

6. Several side paths lead downhill for views of the West Branch of the Black River, but continue to the observation deck, the optimum spot for viewing the falls.

In the spring, rather than two streams flowing over the ledge, the waterfall forms a single torrent. Across the river is spectacular Big Cave (visited on Hike C). The wide arc on either side of the waterfall is evidence of the size of the falls thousands of years ago. Large boulders have fallen into the river as a result of the falls' continual retreat southwestward. Here, again, Berea Sandstone has been undercut by weaker underlying Bedford Formation (shale) that has eroded more quickly, causing overhanging sandstone blocks to break off.

CAUTION: Do not take any of the trails going uphill on the left because they end at private property on Furnace St.

7. Retrace your steps from West Falls to the Old Auto Trail, passing the slag hill on the left. Bear right on the Old Auto Trail downhill alongside the river to its termination. Here are the remains of the automobile ford (washed out in 1969) that was used when the road carried people from one side of the park to the other.

CAUTION: Do not cross the river on this old concrete roadbed as it is extremely slippery due to growth of moss and algae.

Return uphill on the Old Auto Trail.

8. Continue ahead to an unmarked trail on the right that leads downhill to two more park features—Old Quarry and Shelter Cave.

The Old Quarry is on the left. During the 1880s, Berea Sandstone was quarried here for local building purposes. On the ledge above are dynamite grooves in the rock that were created when large sandstone blocks were blasted out for construction.

Continue ahead on this path to Shelter Cave on the left. Note the man-made stone and mortar column that seems to support the roof of the cave. It was built for just that reason—to prevent the collapse of the cracked, overhanging, rocky ledge of the shelter. (According to local history, two skeletons were found in the cave some years ago, the remains of bodies crushed by fallen rock slabs.)

9. Retrace your steps back to the trail junction (Note #8) and continue uphill on the Old Auto Trail. Continue to follow this trail to the park entry road off Hillsdale Ct., passing above the Old Quarry below on the right and private property on the left (1.3 miles).

10. The Berea Sandstone boulder on the park entry road contains a memorial plaque to Elyria Parks Superintendent John P. Machock for his 42 years with the Elyria Park System.

The crossbedding (lines) in the sandstone of this rock was made millions of years ago when the sand was deposited on sloping surfaces along the curving courses of shifting river channels, like wind-blown sand being deposited in the slope of a dune. Extensive deltas of sand were formed as these rivers entered the ancient ocean. Eventually this thick layer of sand solidified into rock (see Appendix A).

Follow the park entry road downhill to the point described in Note #1 and turn right.

11. Again follow the path a short distance toward Ancient Falls, but this time bear left just past a beech tree and go toward the Black River. Here is a scenic view of the wide stream and of an island in its center on the left.

Huge blocks of sandstone have fallen into the river as a result of the underlying shale layer being undercut by erosion. In addition, because the sandstone is porous and holds water, this moisture freezes in winter and causes the rock to crack and break off.

Take the hand-hewn steps carved into the rock on the right and follow the trail along the river to another park feature, Oyster Rock.

12. Oyster Rock is located on the right under Camel's Hump. It is a pale yellow Berea Sandstone ledge with an opening in the rock shaped like an oyster shell. Despite being painted over with graffiti, the cross-bedding in the stone produces a close resemblance to an open oyster.

Walk toward the water to overlook the meeting point where the East and West Branches flow together to form the Black River. On the right see the Old Auto Trail and automobile ford.

Retrace your steps along the riverside trail past the restrooms to the parking area.

HIKE B: ELYWOOD PARK

For the next hike in Elywood Park, drive north on the park road to the automobile ford, on the right. (The road ahead continues to a picnic area, concessions building, playground, and popular fishing area.)

The automoile ford is impassable by car in high water (and in winter), and the gate will be closed then. At other times, two-way traffic over the ford is permitted, one car at a time. At most times, it is not possible, or advisable, to cross the river on foot.

13. Follow signs across the ford on the one-way loop road to the picnic and parking area on the right. Begin the hike at the sign for Lion's Trail, east of the picnic area. The trees are marked with red paint blazes. This path is also marked as the Red Bud Trail. Follow the path through a large bed of blue-flowering myrtle to an intersection.

14. Bear right (east), leaving the red tree blazes. The trail then bends north toward the riverbank. Across the river you can see a park playground on the peninsula.

15. Follow the trail alongside the river. Occasionally you will see blue paint on trees marking the path. Across the creek are dark Cleveland Shale cliffs, the next sedimentary layer below Bedford Formation and Berea Sandstone (see Appendix A).

16. Stay left on the lower trail beside the river, and continue to follow it to a point where you can see the river make a big bend around the peninsula. This is as far as this trail easily penetrates the forest.

Retrace your steps along the river to the intersection described in Note #2.

17. Bear right at this intersection, passing another bed of shiny-leaved myrtle. Cross a small wooden bridge and follow the trail as it bends away from the river.

18. Emerge at the parking area near a sign indicating Indian Trail, where there is also a sign saying "Service Vehicles Only."

Continue ahead to the parking area.

HIKE C: EAST FALLS

To reach the start of this hike from Hike B, recross the automobile ford. Turn left on the park road and follow it uphill to Hillsdale Ct. and Furnace St. Turn left (south) on Furnace St. and go 0.4 mile (3 blocks) to Lake Ave. (also called Lodi St.). Turn left and drive another 0.5 mile (3 blocks) to a city parking lot (free) on the right (south) side of Lake/Lodi St.

19. Cross the street to this entrance to Cascade Park located on another section of the abandoned Old Auto Trail. A sign here reads: "East Falls Observation Deck erected 1989 by Friends of Cascade Park." The sign also informs visitors that the original 15-acre parcel of land for the park was given by the Ely family in 1874.

Near the trail entrance are blocks of sandstone from the Old Quarry that were placed here years ago for an artificial waterfall running over a dip in the ledge.

20. Follow the Old Auto Trail about 150 ft. to the Observation Deck on the right overlooking East Falls and the gorge below.

21. Leave the Old Auto Trail and take the trail to the right (southeast) toward East Falls. Just before the end of the path is a "reflecting rock" that echoes the sound of the falls back to the listener. When you reach the falls, stay behind the fence to view the scene.

The Power Plant Ruins are to the right (west) of the falls. This power generating station diverted water from a dam and spillway above the falls to turbines in the plant, producing electricity for mills, streetcars, and downtown Elyria buildings in the late 1800s and early 1900s. A series of gristmills were powered by these falls as early as 1840. The ruins are a result of the station having been purposely dynamited during World War II to obtain steel for the war effort.

Retrace your steps northwest on the trail to the Observation Deck again.

Bear right to continue on the Old Auto Trail downhill (north) for about 0.5 mile. Stay behind the fence for scenic views of the gorge on the right below. Here there is ample evidence of severe erosion from earlier flooding: old fence posts mark the path of the previous trail and chunks of the Old Auto Trail lie in the river below.

22. Take the steps on the left to go up around a badly eroded area ahead. A set of railroad-tie steps on the left also go down around another eroded embankment. The path continues on parts of the old asphalt/concrete road.

23. Reach a point of land marking the confluence of the rivers seen earlier on Hike A from the opposite side. At a trail junction, stay to the right to go to the tip of the point. The West Branch of the Black River is on the left (west) and the East Branch of the Black River is on the right (east). They join here to form the Black River, flowing north to Lake Erie. Here also is an old concrete pedestrian footbridge (not usable) that formerly connected this side of the park to trails on the other side.

Continue around the point to see the concrete ford of the Old Auto Trail. Again, it is not safe to cross the ford because the moss growing on it is extremely slippery.

Turn around and go back to the stone-lined trail on the right leading toward Big Cave (southwest).

24. On the right just below the slope you may see an old collapsed road with its support rocks fallen away. This old road dates from the 1920s, when the car route extended back to West Falls. A turnaround at the falls enabled cars to return to the main road from there. From this slope there once was a swing footbridge over to the Old Quarry area. Some of the steel footings are still visible on both sides of the water.

Bear right (southwest) on this trail, staying close to the river. (The trail on the left leads uphill to a dead end near private property.)

25. Continue on the trail along West Branch to West Falls and Big Cave. This very large shelter cave contains small limestone stalactites deep against the far wall. Like other shelter caves in the park, it was created by the undercutting and eroding of soft shale layers underneath harder Berea Sandstone. The sandstone collapsed and thus left a cave, which stays cool even on a hot summer day.

Retrace your steps back to the river confluence (Note #5), on past the eroded embankments (Note #4), and along the Old Auto Trail to return to the Observation Deck, trail entrance, and parking area.

This chapter was prepared with the generous assistance of Flora Burkholder.

ERIE COUNTY

Erie County is bisected by two major east-west highways, SR 2 and I-90, and one of its major cities lies in both Lorain and Erie Counties. Downtown Vermilion east of the Vermilion River is in Lorain County; west of the river it is in Erie County.

The county seat, Sandusky, is the gateway port to the Lake Erie Islands, of which Kelleys Island is in Erie County, but North, Middle, and South Bass Islands are in Ottawa County. Numerous ferries transport people and cars to the islands. For information contact Miller Boat Line, P.O. Box 239-FS, Put-in-Bay, OH 43456 (419-285-2421); or Neuman Cruise & Ferry Line, 101 E. Shoreline Dr., Sandusky, OH 44870 (419-626-5557). Sandusky is also home to popular 125-year-old Cedar Point Amusement Park.

Erie County MetroParks comprise six parks and recreation areas: Osborn Recreation Area, Castalia Quarry Reserve, Pelton Park, Edison Woods Reserve, the Coupling Reserve, and James H. McBride Arboretum. Information about the MetroParks, and a quarterly publication, *The Leaflets*, is available from Erie MetroParks Administrative Office, Osborn Recreation Area, 3910 E. Perkins Ave., Huron, OH 44839-1059 (419-625-7783).

Four of Ohio's State Nature Preserves are in Erie County, but two are open only by written permit from the Ohio Department of Natural Resources (ODNR). The two open preserves are Sheldon Marsh, a prime springtime bird-watching wetland of 387 acres in Huron Township, and Old Woman Creek, a National Estuarine Research Reserve with a visitor center (limited hours), three miles east of Huron on Lake Erie. The limited-access areas are Dupont Marsh, a 114-acre marsh on the east side of the Huron River (about three miles upstream from Lake Erie), and Erie Sand Barrens, a 32-acre section of post-glacial beach ridges (sand barrens) in Oxford Township, about 3 miles south of Sandusky. Information about these natural areas is available from ODNR, Old Woman Creek Reserve, 2514 Cleveland Rd., East, Huron, OH 44839; 419-433-4601.

Schoepfle Garden (Ch. 55), though located in Erie County, is maintained and managed by Lorain County Metro Parks. The historical walk in downtown Vermilion (Ch. 54) is west of the Vermilion River and therefore in Erie County.

Of further interest in Erie County is the Milan Historical Museum and Thomas Alva Edison's birthplace in Milan. The museum is at 10 Edison Dr. and is open 1-5 p.m. Tues. through Sun. (419-499-2968).

More information about Erie County is available from Erie County Visitors Bureau, Sandusky, OH 44870; 800-255-ERIE.

54 VERMILION

Distance: 2 miles

Easy

Walking time: 1-1/2 to 2 hours

Description: This easy walk, entirely on sidewalks, begins and ends at the Inland Seas Maritime Museum (216-967-3467). It takes the visitor past historic homes and shops in the Harbour Town 1837 Historic District.

Directions: From I-90/SR2, follow SR 2 after it splits off from I-90. Take the exit for Wakeman-Vermilion. Turn right (north) on SR 60 and continue north 2 miles to Vermilion. Stay on SR 60 (Main St.) past US 6 to the end of Main St. and the Inland Seas Maritime Museum at the Great Lakes Historical Society.

From Lorain go west on US 6 to Vermilion and turn right (north) on Main St. to the Inland Seas Maritime Museum.

Parking & restrooms: On-street parking is available in front of the Inland Seas Maritime Museum, 480 Main St., and at Exchange Park at SR 60 & US 6. A public restroom at the east end of Victory Park on US 6 just east of Main St. is open from Easter weekend to mid-November.

Founded in 1808 and incorporated in 1837, Vermilion reminds one of a small New England seaport. The town, home of the Inland Seas Maritime Museum, has restored many of its old homes and shops along the waterfront to re-create a quaint Harbour Town district. Sailing, yacht racing, and fishing are principal summertime activities here.

Yearly events attract thousands of visitors to Vermilion. The Fish Festival is in mid-June. The Woollybear Festival is the first Sunday in October; its all-day events include a large parade and contests honoring a fuzzy caterpillar whose dark-brown and orange bands are thought to predict the severity of the coming winter. The Great Black-Backed Gull Greeting Party is the third Sunday in October at the Main St. beach. This Audubon Society event accompanied by a pancake breakfast celebrates the migration of these large birds from 1,500 miles away in Labrador. The gulls spend several weeks on the Lake Erie shore.

Vermilion is also known to many for its music box shop, homemade berry pies and chocolates, and pick-your-own strawberry and blueberry farms.

Vermilion was so named because of the reddish clay lining the banks of the river. Early settlers, who first came from New England in 1808-09,

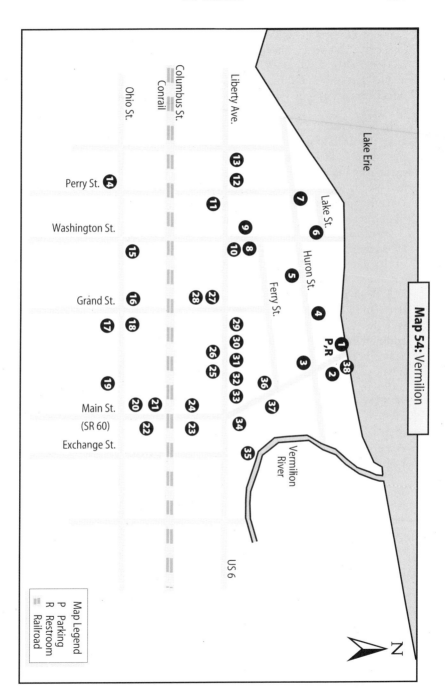

Map 54: Vermilion

cleared the heavily forested land and built cabins and other structures. Many of the original inhabitants were given land by the State of Connecticut as payment for having lost their property in fires during the Revolutionary War. This part of the Connecticut Western Reserve was known as the "Firelands," and its settlers as "Firelanders." Actually, few of the direct beneficiaries themselves came to Vermilion; most sold their claims to others.

In 1840 the U. S. Corps of Engineers built two piers at the mouth of the river, permitting large ships to use the harbor. This improvement helped the fishing industry meet the demand for fish and enabled the establishment of an important and lasting shipbuilding industry. Many fine sailing and fishing vessels, and later steamboats, were constructed in Vermilion. Over the years, as the town prospered and fishing continued to be a very important activity, more than 50 ship captains built their homes here.

More information is available from Vermilion Chamber of Commerce, 5495 Liberty Ave., Vermilion, OH 44089; 216-967-4477, and from Friends of Harbour Town, 5741 Liberty Ave., Vermilion, OH 44089; 216-967-4262.

1. Begin the walk at the museum, which can be visited now or at the end of the tour. The museum, operated by the Great Lakes Historical Society, is in the former Frederick Wakefield House. Built in 1909, it received an addition in 1968. Interesting maritime history of the Great Lakes is presented here. On display are fine ship models, photographs, artifacts, and memorabilia pertaining to lake shipping. Of particular interest are a 1907 restored pilot house from the freighter *Canopus* and a 1992 replica of the 1877 Vermilion Lighthouse. The original lighthouse stood on the west pier of the Vermilion River but was dismantled in 1929 because of the danger of its falling into the channel after ice damage. It was then moved to the east end of Lake Ontario, at the entrance to the St. Lawrence River, where it remains today guarding ships in the vicinity of Charity Shoal.

The museum is open daily from 10 a.m.-5 p.m.; admission is $4 for adults, $2 for ages 6-16, and free for children under 6.

2. Opposite the museum, at 485 Main St. is the remodeled Captain Thompson House, built in 1830.

Turn right (west) onto Huron St.

3. On the corner of Huron and Main (532 Main St.) is the old Steamboat Hotel, also known as Well's Inn. It was originally built in 1838 and enlarged with an 1865 addition.

4. The 1885 Captain J.C. Gilchrist House, on the right at 5662 Huron St., was built by the owner of the largest fleet on the lakes (and honorary captain). It is now listed on the National Register of Historic Places. Converted to Lakeside Hotel around 1900, the house is now a bed and breakfast inn.

5. The Captain Alva Bradley house at 5679 Huron St. was constructed in 1840 in Greek Revival style. At that time, Bradley became captain of the *South America*, and later he initiated substantial shipbuilding in Vermilion. In the 1860s Capt. Bradley moved his shipbuilding business to Cleveland, because thedeeper channel of the Cuyahoga River could accommodate the iron ships that were then being built. His company later became known as the American Ship Building Co.

6. Turn right (north) on Washington St. to number 520, another typical 1840 shipbuilder's home. Since being remodeled, this is one of several houses moved back from the lakefront as the land constantly eroded.

7. Turn left (west) onto one-block-long Lake St. and then left (south) on Perry St. for one block. Many of these small old homes were once summer cottages. Turn left (east) on Huron St. On the northeast corner of Perry and Huron (5750 Huron) is another early house built in the 1840s.

Continue east on Huron St. for one block, then turn right (south) on Washington St.

8. On the southeast corner of Washington and Ferry streets, at the rear of Ritter Library, is a large boulder with the date "1784" and the name "S. Kenton" chiseled on it. Simon Kenton was an explorer and Indian fighter who laid claim to four square miles of land south of the Vermilion River mouth. Daniel Boone called Kenton "the bravest man I ever knew."

Kenton apparently hoped to establish a community here by carving his name on this rock, without filing any legal claims. He is generally considered to have been the first white man in this area. The boulder was found in 1937 on a farm a mile south of Vermilion; it now stands at this spot as a memorial to the first man to recognize Vermilion's potential for settlement. Continue south on Washington St.

9. The 1839 home at 624 Washington (remodeled) was constructed by George Frankenberger, an early cabinetmaker.

10. On the corner of Washington and Liberty is the Ritter Public Library (1958), donated by George Ritter, a Toledo lawyer and philanthropist, to honor his parents, John and Louise Ritter. Containing a bright children's room with a play-sized replica of the sailing ship *Niagara*, the entire library was beautifully remodeled in 1994.

Turn right (west) on Liberty Ave. (US 6).

11. The 1860 Italianate house at 5741 Liberty is headquarters for Harbour Town 1837 Historic District, a local group formed more than 25 years ago specifically to preserve Vermilion's history and historic buildings. This house, also containing a gift shop and restaurant, is identified as Old Jib's Corner, named for Jib Snyder, a sailor, fisherman, and ferryboat operator of the town's early days.

12. Captain Bell's house at 5760 Liberty (now the Victorian House of Flowers) was built in the 1860s.

13. Continue west on Liberty Ave. to 5780, the Pelton House, one of the oldest homes still standing in Vermilion. The original house was built in 1832, but it has had several subsequent additions.

Return to Perry St. and turn right (south) on Perry. Cross the Conrail tracks to Ohio St. (The other east-west railroad going through Vermilion is Norfolk Southern, a subsidiary of Norfolk & Western RR).

CAUTION: Although guarded, this is an active railroad with trains coming through frequently.

14. On the southwest corner of Ohio and Perry streets is the 1870 Baxtine house.

Turn left (east) on Ohio St.

15. The Queen Anne house with triple-peaked roof at 5676 Ohio St. (at the corner of Washington St.) is another ship captain's house. It was built in the 1880s by a Captain Weeks.

16. One of Vermilion's oldest churches is at 752 Grand St., on the corner of Ohio St. The Evangelical and Reformed Church (United Church of Christ) was organized in 1852 by German-speaking people. Its first building was constructed in 1853 and the present building in 1869. A large religious education building was added in 1959.

17. At the intersection of Ohio and Grand streets are more captains' homes. The 1875 red brick at 5583 Ohio is where Captain Gilchrist, Sr., resided. He was captain of the ship *W.H. Gilchrist* that is frequently mentioned in shipping stories. The walls of this home are eight inches thick. Note the interesting Vermilion-kilned white brick window trim and the brackets under the eaves.

18. The 1857 home at 743 Grand St. belonged to Captain Phillip Minch, the owner of the ship *Western Reserve*, which sank in August 1892, taking the lives of many Vermilion residents.

Continue east on Ohio St.

19. At 5559 Ohio St. is the Burton House, built in 1848.

Turn left (north) onto Main St.

20. The Town Hall and Opera House on the corner at 736 Main St. has an interesting history. In 1883-84, when it opened, it became the center of activity in Vermilion. Costing $21,000, the hall contained a courtroom, council chambers, offices, a kitchen, a dining room, and a jail. The opera house on the second floor was the site of musicals, band concerts, minstrels and vaudeville acts, debates, lectures, medicine shows, high school commencements, and of, course, opera. The second floor, closed since 1940, still has the original stage, 450 seats, and its black velvet stage curtain.

21. Next to the Town Hall, at 728 Main St., is another old church building—the former Congregational Church, built in 1886 by the oldest church body in Vermilion. This congregation was first organized in 1818;

in 1956 they built a new church on State St. and this building became a Baptist Church. It is now an antique shop and auction house.

22. Victory Park across the street is noted for its beautiful rose garden. A historic marker describes the settling of Vermilion.

23. Schwensen's Bakery (closed since 1994) at 681 Main St. was a well-known business in Vermilion for 101 years. Founded by a Danish family in 1893, it remained at the same site throughout its existence and was the oldest family business in town.

24. Englebry Dry Goods Store at 686 Main St. was another longtime business, now occupied by other shops. The building at 672 Main St. was built in 1870, and the Baumhart Building in 1916.

Turn left (west) on Liberty Ave. (US 6).

25. This block is the heart of the Vermilion's Harbour Town Historic District. Williams Law Offices at 5581 Liberty are located in a restored 1907 building.

26. The Liberty Theater building at 5591 Liberty was built in 1870 and became a theater in the early 1900s. After it closed, it was a dry goods store for many years.

Turn left (south) on Grand St.

27. The 1870 lighthouse keeper's house at 654 Grand St. is now a business office and living quarters.

28. Vermilion Hardware at 678 Grand St. is in an 1873 building and represents another of the town's durable businesses. At one time the town's only wooden horse collars and baby coffins were sold here.

Return to Liberty Ave., turn right (east) and walk on the opposite (north) side.

29. The Ice Cream Parlour and dining room at 5596 Liberty is a favorite stop for visitors; the business is in an 1850s building that was formerly a funeral parlor.

30. The Harbour Store at 5542 Liberty Ave. (now a dress shop) is the oldest (1847) restored downtown building in Vermilion.

31. The barber shop, the Captain's Chair, has been in business at this location, 5532 Liberty Ave., since 1868.

32. The old Erie County Bank (now a real estate office at 5512 Liberty) was built in the 1890s.

33. Hart's Drug Store occupied this corner at 5502 Liberty from 1920 to 1985; it is now Higgins Pharmacy and still contains an old-fashioned soda fountain. Constructed in 1870 in this prime location, the building has had many occupants over the years—the post office was here, a shoe shop, a dry goods store, a saloon, and, on the second floor, a dentist, a beauty shop, and offices.

A Geological Survey marker on the south side (near the sidewalk) indicates that Vermilion is 597 feet above sea level.

34. Across the street is Exchange Park, so called because it was originally the Farmer's Exchange, where farmers came into town to sell their produce to townspeople.

35. Continue east along Liberty Ave. past the public restroom (modernized in 1995 within a small 1912 building), to a public access path on the left leading down to the river. Here are park benches, a play yard, and picnic tables affording a pleasant rest stop and view of river traffic.

On the west (facing the river) are Fisherman's Bend Condominiums where Kishman Fish Co. was located from the 1880s until 1983. Between 1890 and 1945 there were six large fish companies along the Vermilion River with dozens of fishing boats harvesting the rich abundance of sturgeon, herring, pickerel, and perch from Lake Erie. These have all been demolished.

36. Return to Main St. and Liberty Ave., and continue north on Main St. At 630-626 Main St. are three businesses, one of which is the *Vermilion PhotoJournal* office, located in the former Wagner Hotel (1875). This hotel and others once provided lodging for many travelers and sailors cruising on lake vessels and, later on, for summer visitors arriving by train. The Lake Shore Electric Railway brought many people to Vermilion from Cleveland and other shore towns until it ceased operating in 1938.

37. The Sail Loft Professional Building at 555 Main St. was originally part of one of the early shipbuilding yards and was built in 1840. Chez Francois, a popular French restaurant, is in the lower level of this building.

Between the Sail Loft and the brick building (Water Co. at 537 Main St.) is another public park from which to view the boats passing up or down the river.

On the east side of the river are the Lagoons, lined with Cape Cod-style homes—white with dark roofs and shutters. This development was begun in the 1930s as a work project during the Depression and continued until the 1950s. Originally this land was a great swamp, with a wooden catwalk from Vermilion to Linwood Park, which was a religious, recreational, and residential community established in 1883. (Linwood Park is now reached by car from Liberty Ave., and an entrance fee is charged for use of the beach).

38. At the end of Main St. near the museum is Main St. Beach, where the annual mid-October Great Black-Backed Gull Greeting Party is held on the observation deck. These majestic gulls migrate from their summer breeding ground in Labrador, up the St. Lawrence River to Lake Erie before flying farther south. They are very large birds with black backs and a wing spread of up to 5-1/2 feet.

On the sandy beach you may note some small black patches in the sand. This is not oil but magnetite, a pure, magnetic, naturally-occurring iron ore. When picked up, it feels like sand, though much heavier than ordinary sand. The black iron grains of this sand can actually be separated from the quartz and feldspar grains with a magnet. The light pinkish-purplish mineral grains are garnet—not, however, gem quality. This black sand, with or without garnet, is found on the beaches of western Lake Erie, Kelleys Island, and South Bass Island.

This chapter was prepared with the generous assistance of Flora Burk-holder, and was reviewed by Diane Chesnut, Executive Director, and Roze Smith, Assistant to the Director, Friends of Harbour Town, Vermilion.

55 SCHOEPFLE GARDEN

Distance: 0.6 mile

Easy

Walking time: 1 hour, more or less

Description: The 22 acres of display areas can be viewed from grassy paths in a leisurely manner in any direction, but a loop walk is suggested here. The terrain is generally flat. A dirt path leading down to the river valley is on a gentle slope but the walk is flat along the river. Although the garden can be visited at any time of year, it is especially rewarding to view the special collections seasonally. The highlights are:
April—spring bulbs, wildflowers in the river valley
Early May—dogwood
May—lilacs
Early June—rhododendrons
June through September—roses, hostas, ferns, ornamental gras;
July—daylilies, cannas
Late August—perennials, wildflowers
All seasons—topiaries, evergreens.

Directions: From I-90/SR 2, continue west on SR 2 to Vermilion (not continuing on I-90). Exit at Baumhart Rd. and follow Baumhart south (past I-80) to SR 113. Turn right (west) on SR 113 for 4 miles, going through Henrietta to Birmingham. Turn left (south) onto Market St. (first road after crossing the Vermilion River bridge), and left again onto Mills St. to the Schoepfle Garden parking area.
From SR 58 south, take a right (west) on SR 113 through S. Amherst and Henrietta to Birmingham. Just before entering town, turn left at Market St. and left again on Mills St. to the parking area.
From I-80 (the Ohio Turnpike) take Exit 7A (Baumhart Rd.) going south about 1 mile. Turn right (west) on SR 113 and follow it about 4 miles to Birmingham. Turn left (south) onto Market St. and left again onto Mills St.

Parking & restrooms: Park in the lot off Mills St.; portable restrooms only.

Schoepfle (pronounced Sheff-lee) Garden, a unit of Lorain County Metro Parks, was created by Otto B. Schoepfle on 70 acres of land (22 developed) that once belonged to his grandfather. Schoepfle (1910-1992) was a businessman and former chairman of the *Elyria Chronicle Telegram*. He devoted much of his life to creating his garden in a unique natural setting of woodlands, ponds, sun, and shade—all within the residential area of Birmingham.

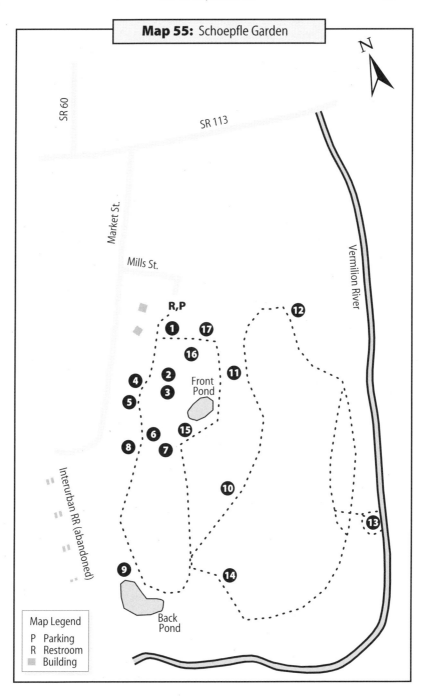

Map 55: Schoepfle Garden

SR 60

SR 113

Market St.

Mills St.

Vermilion River

R,P

Front Pond

Interurban RR (abandoned)

Back Pond

Map Legend
P   Parking
R   Restroom
     Building

The garden, located alongside the Vermilion River in Erie County, contains special collections of trees, shrubs, and perennials, all of which are labeled with both common and Latin names. The entire garden is unexpectedly beautiful and reflects Schoepfle's travels around the world to study and learn about horticultural collections in other lands and climates. In 1969, after major plantings were made, Schoepfle donated his acreage to Lorain County Metro Parks, whose staff now provides maintenance and preservation of the park in its natural beauty.

Schoepfle Garden is open daily from 8 a.m. to dusk, and admission is free. The garden is not handicapped accessible, pets are not permitted on the grounds, and there are no picnicking facilities in the park. If you are interested in a detailed guided tour of the gardens (minimum of 12 persons) or information about videocassettes depicting the four seasons at Schoepfle, call 800-LCM-PARK or 216-458-5121.

1. Enter the garden at the sign west of the parking lot. The house ahead and garden building belonged to the Schoepfle family. The entry path leads to a row of various kinds of clipped hedges and topiaries depicting, among others, a dog sitting in a chair, chickens, and a goose. Some of the oldest topiaries here were started about 1935. One of the youngest is the "terrier," trained since 1985. It is ahead on the right near the ornamental grasses.

The evergreen hedge along the grassy path requires clipping only about once a year. The broadleaf hedge on the right (west) (forming an archway) is actually a series of closely planted beech trees; it is clipped only three times a year.

2. On the left, near the south end of the evergreen hedge, is a large dawn redwood tree (Metasequoia). A deciduous conifer, it bears cones, but its needles drop in winter, unlike evergreen conifers that bear cones and keep their winter greenery. The dawn redwood is often called a "living fossil," because paleobotanists in 1941 identified it in plant fossils found to be 50 million years old. This type of tree is quite likely to have been growing at the time dinosaurs roamed the earth.

3. About 50 feet ahead (south) and on the left (east) is a ginkgo tree, identified by its fan-shaped leaf. (Schoepfle Garden has chosen the ginkgo leaf as a symbol in its publications.)

This tree, too, is considered a "living fossil;" some of its fossilized remains have been found to be 100 million years old. The ginkgo is considered to be the world's oldest living species, because it survives unchanged from its original form. This tree, with both male and female varieties, most probably was also fed upon by dinosaurs. This particular ginkgo is a female, whose unpleasant-smelling seed pods ripen in August.

4. On the right is a collection of modern roses, followed by ornamental grasses, then "old garden" roses. (A nameplate indicates the rose's year of introduction.) Rose breeding began in China about 2,500 years ago. In the mid 1800s, modern rose breeding began in France, and hybridization of tea roses started in 1868.

Schoepfle's "old garden" roses include species that have been propagated and reproduced since 1581 and 1696.

5. Among the ornamental grasses is an unusual black grass alongside a large rock.

6. Just ahead on the left (east), near the daylily path, is one of several summer-blooming kousa dogwood trees. Its leaves resemble the more common flowering dogwood tree, but its small, white flowers develop into pink edible fruit, enjoyed by both birds and people.

7. About 25 feet to the east and downhill is a bald cypress tree, another deciduous conifer. In the spring this tree appears to be dead but soon develops its new, bright green needles.

8. Return to the path and continue south. Just ahead on the right (west), near the edge of the "old garden" roses, is a twin-trunked Cedar of Lebanon tree. According to Biblical tradition, this is the tree used by King Solomon to build his great temple.

9. Continue south to a collection of conifers: pine, hemlock, spruce, and fir. Here are two more bald cypress trees.

At the far end of this collection is a small, tranquil, spring-fed pond (Back Pond) near the edge of the garden's developed area. A patch of bamboo is growing at the upper (western) corner of this small pool. This pond has been here since the late 1800s and was a pleasant rest stop on the electric interurban railway that connected shore towns between Cleveland and Sandusky. In the woods southwest of the pond lies the abandoned railbed of this important transportation system. The old sandstone Vermilion River bridge abutments are still visible on the hillside in the woods.

When Otto Schoepfle was a young child, this pond supplied ice for the family's icehouse. It was considered a "good year" if enough ice remained on the Fourth of July to make ice cream.

10. Turn around to walk north past the daylily collection to the slope on the right where Schoepfle planted many varieties of rhododendrons, creating a gorgeous sight in early June. These plantings are in the midst of a grove of Scot's (commonly called "Scotch") pine planted in 1960. Originally, Front Pond above was created to irrigate the seedling pines; they were intended for Christmas trees, but were never cut for this purpose.

11. Fascinating collections of hostas, ferns, and astilbes are beyond the rhododendrons, all identified. On the left (west) is a shade garden beyond a stone wall. This wall was constructed in 1991 from old foundation stones of demolished local houses.

12. On the right (east) is a split-rail fence, and east of it is a trail leading down to the river. This path through the woodlands offers native dog-woods and many kinds of wildflowers to identify and enjoy in the spring-time.

13. The (unmarked) River Valley Trail leads downhill. At a fork in the trail, stay to the left and soon reach a left turn and a short loop path going to the edge of the Vermilion River. Here is a pleasant view of the river flow-ing north toward Lake Erie.

14. Exit the loop and turn left to continue on the path as it bends uphill to the conifer collection again. As the path emerges from the valley and woods into the open area, note the two bald cypress trees on the right. They are at the edge of the woods about 75 and 125 feet ahead.

Continue north above the rhododendrons to Front Pond.

15. Near the southeast corner of Front Pond is an unusual tricolor beech tree, whose name is derived from the colors of its leaves. Each leaf has three shades of color that differ in different seasons: a shade of green edged with two shades of pink.

The lilac collection is just ahead (north), another beautiful sight in May.

16. Between the lilac and hedge collections to the left (west) is "Holly Harem," where there is one male American holly surrounded by 15 females. These Ohio natives bear fruit—holly berries—and the males supply the pollen.

17. On the right is a border of beautiful annuals and perennials.

Turn right to return to the parking area.

This chapter was prepared with the generous assistance of Flora Burk-holder.

56 KELLEYS ISLAND: GLACIAL GROOVES STATE MEMORIAL AND NORTH QUARRY TRAIL

Easy

Distance: 1.75 miles total. Glacial Grooves State Memorial (Hike 56A) is 0.25 mile; North Shore Loop Trail (Hike 56B) is 1.5 miles.

Hiking time: 1 1/4+ hours total. Hike 56A is 1/2+ hour; Hike 56B is 3/4 hour.

Description: Both hikes are within sections of Kelleys Island State Park. Glacial Grooves State Memorial (Hike 56A) is situated behind a protective fence bordered by interpretive signs. The loop walk to view the grooves is on a paved path and includes short sets of steps. Helpful signs at six stops describe the geologic history of the grooves and different kinds of fossils that can be seen along this walk.

North Shore Loop Trail (Hike 56B) is just north of the Glacial Grooves and begins at the parking lot near the abandoned North Quarry heading west. The trail follows the wooded north shoreline of Kelleys Island where Lake Erie meets the island's limestone base. An old loader from earlier quarrying days can be seen at the beginning of this trail. There are fine views of the water and other Lake Erie islands.

Directions to Kelleys Island: From I-90/SR 2 west, follow SR 2 (after it splits off from I-90) into Sandusky, and to Sandusky Bay Bridge. Follow SR 269 north to SR 163, then continue east to Marblehead. In Marblehead, the Neuman Cruise & Ferry Line and the Kelleys Island Ferry leave from well-marked docks. Neuman Cruise & Ferry Line operates from the Frances St. dock in Marblehead from April 1 through Nov. 19. The Neuman dock on Kelleys Island is near the intersection of Cameron Rd. and Water St. (800-876-1907; 419-798-5800; or 419-746-2595). Kelleys Island Ferry Boat Line operates year round from Marblehead and arrives on Kelleys at the Water St. pier (419-798-9763). Both boats arrive in 20 minutes and ferry cars, bicyclists, and pedestrians. Cruises from Marblehead on the M/V Emerald Empress are offered from Memorial Day through Oct. 28 (800-876-1907 or 419-626-5557).

From Sandusky and Port Clinton, year-round air service is available to Kelleys Island Municipal Airport on the east side of the island. Information is available from Griffing Flying Service (800-368-ERIE; 419-734-3149).

Directions to hikes: Once on the island, walk or drive on Water St. to Division St., then turn north on Division St. Continue north about 1.5 miles to Glacial Grooves State Memorial and North Shore Loop Trail. The Glacial Grooves are on the left, just before Kelleys Island State Park.

Parking & restrooms: Follow signs to Kelleys Island State Park on the north side of the island. The parking lot is east of Glacial Grooves State Memorial and is reached by a one-way road near the fishing pier. Restrooms are located in the campground.

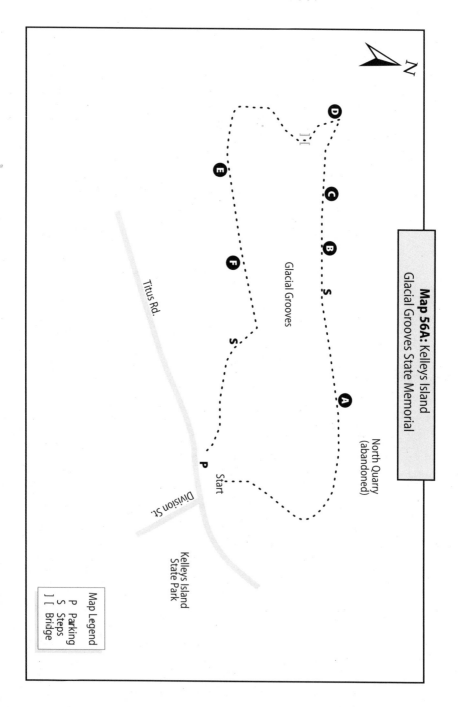

Map 56A: Kelleys Island
Glacial Grooves State Memorial

North Quarry
(abandoned)

Glacial Grooves

Titus Rd.

Start

Division St.

Kelleys Island
State Park

Map Legend
P   Parking
S   Steps
] [Bridge

Kelleys Island, one of the largest freshwater islands in the U.S. at approximately four square miles (2,800 acres), is listed on the National Register of Historic Places. Located in the western basin of Lake Erie, Kelleys Island is 4 miles north of Marblehead and 12 miles north of Sandusky.

Glacial Grooves State Memorial is internationally known as the world's largest and most spectacular display of grooves cut by sliding glaciers. These gouges in solid rock were carved more than a million years ago during the Pleistocene (Ice) Age. The grooves, 396 feet long, 25 to 30 feet wide, and 15 feet deep, lie in limestone bedrock. They reveal a marvelous record of fossilized marine invertebrates that lived in the Devonian Sea 360 million years ago.

In prehistoric times, Kelleys Island was used as a hunting ground by Indians. Archeological studies here have found village sites, burial mounds, and many arrowheads. Inscription Rock State Memorial on the south shore of Kelleys Island shows pictographs carved on a large limestone boulder by Erie Indians about 300-400 years ago.

A man named Cunningham was believed to have been the first white man to inhabit the island between 1800 and 1812. The island became the property of the Connecticut Land Co. in 1817 and was divided into 13 lots given to stockholders in that state. Settlement of Cunningham Island (or Island No. 6, as it was then called) began in 1833 when Datus and Irad Kelley purchased the land for $1.50 an acre and then gave their name to the island. An impressive three-story mansion, built in the 1860s by Addison Kelley for his father Datus Kelley, sits on a spacious shorefront lot in the center of town and is open for tours in season.

Limestone quarrying was once the most important industry on Kelleys Island. Today only one company, Kellstone, Inc., is actively quarrying limestone from the island. Grape-growing and wine-making were at their peak at the turn of the century and were another important source of income for many residents. Now, however, only one company remains—Kelleys Island Wine Co. on Woodford Rd., which is open daily from May to September and on weekends in April and October (419-746-2537).

Fishermen and vacationers crowd Kelleys Island in the summer. Walleye, perch, catfish, and smallmouth and white bass are caught in quantity at peak periods. Boaters enjoy the waters around Kelleys Island because of its ideal lake breezes and small waves. The island is fine for walking because of its isolation, frequent scenic vistas of boats and water, glorious sunsets, and waterfowl, birds, and migrating monarch butterflies.

The Cleveland Museum of Natural History owns 90 acres of prime wetland on Kelleys Island, a popular area for watching migrating birds. Monarch butterflies feed on milkweed and blanket the East Quarry area in September as they rest overnight on their yearly migration to their mountain refuges northwest of Mexico City. In March they head northeast and reach Kelleys Island in late May. Bird-watching information is available by calling 800-255-ERIE or 419-746-2360.

Kelleys Island State Park occupies 661 acres of land on the north shore of the island. The park contains 129 camping sites, available only on a non-reservable basis. Near the campground is a small, sandy, public beach with changing booths and latrines. Picnic tables, grills, a boat launch, and a fishing area are all open to the public. For information call 419-746-2546 in season and 419-797-4530 in the off-season. The Chamber of Commerce (P.O. Box 783, Kelleys Island, OH 43438; 419-746-2360) also provides information to the visitor.

HIKE A: GLACIAL GROOVES STATE MEMORIAL

Glacial Grooves State Memorial is near the corner of Division St. and Titus Rd. Begin the walk at the large Glacial Grooves sign on the west side of the parking area. On this counterclockwise walk you will see letters at stops identified as "A" through "F" (although some of these letters may be missing).

Glacial Grooves State Memorial encompasses 3.5 acres and has been administered by the State of Ohio since 1932. These spectacular grooves were created about 25,000 years ago by the Wisconsinan Glacier, which advanced from the highlands of Labrador, Canada, to this part of Ohio over a 5,000-year time span. As the mile-thick glacier slid forward, it sculpted these grooves under heavy pressure. The ice at the bottom of the glacier dragged slowly over the ground, creating these grooves in the limestone bedrock.

NOTE: Please only *observe* the fossils. *Collection of fossils here or in any other sections of Kelleys Island State Park is strictly forbidden.*

A. The limestone rock at the side of the walkway (and in the grooves) was formed of mud and skeletons of marine invertebrates deposited at the bottom of the warm, shallow sea that covered Ohio during the Devonian Age about 360 million years ago. Deposition of mud on the sea bottom and the creation of limestone (calcium carbonate) from marine animals was a very slow process. Their skeletons, containing calcium extracted from the ocean eventually petrified into solid limestone, as they became buried in sediment.

The fossils in this rock are crinoidea (sea lilies), whose decay left small, round, scattered, plate-like fossils. It may have taken several thousand years for erosion to expose the rock in which these fossils appear.

B. Geologists have discovered 47 different species of ancient fossilized marine animals in the limestone bedrock of this park. In addition to sea lilies, corals are particularly abundant. Tabulate (table-like) corals appear fossilized as a collection of flat, segmented columns; rugose (wrinkled) corals may be found fossilized as round shells with internal divisions or septa; "horn" corals, when viewed from the side, appear to resemble that musical instrument.

Brachiopoda (lamp shells) were sea animals with bivalve shells such as clams have, but with various forms such as fan-shaped, heart-shaped, or wing-shaped. Their folds or creases form vertical lines that resemble lampshades.

The tortuous winding of some of the smaller glacial grooves (as explained at this stop) may be due to pre-glacial or sub-glacial stream flow.

C. The glacial grooves appear as dark and light layers or strata. Crinoid (sea lily) fragments comprise the dark strata; the light strata are composed of a fine, powdery, limy material of broken shells and skeletons called "fossil hash."

The layers underfoot are composed of corals, gastropoda (snails), and cephalopoda—all typical fossilized Devonian Sea animals. Snails often left a cast of their coiled shape rather than the shell itself.

Cephalopoda (nautiloids and ammonoids) grew shells divided into many compartments or chambers. Fossilized cephalopoda show the external sutures (lines) of the many chambers.

D. This stop presents a view of the abandoned North Quarry, which ceased operating around the turn of the century when the glacial grooves were first uncovered in this location. Although geologists have found that the grooves continue underground, no plans exist for any more excavating, in order to preserve those that remain for observation by future generations. It was fortunate that limestone quarry operations ceased when they did, providing this unusual opportunity to study life as it existed in this area millions of years ago.

E. The glacial grooves, deepest at this point, inspire respect for the awesome size and depth of the massive ice shield that slid southwesterly from Canada thousands of years ago. The last glacier retreated permanently about 12,000 years ago, and its meltwater left Lake Erie about 100 feet deeper than it is now. After emptying—and remaining a bog for thousands of years—Lake Erie then refilled and reached its present level about 3,000 years ago. Glacial till left behind covered most of the grooves until their discovery.

You may see glacially polished cross-sections of fossilized tabulate or rugose corals, brachiopoda (lamp or clam-like shells), gastropoda (snails), or cephalopoda (nautiloids and ammonoids).

F. At this stop the grooves below you are deep and straight. But trapped in the mile-high ice were granite-like boulders that, as they were pushed forward, acted as giant grinding and abrading machines. Evidence of different-sized granite rocks frozen into the bottom of the ice as it moved forward is revealed by the smaller winding grooves and striations in the softer limestone.

Fossils that can be identified here are crinoidea (sea lilies), solitary rugose coral, colonial tabulate coral, or brachiopoda.

It is a wonder that these sea organisms, millions of years old, have been uncovered by a glacial process that, relatively speaking, is of such recent origin. These marvelous glacial grooves put the true age of the earth and its geologic processes into new light.

Part of the information in Hike 56A was adapted from *A Glacial Grooves Fossil Walk on Kelleys Island* by L.M. Bowe and C. E. Herdendorf (see Bibliography).

HIKE B: NORTH SHORE LOOP TRAIL

1. The entrance to North Shore Loop Trail begins in the large parking lot used by boaters and fishermen. It is about 200 yards north of Glacial Grooves State Memorial. Enter the trail at the trail marker sign going west. Numbered signposts partially follow the numbered descriptions below.

The first stop provides a view of abandoned North Quarry, where John Clemmons started quarrying limestone in 1830. This was the second quarry to open on Kelleys Island, and operations continued here until about 1900. The stone was of such superior quality that it was used throughout Ohio, Michigan, and the eastern U.S. The first American lock at Sault St. Marie contains this limestone, as does the Cedar Point break-wall and many buildings and bridges in Cleveland.

2. This loader was built in 1888 and used to fill rail cars with crushed stone to be taken to the dock or lime kilns. At one time Kelleys Island Lime and Transport Co. had 16 kilns operating and produced 1,500 barrels of lime per day.

3. Bear right (northwest) at the trail intersection.

This large manmade hill is a spoil bank built to provide workers with access to the stone crusher located in the building next to the loader. The hill is made of fine pieces of stone, a by-product of the stone-crushing process.

Bypass the side trail to the north going up over the spoil bank. Note the small wall on the right made of small pieces of rock left over from stone-crushing process.

CAUTION: Poison ivy is rampant here. The oil (urushiol) exuded from its three leaves and yellowish-white berries can cause an irritating rash when it rubs on skin or clothing, in any season.

4. Bear right (northeast) at the next trail intersection. (The trail to the left passes old stone building foundations of former homes used by quarry workers.)

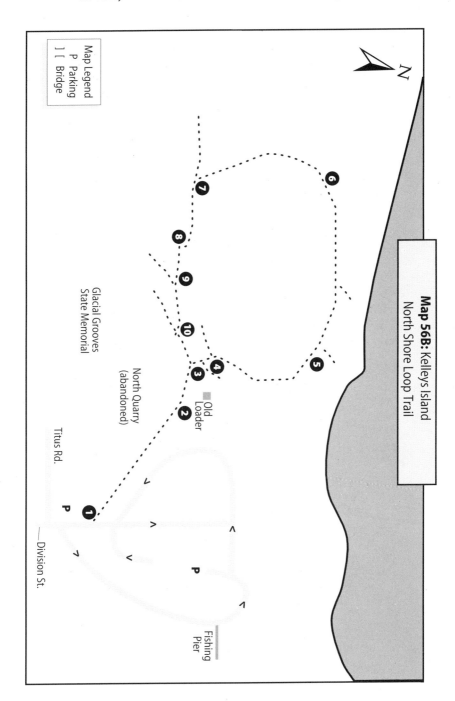

Map 56B: Kelleys Island
North Shore Loop Trail

Map Legend
P Parking
] [Bridge

N

Glacial Grooves
State Memorial

North Quarry
(abandoned)

Old
Loader

Titus Rd.

Division St.

Fishing
Pier

5. At 0.5 mile reach the shoreline of Lake Erie. Turn toward the water on a short spur trail. The rocky shore provides evidence of glaciers in the small grooves in the limestone. There are blocks of limestone left here from old quarrying operations and much evidence of shoreline erosion.

Lake gulls that can be identified here at different times of the year are ring-billed, herring, Bonaparte's, Great Black-Backed, little, and glaucous gulls.

Return to continue on the main trail and turn right (west). At the next opening to the shore, take the short path over to the water for a long view of the islands of Lake Erie. A view to the northwest shows South, Middle, and North Bass Islands eight miles away. To the north and much farther away is Canada's southernmost point of inhabited land, Pelee Island. On South Bass Island is Put-in-Bay, a popular boating destination and home to Perry's Victory and International Peace Memorial and Heineman Winery. Return to the main trail.

6. At about 1.0 mile the trail bends to the left (south).

Among the trees on Kelleys Island are the Eastern cottonwood, a fast-growing species with seeds that look like tiny balls of cotton and leaves that are triangular with marginal teeth. Green and white ash trees can be identified by their pinnately compound leaves, odd in number, and gray bark with diamond-shaped ridges.

Red and sugar maples that grow here are second- and third-generation trees, because maple lumber was used extensively to fuel steamboats traveling on the Great Lakes.

7. Bear left (east) at a "T" junction in the trail. The rocky cliff on the right (south) is thought to represent an ancient shoreline on Kelleys Island.

8. Ohio's state tree, the Ohio buckeye, usually grows 60-80 feet tall and is 2-3 feet in diameter when fully grown. Here it is much smaller, because it is growing in thin soil over limestone bedrock. It is identified by its palmately compound leaves in groups of five and the spiny capsules that surround the shiny buckeye seed. (In contrast, the *yellow* buckeye, which also has leaves in groups of five, is slightly larger, and its seed capsule is smooth rather than spiny.)

9. The foundations is this area once supported buildings occupied by quarry workers who came from Italy, Germany, and other European and Slavic communities to work in the pits.

This hiking trail is a former quarry road; other roads in here are maintained as fire lanes. Continue straight ahead (southeast) when another trail on the right joins this one.

10. Eastern redcedar is a juniper that commonly grows in poor soil and is abundant on Kelleys Island, thriving in the limestone soil. This tree has round or four-sided branchlets covered by closely overlapping, dark-green scales. Its round, 0.3-inch-size cones are green at first, then blue, and are covered with a gray, waxy substance. This slow-growing tree may live for 300 years.

At 1.4 miles meet another quarry road on the right and follow the main trail east to the end of the loop near the concrete loader. Take the same path to the parking lot where the hike began.

57 KELLEYS ISLAND: EAST QUARRY TRAIL AND DOWNTOWN WALK

Distance: 2.35 miles total. East Quarry Trail is 2.1 miles. The Downtown Walk to Kelley Mansion and Inscription Rock State Memorial is about 0.25 mile from the center of town at Water and Division streets.

Hiking time: 1 1/4 hours total. Hike 57A is 1/2+ hour; Hike 57B is 3/4 hour.

Description: East Quarry Trail (Hike 57A) begins near the center of the island off Ward Rd. There are numerous fossils along this trail, but collecting them is forbidden without a written permit from the Ohio Department of Natural Resources (Division of Parks and Recreation, 1952 Belcher Dr., Bldg. C-3, Columbus, OH 43224-1386).
Among the interesting attractions along East Quarry Trail are Horseshoe Lake, with limestone blocks edging it, fossils embedded in the rocks underfoot, some old fence lines of typical island construction, and several varieties of trees. There are many paths here, and several criss cross the main trail, making it necessary to closely follow the descriptions below. NOTE: Near East Quarry Trail is a lilac walk. In the spring, signs for this walk are posted near Estes School on the southeast corner of Ward Rd. and Division St. The lilacs that bloom in this grove are large old specimens that flower each year about the middle of May. Inquire at the Chamber of Commerce for information (419-746-2360).

Directions: (See Ch. 56 for general directions to Kelleys Island.) For East Quarry Trail, go north on Division St. then turn east onto Ward Rd. and continue about 1 mile to the trailhead on the right.

Parking & restrooms: For Hike 57A, park in a small parking area on the south side of Ward Rd. opposite the easternmost buildings of the 4-H Camp. There are no restrooms here.
For Hike 57 B, on-street parking is used. Restrooms are located at the ferry dock.

Kelleys Island State Park occupies 661 acres of land on the north shore of the island. The park contains 129 camping sites, available only on a non-reservable basis. Near the campground is a small, sandy, public beach with changing booths and latrines. Picnic tables, grills, a boat launch, and a fishing area are all open to the public. For information call 419-746-2546 in season and 419-797-4530 in the off-season. The Chamber of Commerce (P.O. Box 783, Kelleys Island, OH 43438; 419-746-2360) also provides information to the visitor. (Please refer to Ch. 56 for an enhanced write-up of Kelleys Island)

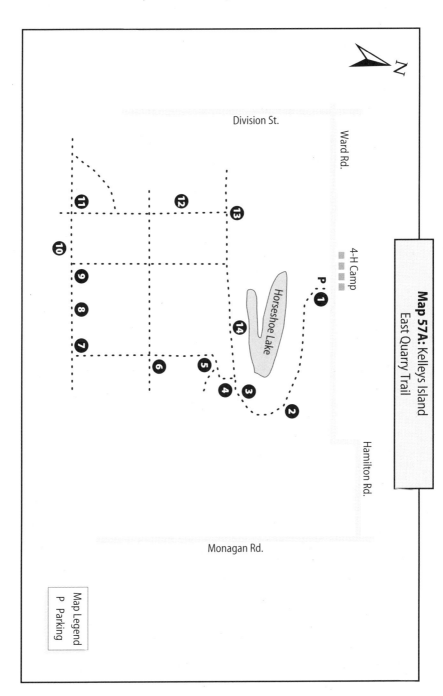

Map 57A: Kelleys Island
East Quarry Trail

Map Legend
P Parking

HIKE A: EAST QUARRY TRAIL

From the center of town at Division and Water streets, walk or drive north on Division St. to Ward Rd. and turn right (east) at Estes School. Continue on Ward for about 1 mile to the East Quarry Trail entrance. Opposite the easternmost buildings of the 4-H Camp there is a very small parking area before the barrier.

East Quarry was (and is) part of a vast limestone quarry that extended westward past Division St. and Bookerman Rd. almost to the western shore of the island. Kelleys Island Lime and Transport Co. began quarrying limestone here around 1933 and continued until 1940. The section called East Quarry extends from Division St. to Horseshoe Lake.

1. Enter the trail on either side of the barrier. Head southeast on a wide path. Horseshoe Lake is just ahead. Stay on the wide path going clockwise (east to west) around the lake. Here you see large slabs of quarried limestone at the edge of the lake.

2. Among the wetlands on Kelleys Island is the swamp located east of Horseshoe Lake. Wetlands like this one are frequently saturated by surface or ground water and thus maintain an environment for rare and endangered plants and provide a habitat for different species of wildlife.

Wetland birds that may commonly be seen here are the red-winged blackbird, common yellowthroat, and marsh wren.

3. Horseshoe Lake is a rapidly aging lake that is smaller than it was originally. The water once was clear but now usually is cloudy, yet plant, fish, and aquatic life is still found in the lake. Fishing for sunfish and small-mouth bass is permitted, with a valid license. Often observed here are great blue herons, egrets, seagulls and other shore birds, fox, and raccoons. (No swimming is permitted in Horseshoe Lake.)

4. At 0.5 mile bear left off the main trail, then immediately right onto a grassy trail going southwest.

Black cherry trees which in other environments eventually grow to 50-60 feet, 1-3 feet in diameter, and may live 150-200 years, cannot reach their full size here because of the thin topsoil on Kelleys Island. The black cherry's oval leaves are 2-6 inches long and contain fine marginal teeth. The bark of these young cherries is smooth, dark reddish brown or black. The wood of the cherry is prized for furniture-making.

5. Pass the trail on the left. Hackberry trees are usually used as ornamentals because of their relatively small size (normally 30-40 feet) and their success in living under adverse moisture and soil conditions. Hackberry bark is characteristically grayish brown with corky ridges and warts. Its ovate leaves are 2-4 inches long with toothed margins.

6. The American basswood tree produces valuable white, straight-grained lumber. It is also valued as a soil improver because its deciduous leaves contain calcium, magnesium, nitrogen, phosphorus, and potassium. The leaves are very large—5-6 inches long and 3-4 inches wide. The small honey-flavored flowers and fruit are attached to a leafy bract 5-6 inches long. Its dark gray bark is ridged and furrowed and was used by Iroquois Indians to make rope.

Cross an east-west side trail (0.6 mile) and continue south.

7. The osage-orange tree, originally a southern species, has been grown extensively for fence rows and hedges. Its ovate deciduous leaves are 3-5 inches long with smooth margins. This tree can achieve a height of 10-50 feet and bears large, round (3-5 inches in diameter), inedible fruit. The wood of the osage-orange tree is characteristically bright orange and yields a yellow dye when soaked in hot water. Since it is used to make archers' bows, the tree is often called "bowwood."

Just past Sign No. 7, turn right at a "T" junction.

8. Continue ahead. The Chinkapin oak, usually 50-80 feet tall in good soil, does not achieve that height in this dry limestone outcrop. Its four-to-seven-inch-long leaves have bluntly pointed marginal teeth with fine white hairs below. Small, ovate acorns are brown to black, and its bark is ash gray, rough, and flaky.

9. Note here the old barrels containing posts with fragments of barbed wire. The method of fencing on Kelleys Island was dictated by the shallow soil above limestone bedrock, which prevented the driving-in of fence posts. Islanders filled barrels with rocks to hold the posts, then strung wire from post to post to form an enclosure or delineate property lines.

Pass a trail on the right, another old quarry road. Here Eastern red cedar grows abundantly in the poor limestone soil.

10. On the left is an Eastern hophornbeam, commonly found in dry soils, which is often called "ironwood" because its wood is extremely hard and tough. The bark has a shredded appearance, with broken, shaggy plates that curve away from the trunk. Its birch-like leaves are three to five inches long and have double-toothed margins. The hophornbeam produces two-inch-long catkins and clustered seed pods with flattened, leafy bladders containing seeds. (In contrast, the American hophornbeam grows in rich soil along streams or swamps and has a smooth, blue-gray, sinewy bark.)

11. Turn right (north) at the four-way intersection (1.2 miles). The crisscrossing trails in this park are former quarry trails and are used by hikers, maintenance personnel, and wildlife. They also serve as fire breaks for the quarry area. (Open fires and motorized vehicles are prohibited here.)

Pass a trail on the left, then an east-west intersecting trail. Note the very thin topsoil layer over the limestone bedrock.

12. On the left is the fast-growing honeylocust tree, growing well in

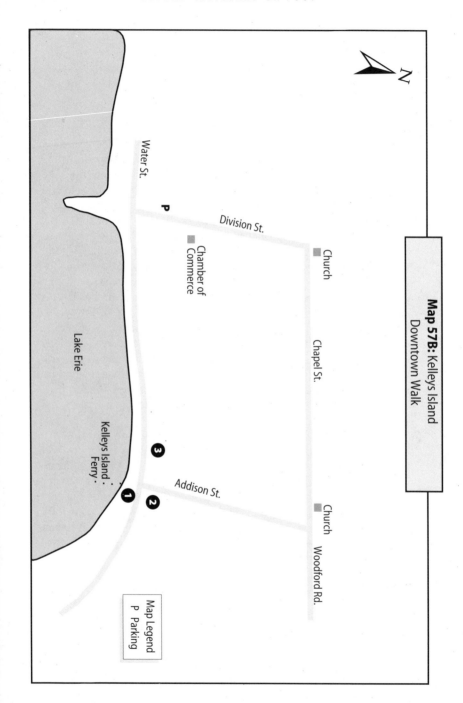

N

Water St.

P

Division St.

Chamber of
Commerce

Church

Chapel St.

Lake Erie

Kelleys Island
Ferry

3

1

2

Addison St.

Church

Woodford Rd.

Map 57B: Kelleys Island
Downtown Walk

Map Legend
P Parking

limestone soil. This tree is distinguished by thorny spines, pinnately compound leaves, and especially its 7-to-18-inch-long brown seedpods. The seedpod contains a sweetish substance similar to honey and is only eaten (when green) by cattle. In other environments this tree can reach 75-80 feet.

Turn right (east) to walk above the old East Quarry.

NOTE: *Fossil collection is not permitted in the quarry or anywhere along the trail.*

13. Here again you may see 360-million-year-old Devonian Sea fossils embedded in the limestone rock underfoot on the trail. Scattered around this area are corals, crinoidea (sea lilies), brachiopoda (lamp shells), gastropoda (snails), cephalopoda (nautiloids and ammonoids), and pelecypoda (clams or bivalves).

14. Reach Horseshoe Lake again and continue on the path past the junction in Note #4. Follow the perimeter trail to the beginning of the hike and the car parking area.

HIKE B: DOWNTOWN WALK

Return from Ward Rd. to Division St. and turn left (south) on Division St. to Water St. Parking is available along the street or at the ferry dock.

1. Inscription Rock State Memorial is on the right near Addison and Water streets. Faint pictographs on the flat-topped limestone boulder were carved, it is believed, by Erie Indians at least 300-400 years ago. These drawings show men, animals, and birds. It is one of the most extensive and best-preserved artifacts of this prehistoric period in the area, though the pictographs are now almost entirely obliterated. A relief of the inscription, drawn from the 1850 original by Capt. Seth Eastman, U.S. Army, shows a human figure with headdress smoking a pipe, animals, and bird forms.

2. Opposite Inscription Rock is Kelley Mansion, a three-story, limestone rock home with a widow's walk, built in the 1860s by Addison Kelley, co-founder of Kelleys Island, for his father Datus Kelley. Inside is a free-standing spiral staircase, handsome woodwork, and rose-colored, cut-crystal windows. Displayed inside is a collection of letters and photos from presidents and dignitaries and a small museum with articles pertaining to the home's residents.

The Civil War-style architecture of Kelley Mansion is similar to several other homes on the island's south shore. It is thought that homes built around the time of the Civil War were constructed by confederate prisoners who were held captive on nearby Johnson's Island in Sandusky Bay. The Mansion is open for tours, with a one dollar donation requested.

3. West of Kelley Mansion is Himmelein House, a three-story, white, wood frame house with dark blue shutters. This handsome home facing the lake on Water St. is a private residence and not open to the public.

A number of other early homes facing Lake Erie are privately owned and occupied but may be viewed from Water St. Of special interest in the downtown area is the small Lake Erie Toy Museum located in Caddy Shack Square on Division St. (admission fee charged).

NOTE: An optional walk follows Division St. north to Chapel St. Take a right turn (east) to Addison St. This route will take you past the Kelleys Island Chamber of Commerce (on Division St.) and two small churches (both on Chapel St). Turn right (south) on Addison to return to the ferry on Water St.

BIBLIOGRAPHY

Banks, P., and R. Feldmann, eds. *Guide to the Geology of Northeastern Ohio.* Cleveland, OH: Northern Ohio Geological Society, 1970.

Blodgett, Geoffrey. *Oberlin College Architecture: A Short History.* Oberlin, OH: Oberlin College, 1979.

Brockman, C. Frank. *Trees of North America.* New York: Golden Press, 1968.

Cameron, Patience and Harry. *Cleveland On Foot.* Cleveland Heights, Ohio: H & P Publishing Co., 1992.

Carlson, E. *Minerals of Ohio.* Columbus, OH: Ohio Department. of Natural Resources, Division of Geological Survey, 1991.

Cuyahoga Valley Trails Council, Inc. *Trail Guide Handbook, Cuyahoga Valley National Recreation Area.* Akron, Ohio: The Council, 1991.

Ellis, William Donohue. *The Cuyahoga.* Dayton, Ohio: Landfall Press, Inc., 1966.

Field Guide to the Birds of North America. Washington, D.C.: National Geographic Society, 1983.

Folzenlogen, Robert. *Hiking Ohio:Scenic Trails of the Buckeye State.* Glendale, Ohio: Willow Press, 1990.

Friends of Harbour Town 1837, Vermilion, OH. Pamphlets and maps. Vermilion, OH: The Friends, nd.

Geauga Park District. Maps and brochures. Geauga County, OH: Geauga Park District, nd.

Gieck, Jack. Personal communication, August, 1995.

Gieck, Jack. *A Photo Album of Ohio's Canal Era, 1825-1913.* Kent, Ohio: The Kent State University Press, 1988.

Grismer, Karl. *Akron and Summit County.* Akron,OH: Summit County Historical Society, 1952.

Hartman, Roy. "History of Carlisle" in *Lorain County Metro Parks Bulletin.* Lorain County, Ohio: Lorain County Metro Parks, 1980.

Hatcher, Harlan. *The Western Reserve.* Kent, OH: Kent State University Press, 1991.

Hudson Library and Historical Society. Leaflets on Hudson History. Hudson, OH: The Society, nd.

Izant, Grace Goulder. *Hudson's Heritage.* Kent, Ohio: Kent State University Press, 1985.

Kelleys Island Chamber of Commerce. Brochure, maps. Kelleys Island, OH: The Chamber, 1995.

Lake Metroparks. Maps and brochures. Lake County, OH: Lake Metroparks, 1988-93.

Linhardt, Becky. *Kelleys Island, An Island For All Seasons.* Kelleys Island, OH: Kelleys Cove, Inc., 1995.

Lorain County Metro Parks. Maps and brochures. Lorain County Metro Parks, 1994.

Lorain County Visitor's Bureau. "African-American Heritage Tour." Lorain, OH: Lorain County Visitor's Bureau, 1995.

Medina County Park District. Maps and brochures. Medina County, OH: Medina County Park District, nd.

Metro Parks Serving Summit County. Mini-maps and brochures. Akron, OH: Metro Parks, 1992.

A Natural History of Lake County, Ohio. Rosemary N. Szubski, Ed. Cleveland, OH: Cleveland Museum of Natural History, 1993.

Newcomb, Lawrence. *Wildflower Guide.* Boston: Little, Brown and Co., 1977.

Oberlin Area Chamber of Commerce. *OBERLIN, A guide to the "most cosmopolitan small town in America."* Oberlin, OH: The Chamber, nd.

Oberlin College, Admissions Office. *Oberlin College of Arts and Sciences.* The Office, 1994.

Oberlin College, Admissions Office. *Oberlin Conservatory of Music.* The Office, 1994.

Ohio Department of Natural Resources. *A Glacial Grooves Fossil Walk on Kelleys Island.* Columbus,OH: Ohio Department of Natural Resources, nd.

Ohio Department of Natural Resources. *Ohio's Trees.* Columbus, OH: Ohio Department of Natural Resources, 1990.

Ohio Department of Natural Resources. *Ohio's Natural Areas and Preserves: A Directory.* Columbus, OH: Ohio Department of Natural Resources, 1987.

Ramey, Ralph. *Fifty Hikes in Ohio.* Woodstock, Vermont: The Countryman Press, 1990.

Rosche, L., ed. *Birds of the Cleveland Region,* 2nd ed. Cleveland, OH: Cleveland Museum of Natural History, 1988.

Weber, Art. *Ohio State Parks, A Guide to Ohio's State Parks.* Saginaw, Michigan: Glovebox Guidebook Publishing Co., 1994.

Western Reserve Academy. *Reserve* (Catalog). Hudson,OH: The Academy, 1994.

APPENDIX A

Generalized Geological Column for Northeast Ohio

Age	Rock Unit	Section	Years before the Present
Quaternary	Glacial Deposits		20,000 or less
Pennsylvanian	Sharon Conglomerate		320 Million
Mississippian	Cuyahoga Formation — Meadville Member		350 Million
Mississippian	Cuyahoga Formation — Strongsville Member		350 Million
Mississippian	Cuyahoga Formation — Sharpsville Member		350 Million
Mississippian	Cuyahoga Formation — Orangeville Member		350 Million
Devonian	Berea Sandstone		
Devonian	Bedford Formation	Euclid Bluestone	360 Million
Devonian	Cleveland Shale		
Devonian	Chagrin Shale		

Legend (right column): conglomerate, siltstone, crossbedding, sandstone, red shale, black shale, gray shale

Source: Joseph Hannibal, Cleveland Museum of Natural History, 1996

INDEX

CLEVELAND
Guides & Gifts

If you enjoyed this book, you'll want to know about these other fine Cleveland guidebooks and giftbooks ...